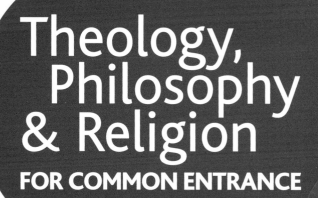

Theology, Philosophy & Religion
FOR COMMON ENTRANCE

13+

Revision Guide

Michael Wilcockson

GALORE PARK

AN HACHETTE UK COMPANY

About the author

Michael Wilcockson was brought up in Cambridge and studied Theology at Balliol College, Oxford. After completing his PGCE at Pembroke College, Cambridge he became Head of Divinity at Aldenham School and later at The Leys School, Cambridge. He was appointed Head of Divinity at Eton College in 1996 and in 2010 became the college's first Head of Philosophy. He was a Farmington Fellow at Harries Manchester College, Oxford in 2003 and Visiting Scholar at Pembroke College, Cambridge in 2010. He is Test Coordinator for A Level Religious Studies for a major examination board and Chief Setter for Common Entrance Theology, Philosophy and Religion for ISEB. He is author of many textbooks for Common Entrance, GCSE and A Level. He is a Fellow of the Chartered Institute of Educational Assessors.

Every effort has been made to trace all copyright holders, but if any have been inadvertently overlooked the publishers will be pleased to make the necessary arrangements at the first opportunity.

Hachette UK's policy is to use papers that are natural, renewable and recyclable products and made from wood grown in well-managed forests and other controlled sources. The logging and manufacturing processes are expected to conform to the environmental regulations of the country of origin.

Orders: **Teachers** please contact Bookpoint Ltd, 130 Park Drive, Milton Park, Abingdon, Oxon OX14 4SE. Telephone: (44) 01235 400555. Email primary@bookpoint.co.uk. Lines are open from 9 a.m. to 5 p.m., Monday to Saturday, with a 24-hour message answering service.

Parents, Tutors please call: 020 3122 6405 (Monday to Friday, 9:30 a.m. to 4.30 p.m.). Email: parentenquiries@galorepark.co.uk

Visit our website at www.galorepark.co.uk for details of other revision guides for Common Entrance, examination papers and Galore Park publications.

ISBN: 978 1 5104 4663 2

© Hodder & Stoughton Ltd 2019

First published in 2019 by

Hodder & Stoughton Ltd

An Hachette UK Company

Carmelite House

50 Victoria Embankment

London EC4Y 0DZ

www.galorepark.co.uk

Impression number 10 9 8 7 6 5 4 3 2

Year 2023 2022 2021 2020

Typeset in India

Printed in Spain

A catalogue record for this title is available from the British Library.

MIX
Paper from
responsible sources
FSC™ C104740

Contents

Introduction

1. ## How to use this book

This revision guide covers the Common Entrance Theology, Philosophy and Religion (TPR) syllabus. The book is set out to correspond to the layout of the examination paper.

- **The first section** covers **Section 1: Theology**. It sets out the content of the Bible texts, the interpretation of the texts and various ways these might be evaluated.

- **The second section** covers **Section 2: Philosophy**. It sets out factual information about four important philosophers and four contemporary ethical issues, the ways the philosophers' ideas and ethical arguments might be understood and various ways these might be evaluated.

- **The third section** covers **Section 3: Religion**. It sets out a summary of the main beliefs and practices of each religion (Buddhism, Christianity, Hinduism, Islam, Judaism and Sikhism), how these might be understood and various ways their beliefs and practices might be evaluated.

The first two sections contain two topics each. Section 3 covers the six religions, and under each religion heading there are two topics. The content of each topic is set out in the same order as the topics in the Common Entrance TPR syllabus.

Read

At the start of each topic you are referred to pages in the two TPR pupil **textbooks** published by Hodder Education (*Theology and Philosophy for Common Entrance 13+* and *Religion for Common Entrance 13+*, both by Susan Grenfell and Michael Wilcockson). You are strongly advised to read these pages first and then use this revision guide, because the textbooks give you more detail with pictures and activities to practise, and, when you have read them, you will have a much fuller understanding of the topics you are revising.

Knowing about, understanding, evaluating

Every sub-topic is set out to correspond to the **three parts** of an exam question:

- **Part a questions** test **knowledge** and **factual** information. Each knowledge topic in this book is introduced as '**Knowing ...**'. The bullet points which follow give a very brief summary of the key information you need to know. The words in **bold** draw your attention to the key points but you should use a highlighter pen to highlight other points.

- **Part b questions** test **understanding** and **interpretation** and meaning of key ideas. Each understanding topic in this book is introduced as '**Understanding ...**', although in the Theology chapter the topics are introduced as '**Interpreting the story**'.

- **Part c questions** test **evaluation** and **your assessment** of a statement. Each evaluation topic in this book is introduced as '**Evaluating ...**'. To help you form an argument there are **two bullet points**: 'On the one hand ...' and 'On the other hand ...'. Each point contains one or two sentences suggesting some ideas you might like to develop or adapt yourself. You may decide that you don't like what is suggested and, if that is the case, you should write your own brief notes on the book and use these to revise from.

Test yourself

At the end of each topic there is a set of 10–14 **Test yourself** questions. Use these to see how much you can remember. Go back over the topic and check you have got the right answers.

Use the book *Theology, Philosophy and Religion for Common Entrance 13+ Exam Practice Questions and Answers* to test yourself further.

Glossary

Each set of two topics ends with a glossary or list of key words. Test yourself by reading each key word and saying out loud how it is defined. Now cover it up and see how much you can remember by writing down the word and its definition. Then uncover and check your answer. In summary:

LOOK, SAY, COVER, WRITE, CHECK

Dates

B.C.E. and C.E. are used throughout this guide. **B.C.E.** means **Before the Common Era** and is equivalent to using B.C. **C.E.** means the **Common Era** and is equivalent to using A.D.

2. Guidance on the exam

The syllabus and your exam

You have **60 minutes** to complete the examination. You must choose **two questions** from **two** of the **three sections**.

- Each **section** has a choice of **four questions**.
- The **first two questions** are from **Topic 1** and the **second two questions** are from **Topic 2**.
- Choose **one question** from either Topic 1 or Topic 2.
- Spend no more than **30 minutes** on each question.

The three sections are:

- Section 1 Theology
- Section 2 Philosophy
- Section 3 Religion

Your teacher will tell you which two sections you have prepared. You should choose your questions from these two sections.

Examination questions

Each question has **three parts** which become increasingly more demanding.

- **Part a** tests factual knowledge. Part a questions are worth 6 marks each.
- **Part b** tests your ability to interpret and explain. Part b questions are worth 6 marks each.
- **Part c** tests your ability to discuss, evaluate and present an argument. Part c questions are worth 8 marks each.

In the examination, spend approximately the following amount of time on each question:

- Part a: 9 minutes
- Part b: 9 minutes
- Part c: 12 minutes

Part c questions are the most demanding because these are designed to test your argument and essay skills. For part c questions:

- Spend at least **two minutes planning** your argument.
- Make sure you start a **new paragraph** for each side of the argument.
- You must end with a **conclusion** in which you **refer to the question** and briefly say whether you agree or disagree with it. Your conclusion must be a separate paragraph. Keep the conclusion **brief** – one sentence is enough.

1 God's relationship with the world

Read *Theology and Philosophy for Common Entrance 13+* pages 4–48.

In this topic we consider how various writers in the Old Testament and New Testament have portrayed and reflected on God's relationship with the world. Such a relationship lies at the very heart of all theological issues and poses some difficult questions. Although the biblical writers considered God to be the all-powerful creator of the universe, they did not think God was remote from the world but that He played a constant part in it. This causes a theological tension between the God who is infinitely greater than humans and beyond their knowledge and the God who reveals Himself as love and the source of justice and mercy.

Themes

As well as knowing the set stories from the Bible, you will also be tested on the following themes:

1 The nature of God – what is God like?

2 The nature of revelation – how does God reveal who He is?

3 God's relationship with Creation – how do God and His Creation interact?

4 God's commands and call to worship – how does God want people to live?

5 The miraculous – how does God act in the world?

6 The divine nature and mission of Jesus

7 Jesus' fulfilment of Old Testament hope

8 God's plans of salvation

You will see that these themes are referred to in each of the stories in this chapter, in the Interpreting the story sections.

1.1 The Creation

Read Genesis 1:1–2:4

Knowing the story

- In the beginning God created the heavens and the Earth.
- Nothing had any shape or form.
- On the **first day** God created **light**, which He called day.
- On the **second day** God **separated the waters** and created the **sky**.
- On the **third day** God created **land**, **seas** and **plants**.
- On the **fourth day** God created the **stars**, the **sun** and the **moon**.
- On the **fifth day** God created **birds** and **sea creatures**.
- On the **sixth day** God created **land animals**. He created **human beings** in His **own image**.

- God gave humans **responsibility** over all creatures.
- God commanded humans to **increase** and **rule** the Earth.
- God completed His work on the **seventh day** and **rested**. He made this a **holy day**.

Interpreting the story

Themes
1, 2 and 3

Most scholars think that the two Creation stories were written at different times and therefore make slightly different points.

There are **two Creation stories** at the start of Genesis: the first (Genesis 1:1–2:4) focuses on **God and the world**; the second (Genesis 2:4–25) on **God and humans**.

The **first Creation** story teaches that there is a **God-given order** and design of the universe.

- God is a majestic **creator** and creates just by **commanding**.
- Humans are given control over Creation because they are made in **God's image** and share in His power.
- Humans have a responsibility to steward and maintain the God-given order of the world.
- Everything has its proper **place** in the Creation.
- Creation is viewed as perfect in its original state, reflecting its creator.
- The **day of rest** is remembered in the fourth of the Ten Commandments as a time of renewal and recreation.

Evaluating the story

Does the theory of evolution suggest that humans are not specially created by God?
Points to consider:

- **On the one hand ...** humans have evolved naturally as part of God's general plan for the world; humans are not specially created but are nonetheless a significant aspect of creation.
- **On the other hand ...** conservative Christians argue there is no firm evidence that humans evolved from lower life forms – that there are many so-called 'missing links' between simple life forms, apes and humans – and therefore God must have specially created intelligent humans.

Does the universe have a meaning?
Points to consider:

- **On the one hand ...** the universe is very well designed so it must have a meaning given to it by God. As Genesis suggests, the world is ordered, beautiful and things appear to work well.
- **On the other hand ...** many atheists and humanists argue that it is we who give the universe meaning and impose order on disorder; that we like to see patterns in nature when in fact there are none and that suffering suggests that if God did design the universe, then He did it very badly.

1.2 The call of Moses

Read Exodus 3:1–17

Knowing the story

- Moses was tending **Jethro's** (his father-in-law's) **sheep**.
- He led them to Horeb.
- God's angel appeared in the **flames of a bush**.

- The bush was **not destroyed** by the flames.
- God called to Moses from the bush '**Moses! Moses!**'.
- Moses said '**Here I am**'.
- God told Moses to take **off his sandals** because he was on **holy ground**.
- God said He was the **God of Abraham, Isaac and Jacob**.
- Moses **hid his face**; he was afraid to look at God.
- God said He had seen the suffering of the Israelites in Egypt and had **come to rescue them**.
- He promised to lead them to a land '**flowing with milk and honey**'.
- Moses was to **go to Pharaoh** and bring the Israelites out of Egypt.
- Moses asked why he should do this.
- God answered that **He would be with Moses** and when he had rescued the people they would worship him at Horeb.
- Moses asked what he should do if the people asked for **God's name**.
- God told Moses to tell the Israelites that '**I am who I am**' had sent him.
- God told Moses to tell the people about **His promise** to take them to a new land.

Themes
1, 2 and 5

Interpreting the story

- This is one of the most important moments in Exodus because **Moses learns of his mission** as prophet and **leader**; also, for the first time **God reveals His name**.
- Taking one's **shoes off** is a sign of respect for God; Moses recognises that this is a **holy place**.
- At first, Moses learns that this God is the **god of his ancestors** (Abraham, Isaac and Jacob). Then he learns that God **is far greater** than this and that He just 'is' – God is **unique** and there is **nothing else like Him**.
- 'I am' can also be translated as '**I will be what I will be**' and implies that God is **eternal** and can **never fully be understood by humans** and that He has future plans for humans which are as yet a **mystery**.
- The ancient Israelites believed that **knowing the name** of a god was a means of being able to call on him to **act**.
- The land '**flowing with milk and honey**' is **Canaan**. God's covenant promise with the Israelites will be to give them a land like Eden. This represents God's generous nature and love.
- Moses is shown as **questioning and unsure**; he needs reassurance from God.

Evaluating the story
Can we ever know God?
Points to consider:

- **On the one hand ...** humans can never know God because He is, by definition, greater than the human mind can imagine. Some argue that we might be able to know about God from miracles or answers to prayer but this never tells us much about who He actually is.
- **On the other hand ...** God reveals aspects of Himself to His leaders such as Moses or to prophets such as Isaiah. Christians believe that in Jesus, humans are able to know about God's love in a new way.

Is the story of Moses at the burning bush the most important moment in the Old Testament?
Points to consider:

- **On the one hand ...** it is the first time God reveals His true nature and calls Moses to start the exodus. Without these two things, the Israelites would not have become a great nation, the Law would not have been given to Moses and this key event would not have inspired the later prophets.

- **On the other hand ...** the burning bush is not the most important moment because it is the giving of the Law at Sinai which is the first moment when the Israelites can think of themselves as a distinct and civilised nation with a code to live by.

1.3 Passover

Read Exodus 12:1–13

Knowing the story

- God told **Moses** and **Aaron** that every Israelite family was to take a **lamb** big enough to feed each person in their household.

- The lamb had to be a one-year-old male **without defect**.

- On the **14th day of the first month** all the lambs were to be **slaughtered** at twilight.

- The **blood of the lambs** had to be painted on the **sides of the door frames** where the family was living.

- The meat had to be **roasted** and eaten with **bitter herbs**.

- The Israelites were to **eat unleavened bread**.

- All of the meat had to be **eaten before morning**.

- While they were eating, they had to be dressed as if **ready to leave** – cloak tucked in, sandals on feet, staff in hand.

- That night God would **kill all the first born** (human and animals) except those of the Israelites who had painted the **blood of the lamb** on their **door frames** – He would **pass over** them.

Interpreting the story

> Themes
> 1, 2 and 8

- Passover marks the start of one of the key events in Israel's history, the **Exodus**. The Exodus is a sign that God sides with those who are oppressed and those who suffer injustice. During the Exodus, Moses received the **Law** at Sinai. Eventually the end of the Exodus was marked when **Joshua** brought the Israelites into the Promised Land.

- The symbol of **exodus** is used by the later prophets to describe God's **covenant relationship** with His people. Isaiah says that although God **punishes** those who stray from His commandments, He also 'leads them out' of suffering and **rewards** those who repent.

- The **first month** in the Jewish calendar is Nisan (March/April in the calendar). Passover night for Jews today begins on 14 Nisan.

- God's command to **eat the lamb** at home stresses the Jewish importance of the **family**.

- Jews today place some of the roasted lamb shank bone on a plate at Passover, but it is not eaten.

- **Bitter herbs** symbolise the suffering of the Jews when they were slaves in Egypt and all the other times when they have suffered (for example, when exiled to Babylon in 586 B.C.E. and during the Holocaust).

- Today the bitter herbs are dipped into **haroset**, a mixture of nuts and dates which symbolises the cement the Jewish slaves used to build Pharaoh's store houses.

- **Unleavened bread** is a reminder that there was no time to bake bread with yeast. It was also eaten at the beginning of the spring barley harvest and therefore symbolises **new beginnings**. The Jews remove leaven as an offering to God and a sign of sacrifice or dedication.

- Rather than eating the Passover **meal in haste**, Jews are now encouraged to lean on the table as a sign of being free. Passover reminds people that **freedom** is one of the most important aspects of human society and is not to be taken for granted.

- God's **passing over** the Israelites is a sign of God's love and **generosity** which the later prophets considered to be a characteristic of His **covenant** relationship with Israel.

Evaluating the story
Should God take sides?
Points to consider:

- **On the one hand ...** God should not take sides because this suggests that He favours some people more than others and He is supposed to love all people equally. Some argue that if God is a god of justice then to be biased towards some people more than others shows that He cannot really be omnipotent (all powerful) because He is acting emotionally, like a human being.

- **On the other hand ...** if justice means righting wrongs, then it is right to treat those who have suffered unfairly first. This is what it means for God to take sides because He is a just and generous God who is prepared to be involved in human history.

Does the Passover, which happened three thousand years ago, teach us anything today?
Points to consider:

- **On the one hand ...** Passover is a powerful story about leadership, bravery, risk-taking and trust and therefore can continue to inspire Jews and non-Jews alike. Some argue that Jesus used the Passover symbols to teach about the meaning of his sacrificial death. Some also point out that Martin Luther King used the Exodus/Passover idea to inspire the people to march to Washington to protest against racial injustice.

- **On the other hand ...** life three thousand years ago was very different from now and the Passover is unrealistic in terms of how we can achieve justice today. For example, painting blood on doorposts and eating unleavened bread sounds more like magic than genuine religious behaviour. It is unfair that innocent Egyptian children and animals should have died simply because they did not carry out these strange commands.

1.4 Crossing the sea

Read Exodus 14:10–31

Knowing the story

- When the Israelites saw **Pharaoh** and his **army chasing them** they were afraid and wished they had **stayed as slaves in Egypt**.

- **Moses** told them to have **courage** and **believe that God** would fight for them.

- God instructed Moses to **raise his staff and stretch out his hand** over the sea to divide it – this would prove to the Egyptians that He was God.

- Then the **pillar of cloud** moved **behind** the Israelites, between them and the Egyptian army.

- Moses stretched out his hand and **all night God made the east wind blow** and **part the waters**.

- The Israelites then walked over the **dry land**.

- The **Egyptians marched after** them.

- Towards the **end of the night** God made the **wheels** of the Egyptian **chariots come off** which threw them into **confusion**.

- The Egyptians realised that **God was on the side of the Israelites**.

- God ordered Moses to stretch out his **hand over the waters again**.

- He did so and at **daybreak** the sea returned and **drowned all of Pharaoh's army**.

- When the Israelites saw this, they put their **trust in God and Moses**, His servant.

Themes 1, 2 and 5

Interpreting the story

- Moses probably passed over the **northern end of the Red Sea or Sea of Reeds** on his way from Egypt to the Sinai desert (and then on to the Promised Land).

- **Moses** is completely **obedient to God's will** and although the people doubt him, by the end of the story they recognise and trust him as **God's loyal servant**.

- The sea here is a reminder of the **waters of chaos** which God separated when He created the **world** or **dry land** (according to Genesis 1).

- The **sea** symbolises both **death and new life**.

- Passing through the sea on **dry land** symbolises a moment of **new creation**, new life and renewed hope.

- The **wall of water** is a symbol of **God's protection** against evil; it does not have to be taken literally.

- **Christians** interpret the passing through the Red Sea as a symbol of baptism when one passes from one's **old life of** sin, washing it away to live a **new spiritual life**.

- The story is about **liberation** and freedom – **politically** and **spiritually**. The Israelites are no longer **political slaves** in Egypt; they are also now **spiritually free** to worship God.

- The **cloud** symbolises God's presence on Earth. The **Jewish** rabbis called this the **Shekinah** of God. The 'cloud' leads the Israelites by inspiring them.

- The crossing of the sea forms a very important moment in the **exodus** from Egypt to freedom. Exodus means **way out** and inspires Jews and Christians today to campaign for **freedom** and **justice**.

Evaluating the story

Does it matter whether the crossing of the sea actually took place?
Points to consider:

- **On the one hand ...** it does matter because it shows how God is actually involved in the world and sides with those who have been unfairly treated and acts to bring about justice. God gave Moses and the people the courage not to be defeated by the Egyptians but to seek freedom.

- **On the other hand ...** it doesn't matter if it actually took place because the story is about individuals and the way they have to overcome their fears and weaknesses to be inspired by God to achieve good.

Is it fair of God to allow the Egyptians to die?
Points to consider:

- **On the one hand ...** God is fair because He is protecting the Israelites who as slaves in Egypt had no power and were used by Pharaoh to make bricks. Many died because of this hard labour. The death of the Egyptians simply reversed the conditions and the Egyptians then experienced what they had inflicted on the Hebrew slaves.

- **On the other hand ...** it is not fair of God because He should care for all humans equally. If it was wrong for the Egyptians to exploit the Hebrew slaves and allow many of them to die or to suffer, then it must also be wrong for God to make the Egyptians suffer and die.

1.5 Elijah at Zarephath

Read 1 Kings 17:8–24

Knowing the story

- God commanded Elijah to go to a place called Zarephath where he would meet a **widow** who would **give him food**.

- Elijah did as he was commanded and met the widow at the **town gate**, where she was picking up sticks.

- Elijah asked her to give him a **drink** and some **bread** to eat.

- She replied that she had no bread and only a **handful of flour in a jar** and some **oil in a jug** – enough to feed her son and **then die**.

- Elijah told her to make enough bread for him and for herself and her son – reassuring her that the flour and oil would **not run out** until the **drought in Israel had ended**.

- The widow did as Elijah instructed, and she fed her family.

- Some time later the widow's **son was very ill** and he stopped breathing.

- The widow **blamed Elijah**, saying that the boy's death was due to Elijah's **judgement of her sin**.

- Elijah carried the dead boy to his room, cried out to God and **stretched himself** on the boy's body **three times**.

- God heard Elijah's call and **restored the boy** to life.

- Elijah returned the boy to his mother and said, **'Look, your son is alive!'**

- The **widow responded** that she now knew Elijah was a **man of God** and the words he spoke from God were **true**.

Interpreting the story

Themes
2 and 5

- The background to the story is that there had been a drought in Israel for some time as God's judgement and **punishment** of the people who were worshipping the god Baal.

- Although **Zarephath** is outside Israel, God had punished the people there because of their worship of Baal.

- The drought explains why the woman says she only has enough flour and oil for one last meal before she and her son die of starvation.

- As a **widow**, the woman is **very poor**. She has no husband to provide for her and her son is too young to earn money.

- The **miracle of the flour and oil** symbolises God's care, love and **generosity** and demonstrates that He is far **greater than Baal** who has none of these qualities.

- The miracle of the bread is also a reminder of God's generosity in the **wilderness** when He provided **manna** (bread) for Moses and the Israelites.

- The second part of the story shows that the miracle of the flour and oil is not enough for the woman to **believe and trust** that Elijah is a prophet of the true God and not Baal. God therefore performs the greater miracle of giving life.

- Elijah touches the boy's dead body even though it would have been considered **unclean**.

- The miracle of the **widow's son's return to life** symbolises the power of God to bring **life out of death** and **hope out of despair** – God **forgives her sins**.

Evaluating the story
Are natural disasters really signs of God's judgement?
Points to consider:

- **On the one hand ...** natural disasters can be explained scientifically and without the need to refer to God. Natural disasters are not disasters unless they affect humans and cause harm. In these cases, humans have to think what they can do to improve how they live alongside nature.

- **On the other hand ...**if God is the creator of the world, then He can use nature as a means of rewarding and punishing humans. If one believes that miracles are signs of God's action in the world, then natural disasters may also be signs of God's judgement.

Is the miracle of the dead boy just a symbol of hope over despair?
Points to consider:

- **On the one hand ...** it is unlikely the boy was actually dead; he was probably in a deep coma. Elijah's actions helped to revive him and he then used this to teach about not giving up and having hope that good can emerge out of suffering.

- **On the other hand ...** we don't know everything about the world, so it is possible that God revived the dead boy. A miracle may be a symbol of hope over despair but it is more than this because as it actually happened, it points to God's presence in the world.

Does the story teach anything about true faith?
Points to consider:

- **On the one hand ...** the story teaches very little about true faith. The woman's faith in God disappears when her son dies and she only believes in God once her son is brought back to life. True faith should not need 'proofs' of this kind – this is also the lesson Thomas learned at Jesus' resurrection.

- **On the other hand ...** the miracle of the bread would not have worked had Elijah not seen the woman's trust in God to provide. The death of her son did not shake her faith in God but showed her that her sins could be forgiven.

1.6 Elijah at Carmel

Read 1 Kings 18:19–39

Knowing the story

- Elijah challenged 450 **prophets of Baal** and 400 **prophets of Asherah** to a contest at **Mount** Carmel.

- Elijah told the people that they had to choose between the worship of **God** and the worship of **Baal**.

- **Two bulls** were cut in **pieces** and placed on two piles of wood but not set alight.
- Whichever **god set the pile alight** would be the **true god**.
- The prophets of Baal called on their god, but **nothing happened.**
- Elijah teased them and told them to shout louder to **wake Baal up**, but nothing happened.
- Elijah built an altar of **12 stones** (one for each of the 12 tribes of Israel) and then poured **four jars of water** on the wood **three times.**
- Elijah prayed to God; God sent **fire to consume the sacrifice.**
- The people shouted, **'The Lord – he is God! The Lord – he is God!'**

Themes
1, 2, 3 and 4

Interpreting the story

- The drought had **lasted over three years**, so many had started to worship the **Canaanite** god **Baal** who was the **god of rain.**
- **Elijah** was Israel's greatest **prophet** and believed that **only God** should be worshipped.
- **Waking up Baal** was part of usual Canaanite worship but Elijah used it to **tease** and taunt the prophets of Baal.
- The **12 stones** Elijah used symbolised the **whole nation** (ten tribes in the south and two in the north).
- Elijah's prayer was **simple** and direct compared to those of the other prophets.
- The people's cry that God is one is contained in the most important **Jewish prayer** today called the **Shema.**

Evaluating the story
Should violence be used to defend one's beliefs?
Points to consider:

- **On the one hand ...** in some extreme cases it is right to defend one's beliefs against those who would be prepared to harm or even kill you. Use of force is also a symbol of the power of belief.
- **On the other hand ...** the use of violence never really persuades people. Oscar Romero believed that true change comes only when people act together in faith and solidarity. Defending one's beliefs might mean having to die for them, as he did.

Are celebrities today's false gods?
Points to consider:

- **On the one hand ...** no celebrity can ever live up to people's hopes and expectations. The 'perfect' lives they live are created by the media and give people false expectations of what can be achieved in life.
- **On the other hand ...** society admires successful people. Celebrities give people hope and they demonstrate what humans can achieve. They are only false when they misuse their success and power.

1.7 The paralysed man

Read Mark 2:1–12

Knowing the story

- **Jesus** was at **Capernaum.**
- There were so many people there that **four men** who carried a **paralysed man** could not get near Jesus.

- They therefore climbed on to the **roof** of the house, dug a hole in it and **lowered the man down**.
- When Jesus saw their **faith**, he said to the paralysed man that his **sins were forgiven**.
- The **lawyers** present **criticised** Jesus and said his words were blasphemy – **only God can forgive sins**.
- Jesus asked the **lawyers** whether it was easier to **forgive sins** or to **heal**.
- To prove that the Son of Man had **authority** to forgive sins, Jesus told the man to **pick up his mat** and go home.
- Everyone was **amazed** as the paralysed man picked his mat and walked.

Interpreting the story

Themes
2, 5 and 6

- In the first century, some **illnesses** were considered to be punishment by God for **sin**.
- Jesus cured the paralysed man because of the **faith** of the **four friends**.
- **Blasphemy** is when a person sets themselves up to be equal with God.
- Jesus was accused by the lawyers of blasphemy. The **punishment for blasphemy** in Jewish law could be the death penalty.
- Jesus' answer was to show his concern for the man's **body** and **soul** equally.
- By saying he was the **Son of Man**, Jesus was not claiming to be God but rather that he was acting with **God's blessing**.
- So, Jesus' command to pick up his mat avoids any **direct** blasphemy, but the lawyers know that **indirectly** he is also forgiving the man's sins.
- The people were **amazed** partly because the **lawyers could not think of a reply** to Jesus' words and partly because the man got up and walked.

Evaluating the story
Do healing miracles happen today?
Points to consider:

- **On the one hand ...** God can and does work in ways that we do not understand. There are many reported healings at Lourdes, for example, which doctors cannot explain.
- **On the other hand ...** there are better ways of explaining unusual cures. The mind can sometimes give people unusual inner strength. In many cases 'cures' turn out to be short term and it is clear there has been no miracle.

Is it wrong for doctors to assist very sick people to die?
Points to consider:

- **On the one hand ...** it is cruel to make someone go through a lot of pain and it would be more caring and loving to end their lives when they want to do so with their family around them.
- **On the other hand ...** it is never right deliberately to shorten a person's life by killing him or her. The hospice movement is a much better alternative: assisting very sick people and allowing them a dignified death.

1.8 The calming of the storm

Read Mark 4:35–41

Knowing the story

- Jesus told his disciples to cross the Sea of Galilee by **boat to the other side**.

- A **storm suddenly blew** up and waves washed over the side of the boat.

- The boat was **full of water**.

- **Jesus** was **asleep** in the stern of the boat.

- The **disciples woke him** and asked him whether he cared if they were to drown.

- Jesus **commanded** the **wind** to be **quiet** and the **waves** to be **still**.

- There was a **great calm**.

- Jesus asked the **disciples** why they were **afraid** and **lacked faith**.

- The disciples were **terrified**.

- They **wondered who Jesus was** that the wind and waves obeyed him.

Themes
3, 5 and 6

Interpreting the story

- This is a **nature miracle**. Nature miracles are often **more spectacular** than healing miracles and usually do not require faith in order for Jesus to perform them.

- Nature miracles illustrate **Jesus' divine powers** because just as God is described in Genesis 1 as creating the **heavens** and the **Earth**, Jesus is also able to control them.

- The wind represents the forces of the heavens, the waves the forces of the Earth.

- This power to control nature led the **disciples to ask who Jesus is** – the only answer is **God**.

- The disciples' **fear** was due to the belief at that time that **deep waters** and **storms** were associated with the **powers of evil** which cause **human suffering**.

- The story might be interpreted more as a parable about our **inner fears** ('storms') and how we can overcome them (faith in God's care).

- The **contrast** is between **Jesus' complete trust in God** (he sleeps) and the disciples' **noisy fear**.

Evaluating the story
Do nature miracles prove that Jesus is God?
Points to consider:

- **On the one hand ...** if nature miracles work by suspending the laws of physics, then only God is capable of doing this without upsetting all the other laws of nature. If we believe Jesus was able to perform nature miracles, then it follows he must be God.

- **On the other hand ...** nature miracles are really stories or symbols about life. In this story, the storm represents all the suffering and evil in the world. Nature miracles are not there to prove Jesus was God but as a parable to contrast his faith in God with our own failings.

Are there evil powers in the world?
Points to consider:

- **On the one hand ...** there are evil powers in the world because there are some people who have done terrible things which no ordinary person would do. As these people are not thinking in a human way, then it is clear they are in some way possessed by an evil power.

- **On the other hand ...** there are no evil powers because as in the story of the calming of the storm, Jesus trusts in God and does not believe in the superstitious 'evil powers' which frighten his disciples. Evil people are not possessed, they are just very bad people.

1.9 The feeding of the five thousand

Read Mark 6:30–44

Knowing the story

- **Jesus' disciples** reported to him all that they had **done** and **taught**.
- There were so **many people** that they **hadn't a chance to eat**.
- Jesus took them in a **boat** to a **quiet place** to be alone, but many people knew where he was going and **got there before him**.
- As it was **late**, the disciples told Jesus to **send the crowd** away.
- Jesus told the **disciples to feed the crowd**.
- They said they hadn't **enough money to buy food** for that many people.
- Jesus asked them what food they had.
- They replied **five loaves** and **two fishes**.
- Jesus sat the people down in **groups**.
- He took the bread and **looked up to heaven**, **gave thanks**, **broke** it and **gave** it to the disciples to **distribute**.
- He did the same with the fish.
- Everyone ate and was **full**.
- The disciples picked up **12 baskets** of leftover bread and fish.
- There were **five thousand men** there.

Themes
1, 5, 7 and 8

Interpreting the story

- Jesus' **disciples** are presented in very **human terms**. They are tired at the end of a long day and want to send the crowds away. Jesus challenges them – it is never too late to enter the Kingdom of God.
- The meal is a reminder of the way God **fed the Israelites in the wilderness** with **manna** or bread (Exodus 16).
- The meal is a **foretaste** of the **heavenly** messianic banquet, the fulfilment of the **Kingdom of God** – the time of **peace**, **justice** and **contentment**.
- The **five loaves** symbolise the **five books of the Torah**; the **12 baskets** symbolise the **12 tribes of Israel**. Both symbols illustrate that the Kingdom of God is the fulfilment of the Torah and the birth a new community (the Church).
- The people were all **full** because in the Kingdom of God everyone will be **mentally** and **spiritually satisfied**.
- Jesus' **actions** of blessing, breaking and giving point towards the Last Supper and **Holy Communion**. Holy Communion is also a foretaste of the Kingdom of God.

Evaluating the story
Did Jesus actually produce more food from nowhere?
Points to consider:

- **On the one hand ...** if God could provide manna for the Israelites in the wilderness then there is no reason why Jesus, as God's son, could not do the same. In both cases, the bread symbolises God's care for His people and His generosity – both signs of the Kingdom of God to come.

- **On the other hand ...** the real miracle was that the people were so inspired by Jesus' teaching on generosity and equality that they all shared the little they had – so much so that they found they had more than enough. The feeding was a dramatic parable of life in the Kingdom of God.

Are miracles just important insights into the world?
Points to consider:

- **On the one hand ...** miracles do not break the laws of nature but are dramatic moments when we see the world in a new way. For example, the birth of a new child is a miracle because we are reminded how extraordinary life is. However, birth is an everyday event in nature.

- **On the other hand ...** miracles have to be more than merely insight. They are extraordinary moments when the most unlikely or even impossible things happen. If God is the creator of the universe, then only He has the ability to do these things; this is why miracles are especially important moments for confirming belief in God.

1.10   The Transfiguration

Read Mark 9:2–13

Knowing the story

- **Jesus** took Peter, **James** and **John** up a **high mountain**.

- **Jesus** was transfigured.

- His **clothes** were **dazzling white**.

- **Elijah** and **Moses** appeared, **talking** to Jesus.

- **Peter** suggested that they **build three shelters** for Moses, Elijah and Jesus.

- A cloud appeared and from it a **voice** spoke.

- The voice said 'This is my **Son** whom I love. **Listen** to him.'

- Suddenly Moses and Elijah had gone and only Jesus was there.

- **On the way down**, Jesus told the disciples **not to tell anyone** what they had seen.

- The disciples asked Jesus why **Elijah** must come first.

- Jesus explained that **Elijah** must come first to **restore society**.

- In fact he had already arrived.

- So now Jesus, as the **Son of Man**, would **suffer** many things.

Interpreting the story

| Themes |
| 2, 6, 7 and 8 |

- The **Transfiguration** reveals to the disciples Jesus' **divine identity** as God's son.

- Transfiguration means a **change in a person's appearance**.

- The event describes the **disciples' spiritual experience** of who Jesus is.

- In their **vision**, the disciples saw Moses and Elijah: **Moses** represents the **Law** and **Elijah** represents Jewish **prophecy**.

- **Jesus** is **greater** than these two figures and therefore is the **fulfilment** of the **Law** and the **hope of the prophets**.

- This is another example of the **Messianic Secret**. On their way down the mountain, Jesus tells the disciples to keep his identity to themselves.

- It was believed that **Elijah** would come to prepare the people for the Messiah. So, if **John the Baptist fulfils Elijah's** role, then **Jesus is the Messiah**.

- Once again Jesus uses the title **Son of Man** to speak of his sufferings, relating back to **Isaiah's** suffering servant.

Evaluating the story

If Peter saw Jesus revealed as the Son of God *at the Transfiguration, why did he later deny knowing him?*
Points to consider:

- **On the one hand ...** Peter may not have fully understood what he experienced in the vision of the Transfiguration. Or he may have thought that when Jesus was being interrogated by the Jewish authorities, if he were God's son he could have easily escaped. He was confused and therefore denied knowing him.

- **On the other hand ...** although Peter may have understood some of the vision, it took a long time for it to make complete sense. It was probably not until the Resurrection when Peter experienced the risen Jesus that he realised that this was the same Jesus he had experienced in the Transfiguration.

Do religious experiences tell us anything about God?
Points to consider:

- **On the one hand ...** a religious experience makes a great impression on a person and they feel they have come into direct contact with God. This means that God is not just an idea but alive and real. Many people feel that they have experienced God's loving presence through nature, music or art.

- **On the other hand ...** religious experience is unreliable; it might just be our own emotional response to something. Often people claim to have experienced God when they are upset and need comforting, so it could be a form of wish fulfilment.

1.11 The Crucifixion

Read Mark 15:22–39

Knowing the story

- The soldiers brought Jesus to Golgotha.

- They offered Jesus **wine mixed with myrrh** but he refused it.

- The soldiers **crucified** him.

- They **cast lots** for his clothes.

- The charge above Jesus' head read: '**The King of the Jews**'.

- **Two robbers** were crucified with him.

- **Passers-by taunted** him by saying that if he was able to knock down the Temple and rebuild it in three days, he could also save himself from the cross.

- Members of the **Sanhedrin** mocked him by saying that although he saved others he could not save himself.

- At **noon** and for three hours the land was plunged into **darkness**.

- At three in the **afternoon** Jesus cried out 'Eloi, Eloi lama sabachthani', which means '**My God, my God, why have you forsaken me?**'.

- Some thought he was **calling for Elijah**.

- One man offered him a **sponge soaked in wine vinegar** on the end of a stick.

- He wondered whether Elijah would now save Jesus.

- Jesus **died** with a **loud cry**.

- The **curtain of the Temple** was torn in **two from top to bottom**.

- When the **centurion** saw how Jesus had died, he said, '**Surely this man was the Son of God**'.

Interpreting the story

Themes
2, 6, 7 and 8

- **Pilate** has just ordered the Crucifixion of Jesus because he probably thought if Jesus was considered some kind of king by his followers, then this was **treason against Caesar** and the Roman punishment for treason was the **death penalty**.

- Jesus refuses the **drugged wine** because he wants to be conscious and for those who have crucified him to see that he is not afraid and for them to be aware that they are killing an innocent person.

- **Dividing up his clothes** shows that the only thing the **soldiers value** about Jesus are his possessions, not him as a person.

- Jesus quotes from **Psalm 22** when he **cries from the cross** and asks for God's help. His cry might sound as though he thinks God has abandoned him.

- Many of the details of Jesus' death are from the **prophet Isaiah's** description of a **suffering servant** (Isaiah 53) who dies at the hands of those who mock him. The servant's death causes those who mock him to repent of their sin.

- Jesus' death is also a **sacrifice** for human **sin**. As the **suffering servant**, his death is an offering to God as a **ransom** to pay off human sin and restore people's relationship with God.

- Jesus' death is therefore an atonement for sin by making humans 'at one' with God.

- The atonement is symbolised by the tearing of the **Temple curtain** in two which shows that the **barrier between God and humans** has been **removed**.

- **The Temple curtain** separated the Holy of Holies from the ordinary people.

- The **darkness** at noon symbolises the **sin of the world**.

- The **centurion** who is guarding the crosses is a Roman and therefore probably not a believer in the one God; however, he is moved by Jesus' dignified death and trust in God and he comes to believe Jesus is either a great **immortal hero** (like Hercules) or actually **God's son**.

Evaluating the story
Was it really necessary for Jesus to die?
Points to consider:

- **On the one hand ...** in an imperfect world the sacrifice of a few is necessary to save the lives of others. This is what happened in the story of the miracle on the River Kwai when a soldier gave up his life to save hundreds of others from being executed. Jesus' death was necessary to take away the sins of the world.

- **On the other hand ...** Jesus did not intend to die and his teachings and healings were sufficient to make his message about God's Kingdom clear. His death was unfortunate but not necessary.

Did the centurion believe Jesus was God?
Points to consider:

- **On the one hand ...** as a Roman, the centurion would have believed that great humans on Earth would be rewarded after death by becoming immortal as sons of the gods. So, although the centurion is impressed by Jesus, he did not think he was God.

- **On the other hand ...** the story intends us to think that the centurion did think of Jesus as the Son of God because he is the first to experience the new relationship Jesus established with God once the Temple curtain had been symbolically torn down.

1.12 The Resurrection

Read John 20:24–9

Knowing the story

- **Thomas** had not been with the disciples when they met the risen Jesus.
- He said he would **not believe** unless he had seen Jesus' marks of crucifixion.
- A week later, Jesus **passed through** the **locked doors** and said, '**Peace be with you.**'
- He told Thomas to put his **finger in the marks on his hands and side.**
- He said, 'Stop doubting and believe.'
- Thomas said, '**My Lord and my God**'.
- Jesus said that those who **believe without seeing are also blessed.**

Interpreting the story

<table>
<tr><td>Themes
2, 4, 6 and 8</td></tr>
</table>

- Various people before Thomas had encountered the resurrected Jesus. Each recognised him in different ways.
- **Mary Magdalene** thought at first the resurrected Jesus was a **gardener** until he spoke her name and then she realised who he was.
- Then the **disciples** experienced the resurrected Jesus in a **locked room** and knew it was him because he showed them the crucifixion marks on his hands and side.
- The purpose of the story of **Thomas** is to show that Jesus **was not a ghost** but **real.**
- The resurrected Jesus teaches Thomas that belief in the Resurrection has to be based on **experiencing God's presence** and the accounts of others, not on direct physical proof.
- Jesus' resurrected body is **not like an ordinary body because** it can appear and disappear. It is hard to know exactly what this means. Some believe the resurrected Jesus had a special **spiritual 'body'.**
- For Christians, the Resurrection is the **climax of Jesus' life and mission** and shows how death, sin, evil and suffering can be overcome.

Evaluating the story

Does belief in Jesus' resurrection require physical evidence?
Points to consider:

- **On the one hand ...** Thomas was allowed to touch Jesus' wounds in order to be convinced that his resurrection was real and that Jesus was not a figment of his imagination. Today people find evidence such as the Turin Shroud and paranormal experiences useful in supporting the idea of Jesus' resurrection.
- **On the other hand ...** the main evidence comes from the long line of Christians who have passed on their experience of the Resurrection to one another. Jesus blessed those who believed without seeing.

Is there any evidence for life after death?
Points to consider:

- **On the one hand ...** humans are more than just bodies – our personalities indicate that we have souls. No one was expecting Jesus to be resurrected but he was, which provides evidence that our souls may continue to exist after death.

- **On the other hand ...** there is no hard evidence for life after death – when a person dies their body rots and that is the end. Anything else is just wishful thinking and an attempt to give us hope that death is not the end.

> Practise answering questions with *Theology, Philosophy and Religion 13+ Exam Practice Questions and Answers* pages 1–2 and 31–35.

Test yourself

1 On which day did God create human beings?

2 What did God say His name was at the burning bush?

3 How were the Israelites to use the blood of the lambs at the first Passover?

4 What happened to the Egyptian chariots at the crossing of the sea?

5 Why did the widow of Zarephath blame Elijah?

6 What did Elijah say would be the sign of the true God at the Carmel contest?

7 What was the lawyers' criticism of Jesus when he said the paralysed man's sins were forgiven?

8 What did the disciples say to Jesus when he was asleep in the boat during the storm?

9 What did Jesus do when he was given the bread at the feeding of the five thousand people?

10 Who appeared with Jesus when he was transfigured?

11 What did Jesus cry from the cross at Golgotha?

12 What did Thomas say when the resurrected Jesus allowed him to touch him?

Human responses to God

Read *Theology and Philosophy for Common Entrance 13+* pages 49–91.

In this topic, you will be looking at another dimension of theology and that is how belief in God affects how people behave. This area of theology is concerned with the nature of human beings – why people do good and evil. It also looks at the nature of belief and what it means to be obedient to God's commands and how we can know what it is that God demands of us.

Themes

As well as knowing the set stories you will also be tested on the following themes:

1 Human nature – what are people like?

2 Human responses to God and His commands – how do people react to God?

3 Human responses to Creation

4 Requirements of discipleship and responding to God

5 Different types of vocation

6 The nature of belief, faith and commitment

7 Consequences of faith and disobedience

You will see that these themes are referred to in each of the stories in this chapter, in the Interpreting the story sections.

2.1a The Garden of Eden

Read Genesis 2:4–25

Knowing the story

- **Before any shrub** had appeared, God created **man** or Adam.

- God made **Adam** from the **dust of the Earth** and **breathed** life into him.

- God planted a **garden** in **Eden**.

- In the middle of Eden there were **two trees**: the tree of **life** and the tree of **knowledge** of good and evil.

- A **river watered the garden**.

- God placed **Adam in Eden** and told him to care for it but **not to eat** from the tree of knowledge.

- God created the **animals from the ground** and brought them to Adam to **name them**.

- God said it was **not good for Adam to be alone** so He would make him a 'helper'.

- But **none** of the animals **were suitable helpers** for Adam.

- So, God put Adam into a **deep sleep** and took one of his **ribs** from which He created a woman, **Eve**.

- Adam and Eve were **naked**, but they were **not ashamed** of their nakedness.

Interpreting the story

- This **second Genesis** story (see pages 2–3 for the first Creation story) focuses on God's **special relationship with humans**. The first Creation story focused on God and His Creation.

- Adam at first is **not a person** or a **human being**, but just dust or a **collection of atoms** as we might say today.

- God **breathes soul** or **spirit** into him which makes him a **person** with thoughts and feelings.

- God's breath shows there is a **special spiritual relationship** between humans and Himself.

- The special relationship between Adam and God is shown by the way Adam **names the living creatures**, just as **God named all the parts** of His Creation in Genesis 1.

- Adam is a **steward** of the world; he has **freedom** to act on God's behalf.

- The command **not to eat from the tree of knowledge** gives man the **freedom** to obey or disobey God.

- The man/woman relationship between Adam and Eve is **very close** – they **complement** each, both being **companions** to each other.

- Men and women have a **natural sexual attraction** to each other which is why they marry and have children.

Evaluating the story

Are men and women equal?
Points to consider:

- **On the one hand ...** men and women are equal because they are both equally intelligent and, given the same opportunities, both can achieve the same results.

- **On the other hand ...** because men and women are physically different and have very different emotions, they are not equal and should be treated differently.

Is the environment there for humans to use as they wish?
Points to consider:

- **On the one hand ...** humans are competitive, so the environment is for them to use to survive and for their own purposes.

- **On the other hand ...** humans are naturally generous and because they are closely related to animals then they have a duty to treat the environment with respect, not only for themselves and animals but also for plant forms which sustain human existence.

2.1b Adam and Eve

Read Genesis 3

Knowing the story

- The **serpent** tempted the woman to eat from the **tree of knowledge**.

- The serpent told Eve that she would not die if she ate from the tree but she would become like God and **know good and evil.**

- **Eve** took some **fruit** from the tree and ate it.

- She gave some to Adam.

- When they ate it they became aware they were **naked** and they made themselves clothes.

- When they **heard God** walking in the garden they **hid**.

- Adam said to God they had hidden because they were **naked**.

- God asked him whether he had eaten from the tree of knowledge.

- **Adam** said that Eve had given him some fruit from it.

- Eve said the **serpent** had deceived her.

- God **punished** the **serpent** by making it crawl on his belly and caused **humans** to be scared of him and try to kill him.

- God punished the woman by making **childbirth** painful and making her husband **rule over her**.

- God punished the man by making **work painful** and declaring that he will **die/ return to dust**.

- God made clothes for Adam and Eve and then **expelled** them from the Garden of Eden.

- God protected the **tree of life** by placing **cherubim** and a **flashing sword** round it.

Themes
1, 2 and 7

Interpreting the story

- **Eden** means **delight** and describes a paradise where everyone and everything works in **harmony**.

- Eating from the **tree of knowledge** means being able to survive on one's own without being **obedient** to God.

- Only God can be self-made without creating evil. Humans are unable to have this knowledge and remain good.

- The **serpent** symbolises **human desire**, **rebelliousness** and **deceitfulness**.

- Eve's act symbolises the human **desire for power**.

- Adam's act symbolises human **weakness** as he gives in to Eve.

- **Nakedness** symbolises **shame** and **conscience**. Adam and Eve know what they have done is wrong.

- The **punishments** symbolise the effects of **sin**. Sin means to cut one's self off from God, which is why Adam and Eve are **expelled** from Eden.

- The physical punishments symbolise the **pain** and suffering of ordinary life; the **inequality** of men and women's relationships; the **struggle** humans have with nature to survive.

- This event is called the Fall, because humans have now **fallen from grace** and their special relationship with God.

Evaluating the story
Are humans naturally generous?
Points to consider:

- **On the one hand ...** humans are naturally good but our environment and upbringing distort our naturally good nature.

- **On the other hand ...** all humans are deeply selfish and because biologically humans are programmed to survive, we never perform entirely generous actions. The story of the Fall indicates that humans are sinful, competitive and sometimes dangerous.

Is obedience to those in authority always good?
Points to consider:

- **On the one hand ...** if we fail to carry out the commands of those in authority then society might fall into chaos. Some think that leaders are there because God appoints them and that therefore society has a duty to obey these people, even if they are bad.

- **On the other hand ...** obedience to those in authority is only good if their commands are good. Some argue that obedience to bad commands is not justified and out of conscience society should disobey them, even if this causes problems.

2.2 Cain and Abel

Read Genesis 4:1–16

Knowing the story

- **Eve** gave birth to **Cain** and **Abel**.

- Abel was a **shepherd**.

- Cain grew **crops**.

- **Abel** offered sacrifices of **animals** to God which **God was pleased with**.

- **Cain** offered sacrifices of **crops** to God which **did not please God**.

- **Cain** was **angry**.

- God told Cain to control his anger otherwise sin, which was '**crouching at the door**', would overcome him.

- In the field **Cain killed Abel**.

- When God asked Cain where his brother was, Cain answered that he was not his '**brother's keeper**'.

- God replied that Abel's **blood** was crying from the ground and He would therefore **punish** Cain by making it impossible for him to grow crops successfully.

- God punished Cain further by making him **wander the Earth**.

- However, God **protected** Cain from being killed by placing a '**mark**' on him.

Interpreting the story

> Themes
> 1, 2 and 7

- Cain and Abel offered **sacrifices** as signs of their **gratitude** to God.

- God **rejected** Cain's offering because Cain's **motives** were bad. Cain is told that his offering will be accepted if he does the right thing. But he is not able to do this and he becomes angry and selfish.

- **Sin** is described as a demon waiting to pounce. Today this might be described in **psychological** terms to mean Cain has deep-seated anger.

- **Abel's blood** crying out refers to his **innocence**. **Blood** is also a symbol of **life**.

- The story teaches us a lot about the **nature of God**. God knows human thoughts and motives. He **desires** genuine worship from the heart. He punishes **fairly** (Cain could have been killed for the murder of Abel). He **cares** for the innocent. He **generously** gives people second chances.

- Cain's example shows the **development** and worsening of human sin from Genesis 3 through jealousy to anger to murder and then lying and denial.

- Cain's **wandering** explains the problems encountered in ancient societies between **city dwellers** and **nomads**.

Evaluating the story
Is jealousy always bad?
Points to consider:

- **On the one hand ...** jealousy can make people act in selfish and foolish ways and can even destroy them.

- **On the other hand ...** jealousy can be sometimes channelled into working harder to succeed and achieve great things.

Do humans ever act with entirely pure motives?
Points to consider:

- **On the one hand ...** humans may have complex reasons for doing things but many people try to overcome any less desirable motives and act for the best.

- **On the other hand ...** it is in human nature to survive and to act selfishly, so however good our motives might appear, they are in fact never pure. Humans have unconscious motives that may not always be clear to the individual.

2.3 Abraham

Read Genesis 22:1–19

Knowing the story

- God decided to **test Abraham**.

- Abraham was told to take his son **Isaac** to Mount Moriah and **sacrifice** him as a **burnt offering**.

- Early in the morning, Abraham set off with **wood** to make the fire for the burnt sacrifice.

- He left the servants behind and took Isaac to worship God.

- Isaac **carried the wood** and Abraham took the **knife**.

- Isaac asked why, when they had wood and fire, there was **no lamb** for the sacrifice.

- Abraham said **God would provide** the lamb.

- Abraham built the altar, **bound Isaac** and put him on top of the wood.

- As Abraham was about to kill Isaac, an **angel** told him to stop and that God now knew of Abraham's faith.

- Abraham saw a **ram caught by its horns in a bush** and he offered the **ram** as a sacrifice instead.

- The angel spoke for a second time and said that God would bless Abraham and make his **descendants as numerous as stars** in the sky and sand on the seashore.

- God also promised that He would give Abraham **land**.

Themes
2, 4 and 6

Interpreting the story

- There were many kinds of **sacrifices** in the ancient world. A sacrifice was a means of pleasing or thanking God by using food, produce or an animal.

- An **animal sacrifice** was the greatest offering because its **blood** represented **life**.

- An **atonement sacrifice** was a special sacrifice to God in the hope that He would **forgive the sins** of a person or people.

- God's command to Abraham was a **test**: it tested his **obedience** to God; it tested whether he was prepared to make the **ultimate sacrifice** of his son as a form of animal sacrifice.

- The action of the **angel** shows that **atonement** sacrifices should be based on **genuine faith**.

- God's agreement or **covenant** with Abraham is a **promise** that He will reward faith by making them a great nation with their own land to live in.

- **God's voice** might be explained today as human **conscience**.

Evaluating the story
Should we always obey our conscience?
Points to consider:

- **On the one hand ...** some, such as Dietrich Bonhoeffer, argue that some situations are so evil, such as Hitler's killing of the Jews, that obedience to conscience means disobeying the law for the greater good.

- **On the other hand ...** others argue that conscience is unreliable and could just be our own selfish desires 'speaking' to us. They argue that if everyone behaved like Bonhoeffer, law and order would break down.

Should we do everything that God commands?
Points to consider:

- **On the one hand ...** it is always necessary to obey God because He is the creator of the universe, He knows all things and He is all loving. Therefore, whatever He commands is good and must be obeyed.

- **On the other hand ...** God gives humans free will and reason to decide what is right so they should never do something that is bad simply because they think God may have commanded it.

Is Abraham a good role model for us today?
Points to consider:

- **On the one hand ...** Abraham's faith and obedience has inspired many, such as William Wilberforce who risked his reputation and helped to abolish the slave trade. He made society a better place to live in by protecting the poor and weak.

- **On the other hand ...** Abraham's blind faith is dangerous; the fact that he was prepared to kill his son shows that he is not a good role model.

2.4a David: David and Bathsheba

Read 2 Samuel 11:1–17

Knowing the story

- One evening in spring, David could see a **beautiful woman bathing** on her roof.

- He found out that she was Bathsheba, wife of Uriah **the Hittite**.

- David had sex with her and then later found she was **pregnant**.

- David told **Joab** to send **Uriah** home to report on the war to him.

- David hoped Uriah would **sleep** with Bathsheba but instead he slept at the **door of the palace**.

- Uriah said he could not go home while his **men were fighting**.

- The next evening David got Uriah **drunk** but Uriah **slept with the servants**.

- David sent a letter to Joab telling him to place Uriah in the **front line of the battle** and then to withdraw his troops so Uriah would be killed.

- Joab did as he was told and **Uriah was killed**.

- David was now **free to marry** Bathsheba.

Themes
1 and 6

Interpreting the story

- The proper role of the king was to **protect**, to be a 'shepherd of the people'. It would have been normal for the king to be leading the army in battle but David **was at home in his palace**.

- David's affair with Bathsheba and his attempt to cover it up show his **misuse of power**.

- David was ruled by **lust** and emotion, **not reason**, when he sent Uriah to his death.

- **Uriah's** virtuous character **contrasts** with **David's selfish** and immoral character.

- Uriah is **loyal**, trustworthy and considers others rather than himself.

- David is lustful, **devious** and dishonest.

Evaluating the story

Should one always obey the law even if the law is bad?
Points to consider:

- **On the one hand ...** people cannot always see the bigger picture and to disobey the law whenever they feel like it might lead to anarchy. Uriah obeyed David for this reason.

- **On the other hand ...** people should protest against unjust laws. Martin Luther King led a campaign of civil disobedience in America because of the unfair laws that discriminated against black people and, in the end, he succeeded.

Is a good leader one who puts people first?
Points to consider:

- **On the one hand ...** a good leader should use his talents to serve others first, just as David should have been a shepherd to the people.

- **On the other hand ...** a good leader is there to put the law, justice, business or the cause first. Business people, for example, have to make their businesses a success, otherwise everyone loses out.

Was David a good person?
Points to consider:

- **On the one hand ...** David was not a good person because he lied, cheated, killed and committed adultery.

- **On the other hand ...** although David was not blameless and he let power lead him astray, he did later repent of his actions and went on to do great things. Perhaps Bathsheba was to blame as she deliberately bathed where David might see her in the hope of seducing him.

2.4b David: David and Nathan

Read 2 Samuel 12:1–14

Knowing the story

- God sent Nathan to **David** to tell him a parable.

- In the parable there were two men, **one rich** and **one poor.**

- The rich man had a **lot of sheep** but the poor man had only **one little ewe lamb.**

- The ewe lamb was loved and part of the family, '**it was like a daughter to him'.**

- One day the rich man had to entertain a traveller but he did not want to use his own sheep so **he took the poor man's lamb** and prepared it for dinner.

- When David heard the parable, he was very angry and said the **rich man should die.**

- Nathan said, '**You are that man!'**

- **Nathan** told David that as king he should **not have killed Uriah** and slept with Bathsheba.

- Nathan told David that **God would now punish him:** he would see his wives taken away by one of his friends.

- David confessed that he had **sinned.**

- Nathan said that **God** would now **forgive** him; he would not die, but his **son would die instead.**

Themes 1, 2, 6 and 7

Interpreting the story

- Nathan was not only a **prophet** but acted as the **king's trusted advisor** and his **conscience.**

- Nathan **protected** David right up until David's death. He plotted with Bathsheba to make Solomon king after David (1 Kings 1).

- Nathan's parable was not intended to be a direct parallel to David's situation but an **example of a gross injustice.**

- Nathan **cleverly** used the poor man's action in the parable to show how **insensitive and crude the rich man is** by comparison.

- Nathan therefore got the reaction he wanted from David by arousing his **conscience.**

- David did not blame Nathan for his **bold criticism** but **admired** Nathan's skill and honesty.

- Nathan pointed out that David's reaction to a lesser crime had implications for him – if the rich man deserves the **death penalty** for stealing, what should happen to David? It is only because David **repented** that he received a **lesser punishment** (not the death penalty but his wives being taken away and the death of his son).

- Nathan teaches that God is **merciful. God does not desire the death of a sinner** but rather that he or she should change his or her way of life.

Evaluating the story

Should leaders and figures in authority be punished more than ordinary people if they misuse their power?
Points to consider:

- **On the one hand ...** leaders should be punished more because great authority means greater responsibility. If this responsibility is abused, then the punishment should be greater.

- **On the other hand ...** the law and punishments apply to all people equally. Although the infamous Dr Harold Shipman killed many of his patients, he was not condemned to death but imprisoned as the law demands.

Was David punished enough for his crimes?
Points to consider:

- **On the one hand ...** David was responsible for Uriah's murder and went out of his way to commit adultery, so both actions should have carried the death penalty. Even David thought that the rich man in Nathan's parable should have been executed.

- **On the other hand ...** kings, like David, and other people with social responsibilities, have much greater duties so we cannot judge them in quite the same way as we do ordinary people. David was punished enough.

2.5 The call of the disciples

Read Luke 5:1–11

Knowing the story

- **Jesus** was **teaching** a crowd by **Lake Gennesaret** (the Sea of Galilee).

- There wasn't enough space to teach. There were two boats on the shore.

- Jesus got into **Simon Peter's boat** and asked him to row out on the water.

- He taught the **people from the boat**.

- Then he told Simon Peter to go into the **deep waters** and put down his **nets**.

- **Simon Peter** said they had worked all night and **caught nothing so far**.

- But he did as Jesus said and caught a **huge number of fish**.

- The **fishermen** in the **other boat** rowed out and also **filled their boat** with fish.

- **Simon Peter** fell at Jesus' feet and said that he was **not worthy of Jesus** because he was a **sinner**.

- Jesus told him **not to be afraid**.

- He said that from now on they were to **'fish for people'**.

- The fishermen **left everything** and followed Jesus.

Interpreting the story

> **Themes**
> 4, 5, 6 and 7

- The story makes a **contrast** between the **faith of the large crowds** and **Peter's lack of faith**.

- The catch of the large number of fish is a **symbol** of the **large number of Jesus' followers**.

- Filling the boat is a **symbol** of the **Kingdom of God bringing fulfilment** and abundant joy.

- **Peter's confession** to Jesus shows that he **understands** the **symbol** of the catch of fish and that he is **not worthy of the Kingdom of God**.

- Peter's **humility** is just what is needed to make him a **good disciple**.

- The disciples are to **transfer** their skills as fishermen to become **disciples** and **preach**.

- Leaving their nets shows the **sacrifice** needed to become a disciple.

Evaluating the story

Does having faith in God mean one should never doubt His existence?
Points to consider:

- **On the one hand ...** doubt implies a lack of faith. If a person doubts God's existence then they are not a true follower. Faith in God does not require proof of His existence.

- **On the other hand ...** doubt is a sign that a person realises that he or she cannot know everything. Peter's humility in front of Jesus was a way of showing that faith also means having to trust in things we do not always fully understand.

Is loving one's family more important than loving God?
Points to consider:

- **On the one hand ...** religion can sometimes break up families and this can never be right. Christianity teaches the importance of marriage and duties to parents so it could never be the case that the love of God means leaving one's family.

- **On the other hand ...** Jesus never taught that a person should not love their family but he did teach that it is important to be clear what values should be placed first. As God is all powerful and all loving, then there may be times when loving and being obedient to God must be more important.

2.6 The Good Samaritan

Read Luke 10:25–37

Knowing the story

- A **lawyer** asked Jesus, 'Teacher, what must I do to **inherit eternal life**?'.

- **Jesus** asked him what the **law** said.

- The lawyer answered that he should **love God** and **love his neighbour** as himself.

- The lawyer asked Jesus '**Who is my neighbour**?'.

- Jesus answered with a parable:

  - A man was travelling from **Jerusalem** to **Jericho**.

  - **Robbers** attacked him, **beat** him up and left him for **dead**.

  - A **priest** saw the man but **crossed** to the other side of the road to avoid him.

  - A **Levite** saw the man and **crossed** to the other side of the road.

  - A **Samaritan** saw him and took **pity** on him, treating and bandaging his wounds.

  - He took him to an **inn** and looked after him.

  - The next day he gave the **innkeeper money** to take care of the man and promised to reimburse him for any further expenses.

- Jesus asked the lawyer who was the **neighbour** to the man.

- The lawyer answered that it was the one who had **mercy** on him.

- Jesus told him to go and **act** in the same way.

Themes
1, 4 and 6

Interpreting the story

- The **traditional Jewish** answer to the question 'Who is my neighbour?' would be '**other Jews**'.

- The point of the parable illustrates the prejudices people have about who is worthy to be considered a neighbour.

- In Jewish law, a **dead body** and blood were considered **religiously unclean**.

- If the **priest** was on his way to the Temple, he could **not touch the body** because he would not then have been allowed into the Temple.

- A **Levite** was an assistant in the Temple. Like the priest, touching a dead body would have made him unclean.

- **Neither man made any effort** to find out whether the man was dead or not.

- The **Samaritans** were **despised** by the Jews and treated as racially and socially inferior; this dated back to the fall of Samaria in 722 B.C.E. when it was thought that they had rejected God's covenant.

- The Samaritan acted **generously**, **mercifully** and out of **love**, which would have been an enormous surprise to Jesus' listeners. The man fulfilled the essence of the Jewish law.

Evaluating the story

Is racism the worst form of prejudice?
Points to consider:

- **On the one hand ...** racism is the worst form of prejudice because it has caused terrible wars and massacres such as the slaughter of Jews in the Holocaust. Racism also causes mistrust and discrimination in local communities based on false views of other people.

- **On the other hand ...** other forms of prejudice such as sexism can be just as destructive for society. Women make up half the world's population but still they find themselves underpaid by comparison with men. Women often fail to get the top jobs and are not always taken as seriously as men.

Is the test of true faith in God love of one's neighbour?
Points to consider:

- **On the one hand ...** true faith in God must mean love of one's neighbour whoever they might be because if we are all made in the image of God, then respect for all humans is also worship and love of God.

- **On the other hand ...** loving one's neighbour is not enough. Some people do things that are not worthy of our love and true faith comes by honouring God through prayer and worship.

2.7 The lost son

Read Luke 15:11–32

Knowing the story

- A man had **two sons**.

- The **younger son** asked to **have his inheritance** immediately, rather than waiting for his father's death.

- The younger son set off to a **distant land** and **spent everything** having a good time.

- When **famine** struck he had to work looking after **pigs**.

- He was extremely **hungry** and could have easily **eaten the pigs' food**.

- He realised his **father's servants** were better off than he was.

- He decided to **return home**.

- He would say to his father **'I have sinned against heaven (God) and against you'**.

- While the son was still some distance from home, his **father** saw him and **rushed to meet him**; his heart was filled with **compassion**.

- His father told the servants to get a ring, a robe and sandals for the son, kill the fatted calf and prepare a **feast**.

- He said that they should rejoice that his **dead son was alive** – **'he was lost and is found'**.

- But the **elder son** was **angry** and told his father that he had never been given a party like this.

- He **refused** to go to the party.

- His **father** tried to **persuade the elder son** to attend and told him that he had **continually enjoyed** everything he owned.

- The father said that it was appropriate to **celebrate the return** of the son who had been **lost and was now found**.

Themes
1, 4 and 6

Interpreting the story

- The parable is aimed at the Pharisees who were critical of Jesus' concern for outcasts.

- This parable is one of a series about the **'lost'** people of Israel (those who were considered to be **sinners** and who were rejected according to the Jewish law) and how there is disproportionate and undeserved rejoicing in heaven when one repents.

- In the parable, the **elder son** represents the **Pharisees** or all those who have kept to the law but are unable to be **generous** to those who have fallen short of its demands.

- The **younger son** represents the **outcasts and sinners** of society.

- **Eating with pigs** is an important idea in the parable. Pigs were considered unclean in Jewish law, so they demonstrate that the younger son had reached an emotional and religious low; he was truly an **outcast from society**. Some consider that this represents sinners such as tax collectors working for the Gentile and unclean Romans.

- The younger son's **return** illustrates the need for all humans to **repent** and to realise their faults.

- The **father** represents **God's** generosity, love and forgiveness for all sinners.

- The **father's generosity** is contrasted with the **elder son's lack of compassion**.

- The **feast** symbolises the **joy** to be experienced in the messianic banquet – especially for those who **repent**.

Evaluating the story
Were Jesus' parables the best way to teach?
Points to consider:

- **On the one hand ...** people remember stories much better than straight teaching. Jesus' parables used events from everyday life to explain complex ideas about the Kingdom of God very effectively.

- **On the other hand ...** however good Jesus' parables were, his most important teaching was done without parables and through his actions. Sometimes parables can confuse as people do not understand their hidden message.

Should the elder son have forgiven his younger brother?
Points to consider:

- **On the one hand ...** forgiveness is at the heart of Jesus' teaching, in the Lord's Prayer and in his treatment of sinners such as tax collectors. The elder son should have been wise and compassionate enough to share in his father's joy and forgive his brother.

- **On the other hand ...** the elder brother was right to be suspicious of his brother. Having squandered all his money, he cannot just turn up and expect everything to go back to normal. Perhaps the younger son needed to prove just how repentant he was before his brother could forgive him.

2.8 Zacchaeus

Read Luke 19:1–10

Knowing the story

- Jesus was passing through **Jericho**.

- Zacchaeus was the **chief tax collector** and very wealthy.

- Because he was **short**, he **climbed** a sycamore **tree** to see Jesus better.

- When **Jesus** came to the tree he told Zacchaeus to **come down**.

- Jesus wanted to **stay at Zacchaeus' house** straight away.

- The **crowd** were **annoyed** that Jesus wanted to stay with a '**sinner**'.

- Zacchaeus immediately said he would give **half his possessions to the poor**.

- He said he would also **pay** all those **he had cheated four times** the amount he had stolen.

- Jesus said that Zacchaeus had received **salvation** and was a son of Abraham.

- Jesus said, 'The **Son of Man** came to seek and save what was lost'.

Interpreting the story

Themes
1, 4, 6 and 7

- **Tax collectors** in Jesus' time were mistrusted because they worked for the Romans and often **overtaxed** the ordinary people so they could become rich. Tax collectors were **not trusted** and were called sinners.

- **'Sinners'** refers to all those **excluded** from the **Jewish law** and therefore shunned by religious people.

- **Jericho** was a **major tax point** for people entering Palestine from the east.

- **Zacchaeus** as chief tax collector was very rich because he had a share **in *all* the taxes** coming into Jericho.

- Zacchaeus' **conscience** led him to make a big effort to see Jesus and listen to his teaching.

- Zacchaeus **repented** because he knew what he had done was wrong, **not because he wanted social recognition**.

- The fact that Jesus stayed with a sinner would have **shocked** the religious people of Jericho because it would have made Jesus **religiously unclean**.

- Despite Zacchaeus being a sinner and working for the Gentile Romans, Jesus declares that he is a true Jew – a son of Abraham.

- Jesus calls himself the **Son of Man** because his role is to **represent all people to God** and prepare them for the **Kingdom of God**.

Evaluating the story
Do we have a duty to help outcasts today?
Points to consider:

- **On the one hand ...** often people are lonely, depressed or lose their jobs and therefore turn to drink, drugs or prostitution which can result in prison. Organisations such as the Salvation Army help these people because the same thing could happen to anyone and all humans are equally important and equally valued.

- **On the other hand ...** often people create their own problems through greed or weakness. Some people think that we do not have a duty to help these individuals and should help those who are genuinely ill, old or disabled.

Did Jesus set a bad example by staying with Zacchaeus?
Points to consider:

- **On the one hand ...** Jesus did set a bad example because it is wrong to mix with people who have low moral standards and who exploit ordinary and vulnerable members of society.

- **On the other hand ...** Jesus judged that Zacchaeus wanted help and he took a risk. Helping those rejected by society is courageous and sets a good example. Jackie Pullinger's work in Hong Kong with drug users required a lot of courage and conviction and was inspired by Jesus' example.

2.9 The centurion

Read Matthew 8:5–13

Knowing the story

- Jesus arrived at **Capernaum**.

- A **centurion** asked him to heal his very **sick servant**.

- Jesus said he would go to his house to heal the servant but the centurion said he was **not worthy enough** for Jesus to enter his home.

- The centurion said all Jesus had to do was to **say the word** and his servant would be healed.

- The centurion said he knew about **authority** because **he was under authority** and his **soldiers were under his authority**.

- So, if he said to his soldiers 'go' they would obey and go.

- Jesus said he had never met anyone **in Israel** with such **great faith**.

- He said **many would come** from east and west and take their place at the **feast** in the **Kingdom of Heaven** with Abraham, Isaac and Jacob.

- But those **already in the Kingdom** would be thrown out into the **darkness**.

- Then Jesus said to the centurion that it would be as the centurion believed.

- At that moment, the **servant was cured**.

Themes
1, 4, 6 and 7

Interpreting the story

- At the time of Jesus, Israel (or Palestine) was occupied and controlled by the **Romans**. A centurion was a **senior officer** in the Roman army and commanded around a hundred men. This centurion had settled in Capernaum along with his family and servants.

- As a **non-Jew** (or Gentile), the centurion knows that it would be wrong for Jesus, as a respected Jew, to enter his house as this would make him **religiously unclean**.

- The **centurion** must have been a **kind man** to care so much for one of his servants.

- The centurion, as an army officer, understands the **nature of authority** and that Jesus doesn't have to be physically present in his home to command his servant to be cured.

- He knows that as God's son, **Jesus has authority** to speak the words to cure, just as the centurion can give commands from a distance to his men and servants to act.

- Jesus' reply shows that even though the centurion is a non-Jew, his faith and understanding of God is **greater than that of many Jewish leaders** who assumed they had a place in the Kingdom of Heaven.

- The **Kingdom of Heaven** is Matthew's equivalent phrase for the Kingdom of God and refers to the **messianic banquet**, the perfect age to come of **peace and justice**.

- The **Jewish leaders** assumed that only Jews, descended from Abraham, Isaac and Jacob, would have places in the Kingdom. Jesus' teaching that it would also include non-Jews would have **shocked them**.

- The **darkness** refers to **hell** where those whom God judges at the Day of Judgement will be sent.

- The purpose of the story is to show that even though God cannot be seen, anyone – Jew or non-Jew – who has **faith in His authority** can ask Him to act for them.

Evaluating the story
Will all good people go to heaven?
Points to consider:

- **On the one hand ...** it is not enough merely to be morally good to be rewarded with heaven. In addition, a person has to believe in God's goodness and forgiveness and to acknowledge their sins. The centurion believed in God and recognised his own sins.

- **On the other hand ...** when Jesus challenged the leaders of Judaism by saying that only certain Jews would enter the messianic banquet, he was rejecting a very narrow view of who would go to heaven. The centurion was not Jewish and it was his good and generous character which Jesus praised.

Is the centurion the model disciple?
Points to consider:

- **On the one hand ...** the centurion is the model disciple. He cares for his servant even though servants in those days were worth very little and he believes in God's word bringing about change in the world. He respects Jesus' authority as a teacher. This is in contrast to Jesus' own disciples such as Peter who denies him and Judas who betrays him.

- **On the other hand ...** although the centurion is a good person, his faith is not tested by hardship, persecution or other difficulties that Jesus' disciples had to undergo – Dietrich Bonhoeffer and Martin Luther King are examples of this in more recent times.

2.10 The rich young man

Read Mark 10:17–27

Knowing the story

- The man asked Jesus what he should do to **inherit eternal life**.

- **Jesus** told him to keep the **Commandments** which focused on human relationships (commandments 5–10).

- The man said he had **kept** these since he was a **child**.

- Jesus challenged him to **sell everything** and give it to the **poor**.

- The man was **sad and left**. He was **very rich**.

- **Jesus** said to the **disciples** that **rich people** would find it **hard** to get a place in the **Kingdom of God**.

- The disciples were **amazed**.

- Jesus told them a **parable**: it would be easier for a **camel to pass through the eye** of a needle than for a rich man to enter the **Kingdom of God**.

- The disciples asked **who** then could be **saved**.

- Jesus answered that **everything is possible** for God.

Themes
1, 2, 4, 5 and 6

Interpreting the story

- In the first century, having **great wealth** was a sign that a person had been **blessed** by God.

- The **man** just **wanted Jesus to praise him** for keeping the Ten Commandments and being a **good person**.

- But Jesus' **challenge** was to **reverse** the man's religious views and ask him to **give to the poor**.

- Jesus showed that the man had **made money an idol**, thus breaking the second commandment, since his money was more important to him than God.

- As **God sides with the poor**, the man is being challenged to see whether he really believes in **justice** and moral goodness.

- Jesus' **disciples** clearly also **fail to understand** the nature of **justice**.

- The parable of the camel and eye of the needle can be interpreted in two ways:

  - All wealth makes it impossible to enter the Kingdom – **all riches must be given to the poor**.

  - Only **attachment** to wealth stops a person entering the Kingdom – **riches should be used wisely** to help the poor.

Evaluating the story

Does love of money cause injustice?
Points to consider:

● **On the one hand ...** there are many examples where love of riches has meant that the poor have suffered great injustices. Mother Teresa in India and Oscar Romero in Latin America both worked to fight against injustice caused by the rich failing to distribute their wealth and exploiting the poor.

● **On the other hand ...** although this could be true, it is only by having money that it is then possible to help the poor and overcome injustice. If there were no love of money, people would not work hard to acquire it.

Is loving one's family more important than loving God?
Points to consider:

● **On the one hand ...** religion can sometimes break up families and this can never be right. Christianity teaches the importance of marriage and duties to parents so it could never be the case that love of God means leaving one's family.

● **On the other hand ...** Jesus never taught that a person should not love their family but he did teach that it is important to be clear what their ultimate values are. As God is all powerful and all loving, then there may be times when loving God must be more important.

> Practise answering questions with *Theology, Philosophy and Religion 13+ Exam Practice Questions and Answers* pages 2–3 and 36–39.

Test yourself

1 How did God create Eve?

2 What did God say would happen if Eve ate from the tree of knowledge?

3 What did Cain say to God when he asked where Abel was?

4 What did Abraham see after God stopped him sacrificing Isaac?

5 What did David tell Joab to do with Uriah?

6 What did David say should happen to the rich man in Nathan's parable?

7 After Simon Peter had caught a large number of fish, what did Jesus tell him to do?

8 What did the Levite and priest do in the parable of the Good Samaritan?

9 In the parable of the lost son, what did the younger son decide to say to his father on his return home?

10 What did Zacchaeus say he would do when Jesus said he wanted to stay at his house?

11 What did the centurion say Jesus had to do to cure his servant?

12 What parable did Jesus tell the disciples in the story of the rich young man?

Glossary

atonement Getting back into a right relationship with God; being at one with God

Baal Canaanite god of fertility and rain, controlled fire and lightning

baptism The symbolic washing away of sin; symbol of becoming a Christian

Bathsheba Wife of Uriah, with whom King David had an adulterous affair

blasphemy Speaking against God or making oneself equal to God

Carmel A mountain range in northern Israel. At the time of Elijah there was a Canaanite holy site on Carmel dedicated to the worship of Baal.

civil disobedience Protesting against the state by disobeying an unfair law

covenant The agreement between God and His people

Creation The world or universe as created by God

crucifixion The Roman death penalty of being nailed to a cross

David Son of Jesse and chosen king around 1000 B.C.E. Ruled Israel until his death in 970 B.C.E.

disciple A follower or student

Eden The garden in Genesis 2 where everything is perfect

evil The absence of good; that which seeks to destroy all goodness; wickedness

Exodus The way out; the departure from Egypt to the Promised Land

faith Having an active trust in someone or in God

Fall The moment when Adam and Eve sinned and fell from grace

Gentile A non-Jew

Golgotha The small hill and rubbish tip outside the walls of Jerusalem where Jesus was crucified

Horeb/Sinai The mountain of God where Moses received the law

image of God The special aspects of being human such as reason and spirit which are God-given

Israelites Another term for the ancient Hebrew or Jewish people

justice Treating others fairly; giving people what is rightly due to them

Messiah The anointed one of God; God's chosen one; Christ

messianic banquet A glorious time in the future of peace and justice. The image of the banquet symbolises a time of plenty attended by the messiah. May also refer to heaven.

miracle An act of God which breaks the laws of physics; a powerful, generous and unexpected moment which is attributed to God

Moses Born in Egypt to a Hebrew mother and brought up as an Egyptian prince. Led the Hebrew slaves out of Egypt in around 1250 B.C.E. Given the Torah by God at Sinai.

Nathan The court prophet who lived at the time of King David. His parable pointed out David's great sin with Bathsheba.

parable A story or short saying comparing everyday human events with the Kingdom of God

Passover The time when the Israelites escaped from Egypt. At the festival of Passover, a special meal is eaten of unleavened bread and other symbolic foods which remember the suffering of slavery and joy of freedom.

persecution Harassment or ill-treatment on grounds of religious beliefs, race, sex, political beliefs, etc.

Peter One of Jesus' 12 disciples who, although he denied knowing Jesus at Jesus' trial, went on to be the chief apostle after his death

Pharisees Jewish religious teachers who taught strict obedience to the law

prejudice Holding an irrational view against someone or some people

prophet Person chosen by God to speak God's message to a person or people

repent To have a sincere change of heart

resurrection Rising to new life from the dead

revelation The means by which God makes Himself known to humans

sacrifice Giving up something for something else of greater value

salvation The process of healing the broken relationship between God and humans; being saved from sin

sin Disobeying God and separating oneself from Him

Sinai/Horeb The mountain of God where Moses received the law

Son of God Jesus' unique relationship with God

Son of Man Jesus' role as the one who would suffer for others

steward To look after the world for God

suffering servant The person in Isaiah 53 who suffers and dies at the hands of his oppressors but whose death causes them to repent of their sinful behaviour

symbol An image used to represent an idea or a relationship. Used theologically, symbols such as fire and darkness may represent sin and evil.

tempt To entice someone to do something wrong

transfigure To change appearance

Uriah The honourable husband of Bathsheba whom King David arranged to have killed

vocation The sense of being called to carry out a task or job; being called by God

worship Giving praise and honour to God

Zacchaeus A tax collector at Jericho whom Jesus met and who promised to give back all the money he had cheated people out of

Zarephath Phoenician city north of ancient Israel on the Mediterranean coast where the people worshipped Baal

1 Great thinkers and their ideas

Read *Theology and Philosophy for Common Entrance 13+* pages 93–122.

Themes

The philosophy section of the Theology, Philosophy and Religion syllabus sets out the following philosophy themes which can be tested in any of the Topic 1 questions:

1 What is a persuasive argument?

2 What is real and what is illusion?

3 Can God's existence be proved?

4 Do the ends justify the means?

5 What is happiness?

6 What is justice?

7 Is civil disobedience justified?

1.1 Plato's life and thought

Plato's life and thought

Knowing about Plato's life and thought

Plato's early life, the influence and example of Socrates

- **Plato** was born in **427 B.C.E.** in **Athens**.

- He came from an **aristocratic** family.

- His brothers included **Glaucon** and **Adeimantus**.

- During most of Plato's early life, Athens was in turmoil because of the **Peloponnesian War** (431–404 B.C.E.).

- **Socrates was an influential philosopher** who inspired the **young Plato** and became his **teacher**.

- Socrates was condemned to death, accused of **treason** for corrupting the minds of young Athenian men and for **impiety (rejection of the gods)**.

- At his trial, Socrates said, 'the **unexamined life is not worth living'**.

- Socrates accepted death nobly and inspired Plato to pursue philosophy.

- Socrates died in **399** B.C.E.

His career as a young man

- Plato worked as a **soldier** and fought in **three campaigns**.

- He lived in **Syracuse**, Sicily.

- He worked as a tutor to **King Dionysius I's son** – but this was not a success.

- He returned to **Athens** to set up the **Academy** (a school/university).

The Academy

- The Academy was founded by Plato to **teach young aristocratic Athenian men** how to become wise leaders.

- His books used **dialogues** to teach his ideas.

- He wrote *The Republic* as a textbook to be used by the students.

- His books also used stories, **allegories** and **parables**.

- An important story in *The Republic* is the parable of the cave.

- Plato learnt from **Pythagorean** philosophers that **mathematics** shows us that this world is just a reflection of the real world.

Understanding Plato's life and thought

- Many Athenians, such as Socrates, wanted a new form of **democracy** and not **oligarchy** (the rule of a **few people** from aristocratic families over the people).

- Plato argued that **democracy** should mean **many well-educated people** leading and ruling the people wisely.

- He rejected **oligarchy** because it had led to bloodshed.

- In Socrates' famous argument with the philosopher **Protagoras**, he showed that there is more to philosophy than just **cleverly winning arguments**. The true aim is to make people think **about ideas and their meaning**.

- The purpose of the Academy was to educate **young Athenian men** to be wise **future leaders** by making them think and philosophise about what is true.

- Plato argued that we know the physical world is **not perfect** because we know what **is perfect**.

- Plato said we can have an **idea** of a **perfect triangle** but there are no perfect triangles in the physical **world**.

Evaluating Plato's life and thought
Should all politicians today be made to study philosophy?
Points to consider:

- **On the one hand ...** they should study philosophy as it will make them clarify their ideas and present much better arguments, which will lead to a clearer idea of justice.

- **On the other hand ...** if politicians studied philosophy, they might spend all their time arguing and trying to define terms and fail to make any practical decisions.

Should Socrates have been killed for teaching philosophy?
Points to consider:

- **On the one hand ...** Socrates was deliberately upsetting society by subverting its laws and making its future leaders reject the gods who represented society's basic values. For this he deserved to die.

- **On the other hand ...** Socrates was not using philosophy to deliberately cause society to fall apart but rather to make its ideas of democracy stronger and fairer. He did not deserve to die.

The parable of the cave

Knowing about the parable of the cave

- The parable or allegory of the cave is found in Plato's book *The Republic*.

- It is told by **Socrates** to **Glaucon**.

  - There is an **underground cave** where **prisoners** have been **chained together**.

  - They can only see the **back of the cave**.

  - What they see are **shadows** of objects.

  - Behind the actual objects there is a fire; the **fire lights up** the objects to create the **shadows** on the cave wall.

  - One day a **prisoner's chains** are **removed**.

  - He is **forced** to **turn around**.

  - He makes his way up a **steep path** to the **entrance to the cave**.

  - He looks into the **sunlight** – at first his eyes find the sunlight **painful**.

  - Once his eyes have adjusted, he looks into the **sun itself**; he is **pleased**.

  - He **returns to the cave**.

  - The **other prisoners** think his journey has been a **waste of time**.

  - When the ex-prisoner attempts to **teach them**, they try to **kill him**.

Understanding the parable of the cave

- The parable is about knowing the difference between **truth and falsehood**; it is about why **philosophy is important**, even if it is **painful** and **difficult**.

- The **shadows** represent the world as we see it through our **ordinary senses**. It is **not the real world**.

- The **prisoners** are ordinary people. They are **not free** because they do not know the truth.

- The **journey out of the cave** symbolises **people starting to think** for themselves and question what they have been taught. It is the journey of the mind or soul.

- The **sun** represents the **source of truth**; it is the **ultimate reality**; it is 'the Good' – the source of all perfection.

- The **treatment of the returning prisoner** shows that many will treat the philosopher as a **trouble maker** because he **upsets beliefs**. It could even cost philosophers their lives, **literally** and **metaphorically**.

Evaluating the parable of the cave

Is the main purpose of the parable of the cave to prove that this world is not real?
Points to consider:

- **On the one hand ...** the main purpose of the parable is to make a distinction between being inside the cave and outside the cave. The parable's purpose is to show that inside the cave the prisoners only see shadows of things which are not real but illusions.

- **On the other hand ...** the parable is about the philosopher's quest for truth, the difficult journey to find it and the happiness and joy of finally grasping it.

Were the prisoners right to try and kill the ex-prisoner?
Points to consider:

- **On the one hand ...** they were right because the ex-prisoner was disrupting their way of life by casting doubt on their beliefs. There was no reason to believe he was right as only he had made the journey and he could have made up what he said.

- **On the other hand ...** they were wrong as what he was offering them was a better way of seeing the world and ultimately knowing about the Good, which is perfect happiness and knowledge of the truth.

1.2 David Hume's life and thought

David Hume's life and thought

Knowing about Hume's life and thought

Upbringing, early life and university

- **David Hume** was born in 1711 in Scotland.

- Some of his family were aristocratic. His father was a successful lawyer.

- His **father died** when David was **two**.

- He went to **Edinburgh University** at the age of 12 to **study law**.

- He **hated law** and left the university.

- At 18 he encountered a group of philosophers who belonged to a '**new scene of thought**'.

- These philosophers were influenced by **Isaac Newton** and his new **science**. They argued for a **scientific basis of all knowledge** including religion, morality and economics.

- His **sceptical** (questioning) views of religion and the existence of God led to **confrontation with the Church**, which accused him of being an **atheist**.

Career, travels and writing

- In 1734, Hume became a **banker** and then **travelled** in **France**.

- He published *A Treatise on Human Nature* in 1739 when he was 25. It was **not a success**.

- His **atheism** meant he was **twice rejected** as a **professor** at Edinburgh University and Glasgow.

- In 1742 he published *Essays, Moral and Political*, which was much more successful.

- In 1745 he became **tutor to the Marquess of Annandale** and in 1746 **secretary to General James St Clair**.

- He became Keeper of the Advocates' Library at Edinburgh in 1752. He then began to publish the six volumes of his *The History of England* (1762), which became the **source of his wealth**.

- In 1757 he published his influential *An Enquiry Concerning Human Understanding* in which he defined what knowledge is.

- As **secretary** to **Lord Hertford**, the British Ambassador to Paris, he mixed with the French philosophers, **Les Philosophes**.

- In 1767 he was appointed **Under Secretary of State**, Northern Department, which was a great honour.

Final years in Edinburgh

- In 1768, Hume **returned** to **Edinburgh** to live and began to **revise his books** on philosophy.

- In 1776, he **died** at his home in St Andrew's Square, New Town, Edinburgh.

Understanding Hume's life and thought

- The 'new scene of thought' had a profound effect on Hume's philosophy and led to his **sceptical method** of reasoning.

- The **sceptical method** involves questioning all beliefs against scientific reasoning. It means that all truth claims must be based on **reason** and **experience**. Beliefs must be **tested** and not held to be true simply because of what is generally accepted.

- Hume argued that there are **no moral laws or facts**. Morals merely express our **feelings** which we treat as if they are moral facts.

- The sceptical method also led Hume to **doubt** whether there is such a thing as **cause and effect**. All we can observe are **events** happening in the world.

- His scepticism led him to **reject the traditional creator designer God** but possibly not God as an underlying principle of the universe.

Evaluating Hume's life and thought

Was Hume's life a success?
Points to consider:

- **On the one hand ...** it was not a success because he failed to become a professor of philosophy at two universities and his books on philosophy were not always well received – his best-selling book was on history.

- **On the other hand ...** he had a wide circle of admiring friends who were greatly influenced by his philosophical method and radical ideas. His intellectual abilities were recognised when he was made an under secretary of state.

Does Hume's philosophy make us uncertain of everything?
Points to consider:

- **On the one hand ...** although Hume uses sceptical reasoning, this does not lead to complete uncertainty about everything. It helps us to be clearer about what we do believe is true about the world.

- **On the other hand ...** his sceptical philosophy does make us uncertain of everything because even if something as basic as cause and effect cannot be proved, then nothing can be known for certain.

Arguments for God's existence and Hume's objections

Hume applied his philosophical sceptical method to one of the most popular and powerful arguments for God's existence, the design argument.

His famous analysis of the design argument appears in his book ***Dialogues Concerning Natural Religion*** (1779). Hume invents **three characters** – Cleanthes, Philo and Demea – to debate the design argument. **Cleanthes** puts forward the design argument.

Knowing about the arguments for God's existence and Hume's objections

Argument for design

- The argument begins by showing that the world **appears** to be **designed**.

- It has design because everywhere there is **beauty**, **purpose** and **order**.

- Hume agrees that the argument **for design** is very strong.

Argument from design

- The argument from design is based on analogy.

- We know, for example, that a **house** has order and purpose and has been designed by an **intelligent mind or designer** (the builder).

- The **world has order** and design (argument for design).

- Therefore, **by analogy**, the world must be designed by an **intelligent mind** or designer.

- The designer must be **very powerful.**

- The designer is what we mean by **God.**

Hume's objections are put forward by Philo and Demea

Philo's objections

- The **analogy** with a house **is poor**. Might a better analogy be with a **vegetable** because the world develops and changes?

- The analogy of the house could suggest it had **several builders**. Might this support polytheism (belief in many gods) rather than monotheism (belief in one God)?

- Human minds like to order and **create patterns**. Might the order we see in nature be an **illusion**? Scholars today call this **apparent design** or **random design**.

- **Our world** may be designed but maybe the **whole universe** is not. If God is too **weak** to design a whole universe, is He God?

Demea's objections

- The design argument **only** points to **God's existence.**

- It does not tell us much about **God's nature.**

- Human minds are too **weak** to know about an **infinite God.**

- The argument suffers from anthropomorphism, that is talking about God as if He were a superior kind of **human being.**

Understanding the arguments for God's existence and Hume's objections

- Hume's objections **don't** necessarily **lead to atheism** but to the **weaknesses** of the design argument which tries to prove that the **all-powerful God** of Christianity exists.

- **Philo's** philosophical objections are **not conclusive**; they **raise lots of questions** which force the **believer to provide good answers.**

- **Demea's** theological objections support a **more traditional Christian** position which is that we can only truly know God through faith not reason.

- One of Hume's **most powerful objections** is that as the world is not static but evolving, then the **design** is constantly changing **according to its own laws.**

- This view is supported by **modern science's theory of evolution.**

- For many people, evolution suggests there is **no external designer** or God.

Evaluating the arguments for God's existence and Hume's objections
Is the beauty and order we see in the world just in our minds?
Points to consider:

- **On the one hand ...** humans like to create order and see patterns. Clouds appear to have faces but we know they do not have actual faces. So, beauty and order are not external to us, they are just part of our minds.

- **On the other hand ...** our minds enjoy order and beauty because they are responding to the order and beauty of the world itself. If there were no order, then the world would quickly collapse into chaos.

Is belief in God just a matter of faith?
Points to consider:

- **On the one hand ...** belief in God relies on God revealing Himself to us. Our minds are far too weak to know God through reason and our own efforts. Faith is the belief that God has revealed Himself through His prophets.

- **On the other hand ...** belief in God is not just a matter of faith, as there have to be good reasons to believe in His existence. The design argument offers many good reasons to believe in God.

1.3 John Stuart Mill's life and thought

John Stuart Mill's life and thought

Knowing about Mill's life and thought

Upbringing and education

- John Stuart Mill was born in 1806.

- His father **James Mill** was a philosopher.

- John's **father** made him study **Greek** and **Latin** at the age of **three**.

- At **12** his father made him study **logic** and **algebra** and at **13** he was made to study **politics** and **economics**.

- He did not have many friends.

- He couldn't go to an **English university** because he was not a member of the Church of England.

- In 1823, he joined the **East India Company** and worked for them for the next **30 years**.

- In 1826, he had a **mental breakdown**. His recovery was helped by reading the **poetry** of William **Wordsworth**.

- Mill was taught by the great legal philosopher **John Austin**.

The Utilitarian Society

- When he **was a child**, Mill's father introduced him to **Jeremy Bentham**.

- Bentham taught Mill his version of utilitarianism.

- Bentham argued that all **laws and morality** should be tested to see if they produce the **greatest happiness or pleasure**.

- After he recovered from his breakdown, Mill realised that there are **higher pleasures**.

- He **rejected Bentham's** idea that humans only seek pleasure.

Career, politics and social reforms

- In 1830, Mill met **Harriet Taylor**; the two became **close friends**.

- Harriet inspired him to develop his ideas about social reforms.

- In 1851, he **married Harriet** after her husband died.

- In 1858, **Harriet died** of tuberculosis.

- Mill published his book ***On Liberty*** in 1859. The book set out his influential liberty principle which supports freedom of speech.

- He published ***Utilitarianism*** in 1863.

- In 1865, Mill was elected a liberal **Member of Parliament** for Westminster.

- He campaigned for **women's suffrage** (women's right to vote) and was **anti-slavery**.

- His ideas about women's rights led to the publication of his book ***The Subjection of Women*** in 1869. He argued that according to the liberty principle, **women** must have the **same rights** and opportunities to education, work and suffrage as men.

- Mill moved to **Avignon**, France, where he was looked after by **Helen**, his step-daughter.

- He died in **1873** and his **autobiography** was published after his death.

Understanding Mill's life and thought

- Mill greatly **admired Bentham** and his rational, scientific analysis of law and morality.

- His **breakdown** and recovery made him realise the **limitations of Bentham's** utilitarianism. He believed that humans are much more than **pleasure-seeking animals** and that **society** needs the **higher pleasures** of art, music, literature and poetry in order to flourish.

- His social reforms were all motivated by his **liberty principle** – the principle that humans are **happiest** when they have the freedom **to choose** how to live their life.

- Because he condemned **slavery** of **all kinds** he was regarded as **being far too liberal**.

- **Harriet Taylor** was a **major influence** on his life, ideas and publications.

Evaluating Mill's life and thought

Should Mill be remembered as a great philosopher or a great social reformer?
Points to consider:

- **On the one hand ...** he should be remembered as a great social reformer. His philosophy was about humans finding happiness and freedom and that is what motivated him to become an MP and fight for social reforms.

- **On the other hand ...** it is as a great philosopher that Mill should be remembered because his books on utilitarianism and liberty still have great influence today. He has shaped the way we think.

Was Jeremy Bentham the greatest influence on Mill's life?
Points to consider:

- **On the one hand ...** without Bentham, Mill would not have been introduced to his ideas which formed the basis of utilitarianism. Later, when Mill modified Bentham's idea of happiness, he didn't reject his basic principles.

- **On the other hand ...** although Bentham was significant, Harriet Taylor played a greater role. She encouraged him to apply his ideas to social reforms, especially to slavery and women's suffrage.

Mill's ethical principles: the greatest happiness of the greatest number

Knowing about Mill's ethical principles: the greatest happiness of the greatest number

- The utilitarian aim is to create the **greatest happiness** for the **greatest number of people**.

- Happiness and pain can be **calculated**.

- Utilitarian calculations take into account the **least amount of pain** caused to the **maximum number of happy people**.

- Mill also argued that through **experience** we know certain actions **tend** to have better outcomes than others.

- These better outcomes can be expressed as **rules**.

- We **don't have to calculate** everything, we can just **follow the rules**.

- Mill is sometimes called a **rule utilitarian**.

- Mill argued that there are **higher pleasures**.

- He said it was better to be a '**human being dissatisfied** than a **pig satisfied**'.

- Bentham argued that **all pleasures have the same value**; it depends on what the individual **likes** or **dislikes**.

Understanding Mill's ethical principles: the greatest happiness of the greatest number

- A moral dilemma is the problem of how to act when two or more **moral rules** or **principles clash**.

- Utilitarians argue that **dilemmas** can be resolved by **calculating** the **greatest overall happiness**.

- Society's **rules** can be revised by **utilitarian experts** who can see when an existing rule is **not producing happiness**.

- If utilitarian social reformers can show that an **existing rule is unfair** and causing pain, then it is **obvious** the rule should be **changed** or **abolished**.

- Rules **protect minorities** by upholding their **rights** and **liberties**.

- Mill argued that **higher pleasures** lead to a more **civilised society**. If Bentham were followed, we would all become like 'pigs' or 'fools'.

Evaluating Mill's ethical principles: the greatest happiness of the greatest number
Does it matter that a few people suffer if the majority are happy?
Points to consider:

- **On the one hand ...** it does matter because the utilitarian principle aims to make as many people as possible happy. Maybe the solution is for the majority to be a little less happy so as to reduce the unhappiness of the minority.

- **On the other hand ...** the utilitarian principle doesn't aim to make all people happy, it simply states that the greatest number should be happy. It is just a fact of life that some people will suffer for the sake of the majority.

Are there higher pleasures?
Points to consider:

- **On the one hand ...** there are no higher pleasures. Bentham was right that we all have different things which give us pleasure and which make us happy and these will depend on who we are; there aren't better or worse pleasures.

- **On the other hand ...** there are higher pleasures because humans are complex and to be happy means that our minds need stimulating as well as our bodies. Higher pleasures stimulate the mind, and minds are what make us truly human.

Mill's ethical principles: ends and means

Knowing about Mill's ethical principles: ends and means

- Utilitarians argue that the **ends justify the means**.

- The ends should achieve **maximum happiness** and **minimum pain**.

- For example, the principle might be used to **torture a terrorist** who holds vital information that will save hundreds of people.

- The **pain** caused by **torture** is **justified** because the information will bring about **happiness**.

Understanding Mill's ethical principles: ends and means

- A **problem** for utilitarians is knowing **exactly the consequences** or 'ends' of an action.

- The **ripple effect** points out that there might be many **negative side effects** that cannot be known in advance.

- Some might argue that even if the **ends justify the means**, that **doesn't** make the means **good**.

- For example, murder is always wrong even if it is justified in an extreme situation.

Evaluating Mill's ethical principles: ends and means
Is stealing from the rich to give to the poor justified?
Points to consider:

- **On the one hand ...** it is justified because the rich have plenty of money to keep them happy so taking some of it to help those in need is justified. Overall, on average, more people will be happy.

- **On the other hand ...** stealing is always wrong. Even if the situation may appear to be unfair, stealing from the rich could cause resentment and in the long term cause greater problems for the poor.

Could telling a lie be good?
Points to consider:

- **On the one hand ...** telling a lie could be good if telling the truth (for example the fact that someone dislikes a certain person) would cause that person a great deal of pain. Lies are only bad when they cause pain.

- **On the other hand ...** even if telling a lie could be justified in a particular situation, it could set a bad example and encourage telling lies in general. It is much better to have a rule that telling lies is always wrong.

1.4 Martin Luther King's life and thought

Martin Luther King's life and thought

Knowing about Martin Luther King's life and thought

Situation and upbringing in the USA

- Since the **1500s**, **black slaves** from **Africa** had been transported to work on the American plantations.

- In **1865, slavery was abolished** but the **southern states** of America got round this by using the **'Jim Crow' laws**.

- These laws said **black people** were 'separate but equal'.

- This meant that black Americans had to create **their own schools**, **universities** and **churches**.

- The facilities used by the black Americans were often **inferior** to those used by the white Americans.

- In **1929**, Martin Luther King was **born** into a **black family** in Atlanta, Georgia (a southern state).

- His father, **Martin Luther King senior**, was a **Baptist minister**.

- Martin Luther King junior attended **Boston University**, where he studied **theology** and was awarded a **doctorate** (PhD).

- He also became a **Baptist minister**.

- **After graduating** he planned to pursue an **academic career**.

Civil rights leader

- In 1955 **Mrs Rosa Parks** refused to move from a seat in a bus designated for white people.

- She was **arrested** and this sparked **outrage** in the **black community**.

- The **Montgomery Improvement Association** was founded to oppose the unfair segregation laws.

- King was persuaded to **lead the association**.

- He led **peaceful protests** such as the Montgomery, Alabama **bus boycott** in 1956.

- In 1957, he and his wife **travelled to India** to meet **Mahatma Gandhi** and see how he had used **non-violent civil disobedience**.

- King carried out many **non-violent acts of civil disobedience** and became a **national civil rights leader**.

- He argued in his **speeches** and **sermons** that the segregation of black people in America was **unconstitutional and illegal**.

- He was **arrested** many times.

- In **1963** he wrote his famous **Letter from Birmingham Jail** to black and white Christian ministers explaining his **reasons for breaking the law**.

- In the same year he led the **march on Washington** where he gave his famous **'I Have a Dream'** speech.

- In **1964** he was awarded the **Nobel Peace Prize** for his civil rights campaigns.

- In **1965** black Americans were given the **same voting rights** as white Americans.

- In **1968** he gave his **'I've Been to the Mountaintop'** speech to three thousand people at the Mason Temple, Memphis, Tennessee.

- Shortly afterwards he was **assassinated** at the Memphis motel where he was staying.

Understanding Martin Luther King's life and thought

- Martin Luther King's teaching was inspired by the **Bible**, the example and teaching of **Jesus** and **Mahatma Gandhi**.

- The prophets **Isaiah** and **Amos** in the Old Testament taught him that it is **against God's laws** to deprive any members of society of **justice** and **love**.

- **Jesus'** teaching and example taught him that protestors should have the courage to **treat their enemies with love not hate** – even if this causes them suffering.

- **Gandhi** showed King how **peaceful non-violent** protest can bring about great changes; Gandhi was a key figure in bringing about Indian independence from Britain (in 1947).

- In his **'I have a Dream'** speech, King:

  - refers to God's **'promised land'** and **'New Jerusalem'** as reasons for **reforming** America into a place of peace, love and justice

  - uses the **Christian Negro spiritual** song of **hope**, **'Free at last'**

  - ends with **Isaiah's** image of a **flattened world** as a **symbol of** equality when all will see God's glory.

- In his **'I've Been to the Mountaintop'** speech, King compared himself to **Moses** in that he knew that he wouldn't see the **promised land** but that God would lead others to redeem America and make it a place of equality.

Evaluating Martin Luther King's life and thought
Was it right for King as a Christian minister to break the law?
Points to consider:

- **On the one hand ...** in the New Testament Jesus teaches that Christians should obey the law as well as being obedient to God. It was wrong for King as a Christian to break the law as he should have been setting a good example by obeying the law.

- **On the other hand ...** he was setting a good example because by disobeying the law and being punished for doing so he was standing up for justice and bringing about social change. He was following the example of the prophets and Jesus in the Bible.

Was King's 'I Have a Dream' speech the most important moment in his life?
Points to consider:

- **On the one hand ...** it was the most important moment in his life because the speech was given to a vast crowd at the Lincoln Memorial statue which symbolises human rights. The symbols of freedom he uses in the speech are very powerful.

- **On the other hand ...** it is not the most important moment because without his other speeches, sermons and protests, his message would not have had a wide impact. There is no one moment in his life which is more important.

King's teaching on justice and fairness

Knowing about King's teaching on justice and fairness

King's teaching on justice and fairness is famously set out in his **Letter from Birmingham Jail**.

- Civil disobedience is justified because:

  - **anytime** is the **right time** to bring about justice

  - **'an unjust law is no law at all'**

  - justice means treating **each person** with **respect**

  - it is **unjust** for white adults to be able to vote but not black adults

  - an **unjust law** is one that fails to conform to **God's eternal law**

  - an **unjust law** is one that does not uphold **human dignity**.

- **Protests are not anti-Christian because they:**
  - are intended to stir up the **consciences** of the community
  - do **not use violence**.

Understanding King's teaching on justice and fairness

- Breaking a law shows **respect for law as a whole** because it is a sign that a particular law has failed.
- Pacifism will sometimes **cause suffering**. This is justified if suffering is the **lesser of two evils** and results in peace – the greater good.
- King called this **realistic pacifism**. Realistic pacifists accept that they must **accept the blame** for breaking the law, for sometimes causing harm and suffering.
- The **means** for justice must **be good**. **Violence** as a means is never justified, however good the outcome.
- The **Bible justifies breaking an unjust law**. In the **Book of Daniel** three Jewish men refuse to obey the unjust law of the king. The king throws them into a **fiery furnace** but God rescues them.

Evaluating King's teaching on justice and fairness
Is breaking a law the best way to change a law?
Points to consider:

- **On the one hand ...** breaking a law draws the attention of the authorities and people in general to the fact that a law is unfair. It gives the lawbreaker an opportunity to explain the reasons for the action.
- **On the other hand ...** protesting, campaigning and writing to the press are much better ways of getting a law changed. If a law is broken, then it weakens the case as it shows the person has no respect for law and order.

Does equality mean treating all people in exactly the same way?
Points to consider:

- **On the one hand ...** by treating all people in exactly the same way one is not valuing one person more than another. Therefore, all people are being treated as equals.
- **On the other hand ...** treating all people in the same way is not equality because different people have different needs and these have to be taken into account. For example, it is not equality to treat an old person as one might a child.

King's teaching on the beloved community

Knowing about King's teaching on the beloved community

- The beloved community is a **reformed America**.
- It is based on **respect**, **love** and **justice**.
- The beloved community will only come about when people overcome their **selfishness**.
- The example of **Jesus Christ's suffering** and **sacrifice** acts as a model of how to establish the beloved community.
- One of King's favourite slogans was **'we shall overcome'**.

Understanding King's teaching on the beloved community

- **Black communities** know what it means to **suffer** injustice.

- **Suffering** can be **redemptive** (it restores freedom); it gives people the courage to struggle for peace.

- Jesus Christ's death and resurrection **stirs up the conscience** of those who have caused suffering and encourages the community to **overcome** evil.

Evaluating King's teaching on the beloved community
Is there any point in struggling for a beloved community if people are essentially selfish?
Points to consider:

- **On the one hand ...** there is no point in struggling for something that will never happen. All it will do is create disappointment, frustration and anger. People are selfish, so it is much better to aim for something more realistic than a beloved community.

- **On the other hand ...** having a vision of what could be a perfect society gives people hope and is certainly worth struggling for. Humans are not fundamentally bad and even selfish people might see the benefits of living in a beloved community.

Does suffering make humans better people?
Points to consider:

- **On the one hand ...** suffering does not make people better because it makes them unhappy and they focus more on their own problems than on the concerns of others.

- **On the other hand ...** learning to deal with suffering can give one strength of character and make one much more aware of the needs of other people.

> Practise answering questions with *Theology, Philosophy and Religion 13+ Exam Practice Questions and Answers* pages 4–5 and 40–44.

Test yourself

1 What is the name of Plato's most famous book?

2 What was the purpose of Plato's Academy?

3 What do the shadows represent in the parable of the cave?

4 What is the title of Hume's first book on philosophy?

5 What is the role of Cleanthes in Hume's *Dialogues Concerning Natural Religion*?

6 Outline two of Hume's arguments against the design argument for God's existence.

7 Name two of J.S. Mill's most influential books.

8 Outline Mill's liberty principle.

9 Why did Mill object to Bentham's utilitarianism?

10 What were the Jim Crow laws?

11 Name two ways in which King protested against Jim Crow laws.

12 Outline two of King's justifications for civil disobedience.

2 Ethics

Read *Theology and Philosophy for Common Entrance 13+* pages 123–62.

Themes

The philosophy section of the Theology, Philosophy and Religion syllabus sets out the following ethics themes which can be tested in any of the *Topic 2* questions:

1 Whether there is existence after death

2 Whether the use of war is justified

3 What is punishment for?

4 What are the limits of freedoms?

5 Who are the marginalised and how should they be treated?

6 Are humans morally responsible for their environment?

2.1 Life and death

Life and death ethics are often judged by two very different principles:

- Some people believe in the sanctity of life principle which believes all human life is **God-given** and therefore sacred.

- Some people believe in the quality of life principle which believes that human life is only valuable when a person can **feel pleasure/pain** and the person experiences more pleasure than pain.

Both principles also depend on whether there is **life after death**.

Nihilism

Knowing about nihilism

- Nihilism means **life has no meaning**.

- Nihilists **don't believe in life after death**.

- **Pessimistic nihilists** teach that life is **meaningless** and death is the end.

- **Optimistic nihilists** teach that it is **up to us** to give **life meaning** and value.

- Albert Camus, the French novelist and philosopher, explored both kinds of nihilism.

- Camus' famous novel which explores nihilism is called *The Outsider*.

- Jean-Paul Sartre, another French novelist and philosopher, taught that people live superficial lives to **escape** the fear of nihilism.

Understanding nihilism

- In Camus' novel *The Outsider*, the chief character, Meursault, is at first a **pessimistic nihilist** because he doesn't care one way or another what happens to him.

- Meursault believes that as there is **no afterlife** and no God to judge and place him in heaven or hell, then it **doesn't matter** when he kills a person.

- Then Meursault **suddenly realises** that as there is no afterlife, he is free to live his life imaginatively as he wants – he is an optimistic nihilist.
- **Sartre** explains that **escapism** is not real life; real life requires making an effort and being **committed to oneself**, one's **job** and other **people**.

Evaluating nihilism

If there is no afterlife and no God, then does it matter how we live our lives?
Points to consider:

- **On the one hand ...** if there is no afterlife and no God to judge us, then there is no fear of eternal punishment and so it doesn't matter how we live our lives, as long as we are doing what we want to do.
- **On the other hand ...** it matters even more how we live our lives if there is no afterlife and no God because if we only have one life and there is no reward or punishment, then we should want to live it as well as we can.

Is being committed to oneself the most important thing in life?
Points to consider:

- **On the one hand ...** being committed to oneself is the most important thing in life as it gives one a purpose and reason to act positively. Lack of commitment means one's life becomes aimless and meaningless.
- **On the other hand ...** being committed to oneself is important but only if one is also committed to something greater than oneself – God, country or other people. Being only committed to oneself is selfish and meaningless.

Resurrection

Knowing about resurrection

- Resurrection is the belief that after death a person's **soul is reunited with its body**.
- **Christians**, **Jews** and **Muslims** all believe in some form of resurrection.
- **Christians** believe in resurrection because the early Christians **experienced the resurrected Jesus**.
- Christians believe that:
  - Jesus' resurrection was a sign that **they too will be resurrected**.
  - Resurrection will take place at the **last judgement**.
  - God will judge all people – the **righteous** will enter **heaven**; the **wicked** will go to **hell**.
  - Resurrection affirms the **value of human life**; it supports the **sanctity of life principle**.

Understanding resurrection

- Christians have **different views** about Jesus' resurrection because it is **not clear what kind of body** the resurrected Jesus had.
- Some think the resurrected Jesus had a **spiritual body** which **wasn't physical** and so could **pass through walls**.

- Some think the resurrected Jesus had a **perfect physical body**.

- Others think the **resurrected Jesus had no body**, he was a **pure soul** and appeared as **a vision** in the minds of the first Christians.

- Some believe **hell** and **heaven** are **not actual places** but **spiritual states** where the soul exists.

- Hell means the soul **exists separately** from **God's love**; heaven means the **soul exists fully** in the presence of **God's love**.

- Belief in resurrection gives **meaning** and **purpose to life**.

Evaluating resurrection

Does belief in resurrection mean that you value life more than a nihilist?
Points to consider:

- **On the one hand ...** belief in resurrection does mean that you value life more than the nihilist because according to the nihilist when you die that is the end, whereas resurrection means that life continues. Resurrection gives meaning to this life.

- **On the other hand ...** the nihilist values life more than the person who believes in resurrection because they are dealing with what we can know for certain which is that we shall all die. Optimistic nihilists value this life because it is the only one we have.

Does resurrection mean having a physical body in the afterlife?
Points to consider:

- **On the one hand ...** in the accounts of Jesus' resurrection, he had a perfect physical body; he spoke with his disciples, ate and could be seen.

- **On the other hand ...** Jesus couldn't have had a body of any kind because the afterlife is not a physical state but a spiritual one. The Resurrection stories are trying to express that Jesus' spiritual resurrection was very real – as if he were actually there in body.

Reincarnation

Knowing about reincarnation

- Reincarnation is the belief that after death a person's **soul returns to this world and inhabits a new body**.

- **Hindus**, **Sikhs** and **Buddhists** all believe in some form of reincarnation.

- In **Hindu** teaching, the jivatman (individual soul) exists in the body as it goes through many stages of life.

  - The cycle through this life and future lives is called samsara.

  - Samsara is controlled by the **law of karma**.

  - **Karma** is the law of **cause and effect**.

  - Living a **good life** creates positive karma which means one is **reborn** into a higher or better form of life.

  - Eventually, once the soul is fully purified, **reincarnation ceases** and the soul achieves total happiness or **bliss**.

- Reincarnation affirms the **value of human life**; it supports the **sanctity of life principle**.

Understanding reincarnation

- Reincarnation explains why some people are **naturally more spiritually** and **morally advanced** from an early age.

- It removes the feeling that one has to **achieve everything in this life** as there will be future lives.

- The promise of **future bliss** encourages people to work hard on becoming **morally good**.

- The **law of karma** means that the **unrighteous** will **justly** be reborn at a lower animal level.

Evaluating reincarnation

Does reincarnation encourage people to be morally lazy?
Points to consider:

- **On the one hand ...** reincarnation does encourage people to be morally lazy because if they get things wrong in this life and create negative karma they can live through many lifetimes to improve in the future.

- **On the other hand ...** reincarnation does not encourage people to be morally lazy because in Hinduism living a good life eventually leads to the end of rebirths and the promise of bliss and everlasting happiness. Being morally lazy could result in living in pain in the next life.

Does reincarnation explain why some people are morally better people than others?
Points to consider:

- **On the one hand ...** it does explain why some people are born with a stronger sense of right and wrong. In their previous lives they lived morally good lives and according to the law of karma they have been reborn as morally superior people.

- **On the other hand ...** reincarnation doesn't explain why some people are morally better people than others. Having a moral sense depends on a person's upbringing, their education and their natural emotional intelligence.

Ethics of war and pacifism

Knowing about war and pacifism

- **War realists** believe that wars are necessary to fight against aggressors and to protect a country's way of life.

- **War militarists** believe wars are a sign of a country's **political strength**.

Just war

- Just war theorists believe war can be justified as a **lesser of two evils**.

- There are **three parts to just war**: justification for going **to war**, justice **in war**, justice **after war**.

- **Justification for going to war:**

  - The **cause** must be **just**.

  - It must be **authorised**.

- The **intentions** must be **good**.
- There must be a **chance of success**.
- It must be the **last resort**.
- Use of force must be **proportionate** to the aim.
- **Justice in war:**
  - Force used **in battle** must be **proportionate**.
  - **Non-combatants** (non-soldiers) must be **protected**.
- **Justice after war:**
  - **Law and order** must be **restored**.
  - The **environment** must be **protected** and restored.

Pacifism

- Pacifists believe that if **killing and violence are morally wrong**, then **war is wrong**.
- **Absolute pacifists** believe **war** is **always wrong**.
- **Weak pacifists** believe that **war is wrong** but may be used as a **very last resort**.
- **Christians are divided**: Jesus taught we should **love our enemies**, but he **didn't condemn soldiers**.

Understanding war and pacifism

- **Utilitarians** and consequentialists who believe that the **ends justify the means** support **war realist** and **just war arguments** because in aiming for **long-term greatest happiness** (ends), some **suffering** may be **necessary** (means).
- Some argue that **not all the conditions** of a **just war** need to be met for a war to be justified.
- Some argue that it is **impossible for all the just war conditions** to be met and therefore **pacifism** is the only moral alternative.
- **Martin Luther King** supported **absolute pacifism** because evil cannot be combatted with the evil of violence. Alternatives to war must be used.
- Some **utilitarians** argue that **absolute pacifists cause suffering** by letting evil leaders act violently and unjustly.
- Some **Christians** argue that pacifism **is an ideal** but in a **sinful world** war is sometimes necessary.
- Some **Christians** argue that **violence** should be replaced by **reconciliation** and people should aim to make the **world peaceful** as **God intended it to be**.

Evaluating war and pacifism
Is a world without war unrealistic?
Points to consider:

- **On the one hand ...** it is unrealistic because humans are naturally aggressive and like power. War is sometimes necessary to stop aggressive rulers from misusing their power and acting unjustly.

- **On the other hand ...** it is not unrealistic because only a few people are aggressive and most people would want to live in a world without war. If countries slowly got rid of their armies, wars would no longer happen.

Can pacifism be morally justified?
Points to consider:

- **On the one hand ...** pacifism can be morally justified because all forms of violence and aggression are wrong. Pacifism respects other people and even if being a pacifist involves suffering, it is better than killing.

- **On the other hand ...** pacifism is a good idea in theory but can't be justified in a world where people use violence against others. Pacifists don't protect the innocent and the weak sufficiently against aggressors, whereas war does.

2.2 Punishment

Aims of punishment

- An **offender** is someone who has committed a crime by breaking the law.

- The **victim** is the person who has had a crime or offence committed against them.

Knowing about the aims of punishment

- There are four **aims of punishment**: retribution, deterrence, protection, reform.

- **Retribution** is paying back to the offender the harm they have caused to others.

- **It is based on the ancient** principle of **lex talionis** – 'an eye for an eye, a tooth for tooth'.

- **Deterrence** punishes those who break the law to **warn** others and **stop** them **doing the same**.

- Examples of deterrence include: **imprisonment, fines, community service.**

- **Protection** removes the offender **from society** so they can't cause harm anymore.

- Protection most commonly uses **imprisonment**.

- **Reform** aims to make the offender see the **error of their ways** and change their behaviour.

- Reform often uses prison to **teach** offenders **new skills**.

Understanding the aims of punishment

- **All punishment** rests on the principle of **just deserts**, that the offender receives the punishment **appropriate to their crime**.

- **Punishment is different** from revenge. Revenge is inflicting harm on someone without authority in retaliation (paying back) for something which was considered to be unfair.

- **Retribution** is based on the idea of **fair play**; it is only fair that if someone breaks the law when everyone else is keeping to it, they should be punished.

- The **problem with retribution** is that the punishment might be judged to be as morally bad as the crime itself.

- The **problem with deterrence** is knowing whether a punishment **actually does stop** others from offending.

- The **problem with protection** is that it is not punishment as retribution and deterrence are; prison might appear to be a **soft option** for the offender.

- The **problem with reform** is that a high number of offenders **reoffend**.

Evaluating the aims of punishment

Should the only aim of punishment be to reform the offender?
Points to consider:

- **On the one hand ...** the aim should be to reform the offender because that shows respect for them as a person. The desire is not to make the offender suffer but to see them change and become a useful member of society.

- **On the other hand ...** reform is not the only aim of prison. The other more important aims are to protect society from offenders and to deter others from committing crimes and show that crime does not pay.

Should the victim of a crime decide how the offender should be punished?
Points to consider:

- **On the one hand ...** only the victim of a crime knows how it has affected their life. If the aim of punishment is to make the victim feel justice has been done, then the victim should select a suitable punishment.

- **On the other hand ...** a victim of crime is not in a good position to decide or select a suitable punishment. This could lead to revenge. A judge is in a much better position to decide what is a just punishment.

Ethics of imprisonment

Knowing about the ethics of imprisonment

- **Prison** is the most common form of punishment.

- The aim of imprisonment is to **protect** society and to **reform** the offender.

- Prison provides a means of **rehabilitation**, to adapt to life back in society.

- Prison as **rehabilitation** is supported by **utilitarians** and **Christian** reformers.

- In 2014–15 in the UK the **reoffending** rate among **adults** released from prison was **23.8 per cent**.

- In 2014–15 in the UK the **reoffending** rate among **juveniles** (10–18 year olds) released from prison was **37.8 per cent**.

Understanding the ethics of imprisonment

- A major challenge is to get the **balance right** between **reform** and **retribution**.

- Many think prisons are **too comfortable** and that conditions should be harsher to make retribution more effective and to be a greater deterrent to others.

- Others argue that **loss of freedom** in prison is an effective punishment.

- The **Prison Reform Trust** argues that prisons should be a **last resort** and only used for **serious offences**.

- Prisons are **overcrowded** and don't protect inmates from bad influences. They are '**universities of crime**' and make offenders worse not better citizens.

- Overcrowded prisons **depersonalise** inmates and this makes it very hard to fulfil the aim of reform and to prepare offenders for the outside world.

Evaluating the ethics of imprisonment

If prisons were harsher, would there be less crime?
Points to consider:

- **On the one hand ...** harsher prisons would certainly make potential offenders think twice about committing a crime. Some think that crime does pay if the prison sentence is only for a short period of time and life inside is reasonably comfortable.

- **On the other hand ...** harsher prisons would not deter potential offenders. A person committing a crime is probably not thinking about being imprisoned and if life inside prison is very harsh it just makes them resentful.

Should prisons only be used for the most serious crimes?
Points to consider:

- **On the one hand ...** prisons are overcrowded and many offences should be punished using community service and fines. Overcrowded prisons create more problems than they solve; prisons should be used only for the most serious crimes.

- **On the other hand ...** the fact that some prisons are overcrowded doesn't mean that prison is not the right punishment. Restricting someone's freedom is a major punishment which prison does effectively and should not just be used for those who have committed serious crimes.

Ethics of capital punishment

Knowing about the ethics of capital punishment

- Capital punishment uses the death penalty to punish offenders.

- It is no longer used in the UK.

- It is **used in countries** such as China, India, Iran, Singapore and USA.

- It is mostly used for **murder**.

- Other offences for which it is used include treason, adultery and selling illegal drugs.

- One of the most famous cases to prompt a debate about the use of capital punishment was that of **Nathan Leopold and Richard Loeb** in 1924 in the USA.

- Leopold and Loeb planned and **brutally killed** 14-year-old **Bobby Franks**.

- **Clarence Darrow**, their defence lawyer, argued that capital punishment was not appropriate because the boys were **mentally disturbed** and **not totally responsible** for their actions.

- They were sentenced to **imprisonment** and not capital punishment.

Understanding the ethics of capital punishment
For:

- When extremely bad crimes have been committed, capital punishment helps the family of the victims **feel justice has been done**.

- The Old Testament states: 'Whoever **sheds blood**, by humans **shall their blood be shed**.'

- Capital punishment **deters** others from committing bad crimes and sends out a message that such acts will **not be tolerated by society**.
- Capital punishment **protects** society from dangerous criminals.
- By accepting capital punishment, the offender shows they are **sorry** for the crime they have committed.

Against:

- **Christians** and many others argue that the 'eye for an eye' aim of punishment is wrong because **punishing a murderer by killing them** is morally **contradictory**.
- The **social background** and **mental state** of the offender often indicate that they are not totally in control of their actions – this is called **diminished responsibility**.
- There is **no conclusive evidence** that capital punishment does deter people from carrying out horrendous crimes.
- **Prison** is as much a **form of protection** as capital punishment and **far less brutal**.
- The **state** is **far from perfect** and has no right to **take away a life**.
- Capital punishment is **irreversible** and makes **reform** and **rehabilitation impossible**.

Evaluating the ethics of capital punishment
Is using capital punishment as morally bad as the crime committed?
Points to consider:

- **On the one hand ...** no one has the right to take away someone else's life even if their crime is horrendous – that is why murder is morally very bad. If the state kills or executes someone in cold blood, this is as morally bad as the crime itself.
- **On the other hand ...** when the state executes someone, it does so because it has the authority to do so as punishment not murder. So, execution for a horrendous crime is retributive justice and is morally justifiable.

Can capital punishment be justified for betraying one's country?
Points to consider:

- **On the one hand ...** betraying one's country by giving secrets to an enemy country is putting the whole country into considerable danger. Capital punishment is justified as it warns others just how serious the crime is.
- **On the other hand ...** life imprisonment is a much better punishment as there is no guarantee that capital punishment will deter others and killing its citizens, however bad their crime, is not a sign of a civilised society.

2.3 Prejudice, discrimination and freedom

Prejudice and discrimination

Knowing about prejudice and discrimination

- Prejudice is holding a belief which is **biased against** a certain group of people **based on little or no evidence**.
- These beliefs are often based on **stereotypes**.

- Discrimination is the **unfavourable treatment** of a person or group.
- **Prejudices are caused by:**
  - **threat** – for example, feeling that the loss of jobs is caused by outsiders
  - **fear** – irrational fear of behaviours that differ from one's own culture, customs, race, gender, sexuality
  - **ideology** – thinking that only one's own political, philosophical or religious view is right.
- The **Stephen Lawrence** case revealed how even the police investigating a racially motivated murder were racially prejudiced.

Understanding prejudice and discrimination

- **Prejudice and discrimination** can lead to many social problems such as:
  - violence and harassment
  - unfair employment and earnings
  - poor housing and living conditions
  - inferior education.
- Institutionalised discrimination occurs when **individuals** are **unknowingly** biased against a certain group because of the way **society or an institution** (such as the police, the army, a school) has **conditioned** them to think.
- The **Macpherson Report** was an important report on racism which highlighted the problem of **unconscious prejudice** and **discrimination** in many areas of public institutions.

Evaluating prejudice and discrimination
Is being prejudiced always bad?
Points to consider:

- **On the one hand ...** people are naturally prejudiced because they are biased towards the beliefs and customs with which they have been brought up and which they value. This is not bad, providing they understand why other people may have different values.

- **On the other hand ...** being prejudiced nearly always leads to discrimination against others because people want to preserve their own values and customs and resist the views of others. This leads to social problems.

Should all forms of prejudice and discrimination be punishable?
Points to consider:

- **On the one hand ...** any form of prejudice and discrimination should be punished because a society that values all its citizens must send out a strong message that sexism and racism, for example, are deeply disrespectful and reduce the freedom of people to live happy lives.

- **On the other hand ...** not all forms of prejudice and discrimination are necessarily intentional. Some people might unknowingly discriminate because of the institution they belong to. They should be educated to see the nature of their prejudice rather than being punished.

Freedom

Knowing about freedom

Freedom

- **J.S. Mill** argued that freedom is a **basic human necessity** to live a **happy life**.
- He called this necessity the **liberty principle**.
- The only reason why liberty may be **interfered with** is **harm to others** and **harm to oneself**.
- The liberty principle has led to more **tolerant societies**.
- Freedoms are supported and protected by **human rights**.
- The **Universal Declaration of Humans Rights** (1948) states that 'All humans are born free and equal in dignity and rights.'
- Rights imply **duties**, duties to **respect** the **rights** and **freedoms of others**.

Freedom of speech

- Freedom of speech is the basis for modern democracy.
- Slander is **speaking untruths** about someone in public.
- Libel is **writing** and **publishing untruths** about someone.
- A **major** problem today is how the **internet** is to be controlled.

Freedom of action

- **Freedom of expression** also includes expressing one's views through **actions**.
- **Political freedom** of action includes: holding meetings, conducting marches, protesting.
- **Interventions** reduce someone's actions in their **best interests**.
- **Carers** may use **interventions** to limit the freedoms of those with **disabilities** (physical and mental) for their own good.

Freedom of belief

- Freedom of belief is also referred to as intellectual freedom.
- Freedom of belief includes being **free to hold** a variety of **religious**, **political** and **moral** beliefs.

Understanding freedom

- A central moral issue is where to set the **limits of free speech**.
- The **liberty principle** is against censorship unless it is for the **greater good**.
- For example, the press might **not be allowed to publish** information if it is against the **national interest**.
- Not having freedom to perform political actions would be a form of imprisonment and might lead to a **police state**.
- **Limiting freedom of action** poses the problem of **who decides** what is in the **best interests** of someone and when this **justifies an intervention**.

- **Freedom of belief** is important in a **multicultural society** and leads to a greater **variety** of ideas.

- Freedom of belief leads to **healthy political debates** and **intellectual discussions** at schools and universities.

- **Restrictions** on **freedom of belief** might, for example, be to:

  - make it illegal for someone to express sexually or racially offensive ideas by punishing them

  - state that it is unprofessional for teachers to express their political views to their pupils.

Evaluating freedom

Should the press regulate itself?
Points to consider:

- **On the one hand ...** the press should regulate itself because of the right to freedom of expression. If the press is regulated by the state, then citizens are not going to have access to a wide range of information, which reduces their freedom of belief.

- **On the other hand ...** the press should be regulated externally because often it fails to respect people's privacy because it is motivated by selling copies and making money. Even if what is published is not libel, it can badly damage someone's reputation.

Are people free to believe whatever they wish?
Points to consider:

- **On the one hand ...** people are free to believe whatever they wish, however absurd, as long as these beliefs don't directly discriminate against others and reduce their freedom of belief.

- **On the other hand ...** people are not free to believe whatever they wish because society does not tolerate ideas that express hatred towards certain groups of people based on gender, race, religion or disability, for example.

Treatment of the marginalised in society

Knowing about treatment of the marginalised in society

- The marginalised might include:

  - people who **do not contribute to society**, for example the poor, drug/alcohol abusers

  - those whom **society marginalises** because of **prejudice**, for example disabled people, women, immigrants, ethnic minorities.

Understanding the ethical issues surrounding the treatment of the marginalised in society

- An important moral aim is to **shift attitudes** to the marginalised and **change their status** in society.

- Changing attitudes may come about through **conscious direct action** by:

  - **positive action** – acting in favour of a marginalised group over the non-marginalised

  - affirmative action – combating the conditions that have caused a group to be marginalised through legislation.

- The **moral problem** with positive and affirmative action is that it could be thought to be **unfair** to the non-marginalised and cause **resentment**.

- The marginalised may **not want special treatment** through positive action.

Evaluating the ethical issues surrounding the treatment of the marginalised in society
Will there always be marginalised members of society?
Points to consider:

- **On the one hand ...** with proper education and anti-discrimination laws over time it will be possible to eliminate prejudices that marginalise certain members of society.

- **On the other hand ...** it will always be a risk that in allowing people freedom of expression, some will have prejudices which will marginalise other members of society. Some people marginalise themselves because of their anti-social behaviour.

Is positive action unfair?
Points to consider:

- **On the one hand ...** positive action is not fair because it favours a group based not on their appropriate skills or qualifications but because in the past they have been discriminated against. It is patronising to the marginalised group.

- **On the other hand ...** it is fair because it compensates the marginalised group for the injustices of the past. Favouring the marginalised group will also help shift attitudes and create greater equality in the future.

2.4 The environment

The human treatment of the environment

Knowing about the human treatment of the environment
There are many ethical responses to environment issues. Two broad responses are those of the environmentalists and environmental sceptics.

Environmental issues

- Environmental crisis refers to major changes in the natural world which **threaten human life** and **other forms of life**.

- Environmental **issues** include:

  - climate change

  - production of greenhouse gases

  - depletion of the ozone layer

  - use of fossil or natural fuels

  - rise in world population

  - pollution.

Environmentalists

- Environmentalists argue that there is an **urgent need to act now**.

- **Extreme global weather** conditions are causing **catastrophic effects** in the environment.

- **Humans** are **largely to blame** and have a **duty to future generations** to **act now**.

- Al Gore's film *An Inconvenient Truth* (2006) presented the **catastrophic impact** of **human activities** on the environment.

- Major world players such a **multi-national corporations** (MNCs) have a key role in developing **responsible environmental policies**.

Environmental sceptics

- Environmental sceptics are **not climate change deniers**.

- They are **sceptical** or **cautious** about the **extreme views of environmentalists**.

- **Science** has **not proved humans** are **totally to blame** for climate change.

- The **catastrophe** position works on **fear** not **genuine moral concern**.

- Humans have to **balance their needs** against the **needs of nature**.

- For example, **hydroelectricity** is good because it **reduces the use of fossil fuels** but it **causes loss of natural habitats**.

- The philosopher **Arne Næss** (1912–2009) argued that in future we should develop **small sustainable communities**.

Understanding the human treatment of the environment

- **Environmental ethics** depend on how the environment is viewed and the part played in it by humans.

- Shallow ecologists, such as **utilitarians**, believe humans should look after the environment because it is in **their best interests** in the long term to do so.

- **Middle ecologists**, such as **Christians**, believe **God created** the world to be good and humans have a **duty** to maintain it responsibly as His **stewards**.

- Deep ecologists, such as **Buddhists**, believe that every aspect of the world is connected and therefore humans have a duty to animals, plants and even rocks to treat them with respect.

Evaluating the human treatment of the environment
Are humans only concerned for the environment for selfish reasons?
Points to consider:

- **On the one hand ...** humans only care for the environment for selfish reasons but there is nothing wrong with this from a utilitarian point of view because if they don't care for the environment, then it will cause them harm.

- **On the other hand ...** humans care for the environment for other reasons. They may act for Christian reasons as they have a duty to be good stewards of the world and to look after its ecosystems because that is the God-given order of things.

Are deep ecologists the only people who treat the world with genuine respect?
Points to consider:

- **On the one hand ...** deep ecologists consider humans to be part of the ecosystem and not superior to it. This means they have genuine respect for all aspects of the world.

- **On the other hand ...** shallow ecologists respect the world because they know what will happen to it if they don't. They believe that environmental catastrophes resulting from climate change are the result of human activity.

Ethical treatment of animals

Knowing about the ethical treatment of animals

- **Over-farming** can cause **loss of biodiversity** and reduction of food chains.
- Cows **excrete methane** which damages the **ozone layer**.
- Some philosophers, such as **Descartes**, argued that animals **don't have souls**.
- If animals don't have souls, then they are **no different from machines** and humans can **use them as they wish**.
- The **utilitarian** philosopher **Bentham** argued that **animals can suffer** and so humans should treat them with **care**.
- Animal ethical issues include:
  - **testing drugs** on animals before giving the drugs to humans
  - using animals for **human entertainment** in zoos and circuses
  - using animal **tissues** for humans.

Understanding the ethical treatment of animals

- A major moral issue is whether humans should eat animals or be vegetarian.
- Arguments **against meat eating**:
  - Humans can live **healthy lives** without eating meat.
  - Killing animals to eat them causes them **pain**.
  - Far too many animals are **intensively farmed** and killed just to give humans **pleasure**.
  - If **eating human animals** is **morally bad,** so is eating non-human animals.
  - **Vegetarianism** is better for the planet.
- Arguments **for meat eating**:
  - Humans are **designed** to eat meat.
  - Humans get **pleasure** from eating as do **non-human carnivores**.
  - Humans are **morally superior** to animals, so eating them is **not equivalent** to eating humans.

Evaluating the ethical treatment of animals
Is it wrong to use animals for human entertainment?
Points to consider:

- **On the one hand ...** many animals have a close relationship with humans and enjoy their company and like performing for them. If animals are looked after properly, there is no reason why they should not be used for human entertainment.
- **On the other hand ...** some animals are used to fight each other and are trained to do unnatural things simply for human entertainment. This shows very little respect for non-human animals and their right to live in their natural habitat.

Is eating meat morally acceptable?
Points to consider:

- **On the one hand ...** eating meat is natural for humans just as it is natural for non-human carnivores to eat other non-human animals. Providing the animals are looked after well and killed humanely, then there is no strong moral objection.

- **On the other hand ...** humans can live healthy lives without eating meat. If it is wrong to kill human animals, then it also morally wrong to kill non-human animals. There is no humane way of killing animals.

Ethical treatment of the material world

Knowing about the ethical treatment of the material world

- **Conservation** is the management of natural resources to avoid loss and damage.

- This can be done through **political agreements** at **world summits**.

- Summits are meetings of **world leaders**.

- Examples of world climate summits are **Kyoto** (1997) and **Copenhagen** (2009).

- At the **Paris Climate Agreement** (2015) countries agreed to reduce global temperature rises.

- 'Thinking green' means changing people's attitudes through, for example, education, change in building regulations and recycling.

Understanding the ethical treatment of the material world

- There are two main approaches to dealing with the material world:

  - political and on a **large scale**

  - personal and at a **local level**.

- **Shallow ecologists** tend to stress the global and political environmental issues.

- **Deep ecologists** prefer to get people to think at a local level about their relationship to the material world.

Evaluating the ethical treatment of the material world
Do we have a responsibility to future generations to care for the material world now?
Points to consider:

- **On the one hand ...** we do have a responsibility to future generations because although they don't yet exist, they rely on us to look after the material world as best as we can so they can enjoy the world as we do.

- **On the other hand ...** we can't be responsible to people who don't yet exist. We can care for the material world for ourselves but there is no law or duty to say we should do more than this.

Is thinking green at a local level the best way of caring for the environment?
Points to consider:

- **On the one hand ...** thinking green at a local level is the best way because people care more for the local environment and see the effects of caring for it more immediately.

- **On the other hand ...** thinking green at a local level is a good start but it does not deal with global problems which are much more dangerous and could be catastrophic. The best way of caring for the environment is for governments to make their policies greener.

Practise answering questions with *Theology, Philosophy and Religion 13+ Exam Practice Questions and Answers* pages 5–6 and 45–49.

Test yourself ✓

1 What does nihilism mean?

2 What is resurrection?

3 What is reincarnation?

4 Outline the three main parts of the just war theory.

5 Define retributive punishment.

6 Outline two aims of imprisonment.

7 Give one reason for and one reason against capital punishment.

8 Give a definition of prejudice and discrimination.

9 Give two examples of freedom of action.

10 What is positive action?

11 What do environmentalists believe?

12 What do deep ecologists believe about the environment?

Glossary

affirmative action Combating the conditions that have caused a group to be marginalised through legislation

Al Gore Vice-President of the USA (1993–2001). Produced the film *An Inconvenient Truth* (2006) presenting the catastrophic impact of human activities on the environment.

Albert Camus French novelist and philosopher (1913–60), explored various kinds of nihilism

analogy Using something that is known to explain something new

anthropomorphism Describing an animal or object in human-like terms

censorship Prohibiting all or part of a book, film, speech, etc.

civil disobedience Protesting against the state by disobeying an unfair law

consequentialist Someone who practises consequentialist ethics, who judges the rightness of an action by its outcome

David Hume Scottish philosopher and historian (1711–76) influenced by Isaac Newton who developed a version of sceptical (questioning) reasoning

death penalty A punishment used by the state when it executes someone who has performed a grossly offensive act

deep ecologists Ecologists who focus on the close relationship humans have with the material world

design argument An argument which concludes that because the world appears ordered and designed that this indicates the existence of God who has designed it

discrimination The unfavourable treatment of a person or group

environmental crisis Major changes in the natural world which threaten human life and other forms of life

equality Treating people in a fair and equal way

freedom Being able to act according to one's wishes without interference

institutionalised discrimination Occurs when individuals are unknowingly biased against a certain group because of the way society or an institution has conditioned them to think

intellectual freedom Freedom of belief

John Stuart Mill Philosopher and social reformer (1806–73) who developed his ideas of liberty and utilitarianism

Jean-Paul Sartre French philosopher and writer (1905–80) who developed a philosophy of positive nihilism

just war War that is justified according to various conditions: justification for going to war, justice in war, justice after war

libel Writing and publishing untruths about someone

liberty principle The principle that humans are happiest when they have the freedom to choose how they wish to live their life

Martin Luther King Christian minister and civil rights campaigner (1929–68) who led many protests for black rights

monotheism Belief in and worship of one God

moral dilemma The problem of how to act when two or more moral rules or principles clash

pacifism The view that if killing and violence are morally wrong, then war is wrong

parable of the cave Plato's analogy or story comparing the world of illusion as existence in a cave and reality as life outside a cave

Plato Greek philosopher (427–347 B.C.E.), taught by Socrates, who lived in Athens and founded the Academy

polytheism Belief in and worship of many Gods

prejudice Holding a belief that is biased against a certain group of people based on little or no evidence

quality of life principle Human life is only valuable when a person can feel pleasure/pain and the person experiences more pleasure than pain

revenge Inflicting harm on someone without authority, in retaliation (paying back) for something that was considered to be unfair

samsara Reincarnation or the process of birth and rebirth over many lifetimes

sanctity of life principle The belief that all human life is God-given and therefore sacred

shallow ecologists Ecologists who focus mainly on environmental issues if they impact on humans

slander Speaking untruths about someone in public

Socrates Greek philosopher (died 399 B.C.E.), who developed a method of argument based on questioning. He was condemned to death for treason by corrupting the minds of young Athenians.

utilitarianism Consequential ethical system based on the idea of the greatest happiness of the greatest number

RELIGION

The following chapters in Section 3, cover the six world religions prescribed in the syllabus:

- Buddhism

- Christianity

- Hinduism

- Islam

- Judaism

- Sikhism

If you are answering a question from Section 3 for the examination, then you only need to revise **one** religion. If you are not sure which one to revise, then check with your teacher.

A: Buddhism

1 Buddhist beliefs and teachings

> Read *Religion for Common Entrance 13+* pages 1–16.

1.1 The Buddha

Siddhartha's early life

Siddhartha, who became the **Buddha**, is the central figure of Buddhism. His example is sometimes used as a parable to show people how to live and aim for enlightenment.

Knowing about Siddhartha's early life

- Siddhartha Gautama was born **563 B.C.E.** in Lumbini.

- Siddhartha's father, **King Shuddhodana**, was **ruler** of a **Northern Indian** clan.

- His mother gave birth to him **painlessly** and he was able to **walk immediately** afterwards.

- Asita, a holy man, predicted that Siddhartha would grow up to be either a great **religious teacher** and would give **away all his possessions** or a **great ruler**.

- His **father** lavished great **luxury** on Siddhartha so he would **not be interested in religion** and avoid seeing suffering and decay.

- But, deep down, Siddhartha was **not happy** with all this luxury.

- At a **ploughing festival** he was able to use the movement of the plough to meditate with ease.

Understanding Siddhartha's early life

- Stories and **legends** of Siddhartha's early life are intended to show that he was always going to be a **great spiritual leader** of great compassion.

- His **painless birth** showed how he had overcome **pappa karma** (negative karma).

- The appearance of a **rainbow** and **lotus flowers** at his birth are symbols that Siddhartha was to be an **enlightened person**.

- This was his **last reincarnation** because he was to become **the Buddha** and achieve parinirvana.

- The **ploughing festival** showed how **naturally** spiritual Siddhartha was and his natural **compassion** (karuna) for all creatures (he was upset that the plough would be killing insects and worms).

Evaluating Siddhartha's early life
Does it matter if the story of Siddhartha's early life is made up?
Points to consider:

- **On the one hand ...** it does not matter because his later life shows that he was a great person who showed compassion and love for all creatures. The stories are intended to emphasise how special he was.

- **On the other hand ...** it does matter because if it is made up we cannot trust anything else about his life. Many strange things happen in nature – rainbows and flowers can appear when we do not expect them.

Was the ploughing festival the most important event in Siddhartha's early life?
Points to consider:

- **On the one hand ...** it was the most important event because it was then that he found how to meditate, which is central to Buddhism. It also made him realise that his future was probably as a teacher and holy person.

- **On the other hand ...** it was more important that he discovered that there is more to life than what he experienced in the palace and his gradual realisation that great material luxury does not bring happiness.

The four sights

Knowing about the four sights

- Siddhartha was not happy with his life and **wanted to see life outside** the palace.

- At the **age of 29** he set out with **Channa**, his chariot driver, from his palace and saw **four sights**:

  - an **old person**

  - a **sick person**

  - a **dead person**

  - a wandering **holy man**.

Understanding the four sights

- The four sights contrast with Siddhartha's life in the palace.

- They form the basis of the **three marks of existence**.

- Becoming **old** shows that **everything changes** and decays (anicca); decay/anicca cannot be avoided.

- **Sickness** shows that the physical life is fragile and **subject to pain** (dukkha).

- **Death** indicates what inevitably happens to all physical life; it comes to an end – this causes **mental suffering** (dukkha) as we know even happy lives will come to an end.

- The **holy man** shows that despite suffering and change, life can offer **spiritual satisfaction** and happiness.

Evaluating the four sights

Is seeing the dead person the most significant of the four sights?
Points to consider:

- **On the one hand ...** it is the most significant because it is the one thing that happens to all living things and cannot be avoided. Facing up to the reality of death puts all the three other sights into perspective.

- **On the other hand ...** the most significant sight is the sick person because sickness is a more common everyday experience and illustrates dukkha better than the prospect of death.

The journey to enlightenment, teaching and death

Knowing about the journey to enlightenment, teaching and death

Journey to enlightenment

- Siddhartha first lived an ascetic life, avoiding physical pleasures, **eating almost nothing** and practising some extreme yogic exercises like breath-control.

- He was joined by **five ascetics** who also practised extreme forms of fasting.

- **After six years** he realised that this did **not bring enlightenment**.

- He almost died but a young girl, **Sujata**, gave him some **milk rice** to eat.

- He followed his intuition that the true path to enlightenment was a **middle way** – avoiding the extremes of **asceticism** and sensual **pleasure**.

- Siddhartha's **five ascetic companions** were disappointed by his weakness and left him.

Enlightenment

- Siddhartha sat at the foot of a **great tree** in a forest near a village. Later the tree became known as the Bodhi tree (Bodhi meaning enlightenment) and the village was named **Bodh Gaya**.

- He **vowed** he would **stay there** until he had **discovered** the **truth**.

- He experienced many **temptations** throughout the **night**.

- The **god of illusion**, Mara, tried to stop him meditating by **tempting** him sexually with his daughters and **frightening** him with his army of sons.

- At **dawn** Siddhartha believed he had achieved **enlightenment** by gaining true **knowledge**.

- He was now called the **Buddha** or **Enlightened One**.

- He gained Three Great Knowledges.

- Out of **compassion** he decided to communicate to others what he had discovered.

Teaching and death

- After a few weeks at **Bodh Gaya**, the Buddha went to **Sarnath** where he began to **teach the** dharma.

- His first sermon is called '**Turning the Wheel of Dharma**'.

- The **five ascetics** returned and became his first monks or **bhikkhus**.

- At the age of **80**, the Buddha's **physical body passed away** and he achieved **final nirvana** (parinirvana) at a place called **Kushinara**.

- His body was **cremated** and his remains divided up and placed in **eight** stupas (monument buildings).

Understanding the journey to enlightenment, teaching and death

- There was a tradition of wanderers searching for the truth in India. Siddhartha at first followed what they taught but realised their extreme methods only made him more unhappy.

- **Sujata's** generosity (or dana) showed Siddhartha that he had been **selfish** in his quest; she recognised he was a **spiritual person** and would **become enlightened**.

- **Mara** is a **symbol** of all the obstacles to enlightenment which the Buddha could overcome by transforming the forces of **craving**, **hatred**, **fear** and **doubt** into positive states of mind.

- There are many ways in which the Buddha's enlightenment may be explained; one way is called **the Three Great Knowledges**.

- **First knowledge** – he confirmed that we have all lived many previous lives in various forms.

- **Second knowledge** – he saw how people's many previous lives and deaths are governed by their actions (karma).

- **Third knowledge** – the Four Noble Truths (see page 76) showed how anyone can overcome suffering (dukkha) using the right methods.

- The Buddha's **parinirvana** shows that although the historical Buddha is dead, he **lives on** through his **dharma** or teaching of the truth.

- The Buddha's **life is a parable** and example of how the **middle way** is to be achieved between the **extremes** of material **luxury** and **ascetism** (religious denial of food and material things).

Evaluating the journey to enlightenment, teaching and death
Would Siddhartha have achieved enlightenment without Sujata's offering?
Points to consider:

- **On the one hand ...** her action saved Siddhartha from near starvation and made him realise how rejecting food and other ordinary things of life makes one more self-centred. Had she not acted, Siddhartha might either have died or given up in despair.

- **On the other hand ...** Siddhartha had probably already realised that the ascetic life was not going to work; Sujata was one of several people who confirmed what he already thought.

Did Mara actually tempt Siddhartha?
Points to consider:

- **On the one hand ...** Siddhartha believed there were gods or spirits and the experience of the temptations which Mara offered him would have felt very real. He might have literally felt he was battling between Mara's sons and being sexually enticed by his daughters.

- **On the other hand ...** as Siddhartha's enlightenment was spiritual and in his mind, the temptations were no more than his own powerful negative desires which he had to turn into positive thoughts.

1.2 Dharma: three marks of existence

The dharma is the Buddha's teaching and is also called the **Path to Awakening**. The three marks of existence are that there are three universal true things about existence; these are the basis of the dharma.

Knowing about the three marks of existence

- **The first mark** is **anicca** – all conditioned things are **impermanent**, everything **changes**.

- **The second mark** is anatta – no one has **permanent self** or **soul**.

- **The third mark** is **dukkha** – there is **suffering** in the world. Life is unsatisfactory because everything changes and things **die**. The different types of suffering are:

  - **physical** and emotional suffering

  - **anxiety** and regret caused by change

  - **psychological** suffering caused by feeling there is no meaning to life.

- Accepting that the three marks are true is the first stage on the path to **enlightenment**.

Understanding the three marks of existence

- Anicca **cannot be stopped** (as the Buddha's father found when he tried to do this); trying to stop change causes suffering.

- **Change is good** as it allows people to develop.

- Anicca means that as **everything changes** there cannot be an **unchanging creator God**.

- Realising that everything is impermanent, that there is no fixed self and that there is suffering means that humans can see **life as it really is**.

- What I call 'I' is **constantly changing**, just as a river changes as it flows through its banks.

- Having **no fixed soul** gives humans **freedom** to change.

- Suffering (dukkha) is not negative once we understand what kind it is and so how to deal with it.

Evaluating the three marks of existence
Is having a soul what makes us a person?
Points to consider:

- **On the one hand …** having a soul is the special part of a person which makes one unique. It is our essential self which does not change, unlike the body, and is the source of our thoughts.

- **On the other hand …** having a soul is not what makes us a person, because we have a physical body, emotional experiences, thoughts and reason. All these elements combine to make us a person.

Does Buddhism focus too much on suffering?
Points to consider:

- **On the one hand …** it does not focus too much on suffering because suffering is part of life and although suffering can be terrible, coping with it enables us to live fuller, more creative and imaginative lives.

- **On the other hand …** given a choice between suffering and not suffering most people would choose not to suffer. Buddhism does focus on it too much; it should focus more on things that make us happy and fulfilled.

1.3 Dharma: Four Noble Truths

The Four Noble Truths are the Buddha's ways of dealing with mental and spiritual suffering just as a doctor might deal with physical suffering.

Knowing about the Four Noble Truths

- **The First Noble Truth** is that all life involves **suffering** or **dukkha**.

- **The Second Noble Truth** is samudaya – the cause of suffering which is craving or tanha. Tanha is caused by the three poisons:

  - **greed** – wanting more to satisfy desires (symbol: cockerel)

  - **hatred** and destructive behaviour (symbol: snake)

  - **ignorance** of the world as it really is (symbol: pig).

- **The Third Noble Truth** is nirodha, that if craving is overcome then so is suffering.
- **The Fourth Noble Truth** is magga or the Noble Eightfold Path, based on the principle of the **Middle Way** between the **extremes** of **luxury** and **hardship**.

The Noble Eightfold Path

- The path also helps **train the mind** to develop:

  1 **Right view** – progressively understanding the **dharma** and teaching of the Buddha

  2 **Right intention** – making a firm **commitment** to follow the path

  3 **Right speech** – making a moral commitment to **speak truthfully**, **kindly** and **harmoniously**

  4 **Right action** – making a moral commitment to the Five Precepts (see page 80)

  5 **Right livelihood** – making a moral commitment not to do any job which harms or **exploits** other **humans**, **animals** or the **environment**

  6 **Right effort** – cultivating through meditation **ethical mental states** such as **loving kindness** (metta), generosity, patience and **compassion** (karuna)

  7 **Right mindfulness** – developing continuous **presence of mind** by being aware of the body and its sensations; being mindful of the environment and other sentient beings

  8 **Right concentration** – through **meditation** by dwelling on higher states of consciousness free from the **three poisons**.

Understanding the Four Noble Truths

- The principle of **samudaya** is **optimistic** that despite the problems life throws at us, these can be overcome eventually (perhaps over many lives).
- **The Middle Way** teaches that extremes **do not bring enlightenment**. Life is about achieving a balance. The **Buddha's life** illustrates this well.
- **The Noble Eightfold Path** develops three important aspects of oneself:

  - **wisdom** (ways 1 and 2) – the ability to develop a right understanding of the world and one's place in it

  - **ethics** (ways 2–5) – the ability to make the right moral choices in day-to-day life

  - **meditation** (ways 6–8) – the ability to develop the right mindset and personal qualities such as compassion, love, generosity and selflessness.

- **The magga** is designed to deal with **everyday life**.
- Living the magga (way) takes practice and effort; Buddhism is realistic that not everyone may be able to do this.

Evaluating the Four Noble Truths

Is right intention the most important path in the magga?
Points to consider:

- **On the one hand ...** it must be the most important because without the right intention then all the other paths within the magga would be meaningless. The magga is based on the idea of 'right' action, speech and so on; right means intending to do these things well.

- **On the other hand ...** without having the right mindset then the intention could be wrong or confused. All the different parts of the magga work together to ensure that the person who follows it does so in the best possible way.

Does the magga really help in everyday life?
Points to consider:

- **On the one hand ...** the magga does help because the first two stages of the Four Noble Truths help isolate the source of a problem, then it looks at one's own motives such as greed or ignorance and then the various paths of the magga help one to develop the right attitude and act in the best interests of oneself and others.

- **On the other hand ...** the magga is not practical and is too abstract. In everyday life, there is not time to meditate and reflect when making decisions. The magga may be helpful for Buddhist monks and nuns who have the time to practise it, but not for ordinary people.

1.4 Ethical teachings

Buddhist ethics are not just theoretical but practical. Being moral also means developing one's character and spiritual awareness just as one might cultivate a garden so that all the plants grow well. Developing one's moral life is called bhavana.

Karma

Knowing about karma

- **Karma** means intentional **action**.
- It is the moral law of the universe and describes the **relationship** of **cause** and **effect** in nature.
- Actions that are **skilful** bring about **punna karma** – beneficial results for oneself and others.
- Actions that are **unskilful** bring about **pappa karma** – harmful results for oneself and others.
- Actions have **consequences** for **oneself** and **others now** and in **future lives** after **rebirth**.
- The **Noble Eightfold Path** gives **guidance on** how to perform **skilful actions**.

Understanding karma

- Karma is based on **observation of nature** which shows that all causes have effects.
- Understanding karma is essential to **behaving well** as we know that we **cannot escape the consequences** of our actions at some time (perhaps a future life).
- The best we can do in **difficult situations** is to ensure our intentions are good and our actions are skilfully done.
- Practising the Noble Eightfold Path means we are more likely to develop punna karma and **reduce dukkha**.

Evaluating karma
Does karma really explain why good people suffer bad things?
Points to consider:

- **On the one hand ...** it does explain why good people suffer bad things because we cannot know exactly what their intentions were in the past, either in this life or a previous life. Sometimes appearances may deceive us and someone who may appear to be good, is not truly so.

- **On the other hand ...** karma does not explain why good people suffer bad things. Their suffering could simply be bad luck or misfortune. It is hard to accept that a bad action in a previous life could specifically affect a person in a totally new life.

Re-becoming (samsara)

Knowing about re-becoming

- **Samsara** or re-becoming is the cycle of life–death–rebirth.

- The Buddha had **lived many previous lives** as a non-human animal.

- All **intentional actions** (karma) condition what one becomes in this life and the next life.

- The Buddha taught that this life and the next one might be compared to **lighting a candle from another candle**: the second candle/flame is different from the first, but it could not exist without the first.

- Samsara is represented by the image of the Wheel of Life. The six realms it represents are:

  - **god** world

  - **human** realm

  - **animal** world

  - **hell** realm

  - **hungry ghost** realm

  - **aggressive** god realm.

Understanding re-becoming

- Samsara is not a theory as it describes the **observable processes** of **nature**.

- Re-becoming, re-birth or reincarnation **cannot be proved** but it explains how in some way all **sentient** beings (beings who are able to think and feel) live many lives and are affected by their **previous actions**.

- The different realms in the **Wheel of Life** might **not be actual realms** but explain different aspects of our characters.

- The **Wheel of Life** might describe **actual realms** which sentient beings pass through on their journey to enlightenment.

- For example, the **animal world** could refer to actual animals which we might have lived in during another life or to our human animal self when we only crave food and sex and not spiritual things.

Evaluating re-becoming
Is there any evidence that re-becoming is true?
Points to consider:

- **On the one hand ...** although some people think they can recall previous lives, there is no way of proving whether these are actual memories or the result of something they have read about and forgotten.

- **On the other hand ...** some people under hypnosis can be taken back to earlier lives which they describe in detail. The detail is often found to be true. Knowing who one was in a previous life helps explain who one is now.

Does the Wheel of Life describe actual realms of existence?
Points to consider:

- **On the one hand ...** the realms actually exist because we can observe animal and human realms. There are reasons to suppose other realms may exist which we cannot see as they are inhabited by spiritual beings who are different from ourselves, such as gods and spirits.

- **On the other hand ...** it is more helpful to think of the realms as being sides of our character. By reflecting on each of them we can think where we have got to in our journey through life.

Compassion and loving kindness

Knowing about compassion and loving kindness

- Compassion or **karuna** is the desire for all sentient beings to live well.

- Loving kindness or **metta** is the experience of oneness with all living things.

- Metta and karuna are closely related.

- The Buddha gives the **example of a mother saving her child** without concern for her own life.

- The metta and karuna are the basis of the **Five Precepts** or pansils:

  - Avoid harming **sentient life**.

  - Avoid taking what is **not yours**.

  - Avoid committing any **sexually harmful** act.

  - Avoid **harmful speech**.

  - Avoid clouding the mind with **intoxicants**.

- The **metta meditation** may be used to develop metta and karuna.

Understanding compassion and loving kindness

- Metta and karuna are at the **heart of Buddhist ethics** because all sentient beings are dependent on each other.

- People must be **generous** to those who are weaker than themselves and depend on them.

- The pansils expand the ethics paths in the **Noble Eightfold Path**. Avoiding harmful acts develops **personal** punna karma, harmonious **societies** and a cared for **environment**.

Evaluating compassion and loving kindness
Would the world be perfect if everyone practised metta and karuna?
Points to consider:

- **On the one hand ...** the world would be transformed because everyone would genuinely care for everyone else and be sensitive to their needs. Metta and karuna would help overcome differences because we wouldn't be acting out of self-interest.

- **On the other hand ...** not everyone is capable of practising metta and karuna because they are not motivated to do so. It is simply unrealistic to suppose perfection is possible.

Are the pansils obvious?
Points to consider:

- **On the one hand ...** they are obvious because all humans know that failure to respect other people – their bodies and minds – causes harm and makes life unhappy. Most cultures have similar rules.

- **On the other hand ...** the pansils are not obvious because if they were then more people would carry them out and respect them. The fact that the Buddha had to teach them shows they do not come naturally to many people.

Nirvana and parinirvana

Knowing about nirvana and parinirvana

- Nirvana literally means **blowing out**.

- It is liberation from **samsara**.

- What is blown out are the three poisons of **hate**, **greed** and **ignorance** which drive the Wheel of Life.

- **Nirvana** is the positive state of **freedom**, **unconditional love**, **contentment**, **joy**, **peace**, **energy** and **fearlessness**.

- **Nirvana** is the term used to describe the **enlightened state**.

- **Parinirvana** occurs once the physical body has passed away. It cannot be described.

- The **Buddha's death** is known as his parinirvana.

Understanding nirvana and parinirvana

- Nirvana is very hard to describe because it is **beyond ordinary thought**.

- Nirvana can be achieved by developing **metta** and **karuna** for all sentient beings.

- Only in **meditation** can nirvana be **experienced**.

- Nirvana is **freedom** from **dukkha** and utter contentment; the experience is beyond ordinary language.

- **Parinirvana** is achieved only when a person has no **pappa karma**. We cannot know what this state is like, but we assume it is one of complete bliss.

Evaluating nirvana and parinirvana
Is nirvana desirable?
Points to consider:

- **On the one hand ...** one cannot actively desire nirvana as desire is a form of tanha or attachment. Nirvana should emerge naturally from being kind and generous. Bodhisattvas are good examples of beings who don't desire nirvana but the happiness of others.

- **On the other hand ...** nirvana is desirable as an ultimate goal as it is a state of complete contentment. Desire in this sense does not have to be attachment, but the result of metta.

Is nirvana an illusion?
Points to consider:

- **On the one hand ...** it is an illusion because it can't be described and we can only take other **people's word** for it that they have experienced it. As it can only be experienced in meditation, it could just be a **figment of a person's imagination**.

- **On the other hand ...** nirvana is not an illusion because the **Buddha was inspired** by it; it formed the basis of all his **teaching**. It can't be an illusion for **so many people** over **so many years** to have experienced and changed the way they see the world.

Practise answering questions with *Theology, Philosophy and Religion 13+ Exam Practice Questions and Answers* pages 7–8 and 50–54.

Test yourself ✓

1 What was Asita's prediction at Siddhartha's birth?

2 Name the four sights.

3 What was the role of Mara in Siddhartha's enlightenment?

4 Name the three marks of existence.

5 What is nirodha?

6 Name any three paths in the Noble Eightfold Path.

7 What is karma?

8 Name any three of the six realms of the Wheel of Life.

9 What do metta and karuna mean?

10 What are the three poisons which are blown out in nirvana?

11 What is parinirvana?

2 Buddhist practices and ceremonies

Read *Religion for Common Entrance 13+* pages 17–29.

You should be aware that there are different Buddhist traditions. The main two are: **Theravada Buddhism** and **Mahayana Buddhism**. In Theravada there is more emphasis on being a bhikkhu (monk) or bhikkhuni (nun) and in Mahayana the spiritual ideal is the **bodhisattva** – a person or being of great compassion. There are many forms of Mahayana; **Zen Buddhism** is one example which you should know about.

2.1 Mettation

2.1 Meditation

Knowing about meditation

Aims of meditation

- Meditation is the third element of the Noble Eightfold Path.
- Meditation is **bhavana** which means **cultivating the mind** or developing the mind.
- It makes the mind and heart clearer so as ultimately to achieve enlightenment.

Samatha meditation

- Samatha means **concentration** and tranquillity.
- It can be practised using a breathing exercise to achieve **mindfulness**.
- It might use the **metta meditation** practice.

Vipassana meditation

- Vipassana means **insight**.
- It is often done under supervision of a **spiritual master**.
- It uses **visualisations**, such as bringing to mind a **buddha** or **bodhisattva**.
- By reflecting on a buddha's or bodhisattva's **qualities** a person can become more like them.

Zen meditation

- Zen Buddhists believe that all humans have Buddha nature.
- Buddha nature means that humans all have the **potential to become enlightened**.
- A koan is a **short story** or **sentence** or **haiku** which at first makes very little sense.
- An example of a koan is the **story of the muddy road**.
- Koans are used to make someone **think differently** about the world and achieve satori, spiritual awakening.
- Zen meditation might include special ceremonies such as **tea-making** and **flower arranging**.

- **Zazen** means **just sitting**. The person sits upright and focuses on the area below the navel.

- **Kinhin** means **walking** and is used between zazen sessions. The person focuses on their walking and breathing.

Understanding meditation

- Meditation is more than **just relaxing**, it requires **effort**, **determination** and **practice**.

- Meditation means becoming more **open to life** and to **loving kindness** (metta) by focusing the mind on others.

- Caring about the heart and mind helps develop more **happiness**.

- Meditation helps to **overcome** the **three poisons**.

- The purpose of vipassana meditation is to learn that the dharma is **not theory** but an **insight** into how things in existence **actually are**.

- Having Buddha nature means that enlightenment is **not restricted** to a few special people (such as monks) but is for **everyone**.

- All Zen meditation is designed to make a person more **mindful** so that ordinary things such as walking and making tea may be used to become conscious or mindful of one's **Buddha nature**.

Evaluating meditation
Is meditation no more than relaxation?
Points to consider:

- **On the one hand ...** meditation is a form of relaxation but this is only so that the mind can overcome the desires of the body and focus on higher thoughts and develop compassion for others.

- **On the other hand ...** meditation is no more than relaxation and a means of becoming calmer and more content with one's self. There are no higher thoughts.

Can koans really develop metta?
Points to consider:

- **On the one hand ...** koans develop metta because they force a person to think differently about the world and see it from the perspective of other people. This means that they become more compassionate to the situation of others and less focused on themselves.

- **On the other hand ...** koans are just brain teasers. They might confuse people; there is no reason why they should necessarily develop metta.

2.2 Buddhist places of worship

Temples, shrines and monuments

Knowing about temples, shrines and monuments
The Buddha and his monks at first had nowhere permanent to live. Their monasteries were created during the rainy season and gradually were used all the year round. Today Buddhist monks and nuns live in permanent viharas or monasteries/temples.

Temples and shrines

- The temple might include a **shrine room** which:

  - is the most important room in the temple

  - is used for **meditation**

- contains **Buddha** or **bodhisattva** images or **rupas**, in front of which are **seven offering bowls**

- contains **flowers**, **candles** and **incense** which are traditional **offerings**

- contains **cushions** for use in **meditation**.

- In the **temple grounds** there might be a **large Buddha rupa**, a **bodhi tree** and a **stupa** or monument.

Monuments

- **Monuments** or **stupas** are buildings which were originally built to contain the **ashes** of the **Buddha** after his death.

- The **important stupas** now commemorate significant places in the **Buddha's life** such as: **Lumbini**, **Bodh Gaya**, **Sarnath** and **Kushinara**.

- Stupas may also contain the ashes of bodhisattvas and great Buddhist teachers.

- **Pilgrims** walk **round the outside** of monuments as a form of **meditation** and respect.

- Stupas have inspired **Buddhist art** and architecture such as the pagoda in Japan.

Understanding temples, shrines and monuments

- **Shrine rooms** don't have to be part of a temple or vihara. Many people set up a shrine in their **home** so they can carry out meditation and **puja**.

- Shrine rooms at home may have the advantage of **fewer distractions** from other worshippers.

- Buddhist art contains many symbols which help worshippers focus on important Buddhist ideas such as:

  - the **eight-spoked wheel** which symbolises the dharma

  - the **bodhi-tree** which symbolises the Buddha's enlightenment

  - an **empty throne** which symbolises the Buddha's royal early life which he abandoned in his quest for enlightenment.

Evaluating temples, shrines and monuments

Do stupas of Buddhist teachers encourage hero worship?
Points to consider:

- **On the one hand ...** stupas are there to pay respect to great Buddhist teachers and to help Buddhists think about their teaching and example. Stupas, like rupas, are not there to be worshipped.

- **On the other hand ...** many stupas attract pilgrims and others who travel long distances. Inevitably this makes the teacher or bodhisattva far too important and encourages people to worship them as heroes.

Should shrines only be in temples?
Points to consider:

- **On the one hand ...** shrines should only be in temples because they can be administered properly by monks and nuns who will also make sure the shrines are treated with respect and puja is carried out properly.

- **On the other hand ...** having a shrine at home means a person doesn't have to find a shrine to meditate and carry out puja. It can be used at any time of the day.

Worship

Knowing about worship

For details about what is in a shrine room see page 84.

- **Worship** is called **puja**.
- **Puja** take place at a home shrine or in a temple shrine.
- A worshipper might make **offerings** of flowers and food.
- Puja begins by **lighting incense** and ringing a **bell** or gong.
- A person **bows three times** at the shrine itself and to the rupa.
- They also perform the mudra **of respect**.
- Worshippers sit on **cushions**.
- They chant and recite mantras together or individually.
- This may be followed by silence.

Understanding worship

- Offerings such as flowers and food treat the Buddha as an honoured guest.
- Light from **candles** represents the **presence of the dharma**.
- **Incense** creates a sense of **peace and calm** and symbolises good deeds.
- **Mudras and mantras** help by **controlling** body and mind; repeating words releases the mind from **attachment** to the words themselves and on to a higher meaning.
- **Silence** is essential as it aids meditation and **creates calm** in which to focus the mind.

Evaluating worship

Is puja at home more effective than in the temple?
Points to consider:

- **On the one hand ...** puja at home is more intimate and can be carried out at a person's own pace and at a time of their own choosing. Puja at home is probably quieter with fewer distractions than in a temple.
- **On the other hand ...** puja in the temple done with others with a common purpose can help concentration and give a greater sense of belonging to the sangha and metta for others.

Should all Buddhist worship be in silence?
Points to consider:

- **On the one hand ...** silence helps a person to become more aware of their thoughts and this helps them to become more conscious of all the distractions which stop them living a spiritual life.
- **On the other hand ...** silence itself can be a distraction and the mind can wander without direction. Chants and mantras can therefore help refocus the mind. So, not all Buddhist worship should be in silence, just some.

Buddha and bodhisattva images and symbols

Knowing about Buddha and bodhisattva images and symbols

Images or rupas

- An **image** is called a **rupa**.

- **Some** images are of the **historical Buddha**, some of **bodhisattvas** (enlightened beings).

- **Some** Buddhists like to **meditate** using **several images**.

- **Some** meditate just using an image of the **historical Buddha**.

- An **angry Buddha** rupa helps to direct **anger** in a **positive way**.

- The **flame** on a Buddha's head is a symbol of **enlightenment**.

- The **dot** in the middle of the Buddha's **forehead** is a symbol of **energy** and wisdom.

- Buddha's **long ears** symbolise his **royal origins**.

Symbols

- The **lotus flower** represents **enlightenment**, wisdom and compassion.

- The symbol of **stepping down** is a symbol of the way a **bodhisattva** comes to **help** people.

- The bodhisattva Avalokiteshvara has a **thousand arms** to represent **compassion** and love for all.

- **Vajra** means both **thunderbolt** and **diamond**. A vajra was originally used in war as a club. It symbolises **overcoming ignorance**.

- A **lotus flower** is a sign of **enlightenment** and of the journey of the mind from **ignorance** to **wisdom**.

- The **eight-spoked wheel** represents the **Noble Eightfold Path** and is a very common **symbol of Buddhism**.

Understanding Buddha and bodhisattva images and symbols

- The Buddha is never worshipped in Buddhism but various images are very helpful for **education** and **mediation**.

- Rupas are **never worshipped** but they represent the qualities of the bodhisattva or Buddha which the worshipper wishes to contemplate.

- Rupas are often used in puja and meditation to **develop tranquillity** and inner peace.

- Symbols serve a similar purpose as rupas in worship and meditation.

- The **eight-spoked wheel** or wheel of dharma reminds Buddhists of the Buddha's first sermon, '**Turning the Wheel of Dharma**', in which he outlined the basic principles of Buddhism.

- The **vajra** reminds us that, like a diamond, the **dharma can never be destroyed**. As a club, it symbolises **spiritual energy** and determination.

Evaluating Buddha and bodhisattva images and symbols
Are rupas a distraction in worship?
Points to consider:

- **On the one hand …** properly used and understood, rupas help a person become closer to the qualities a rupa represents. It helps them visualise these values as they are represented by the rupa. A much loved rupa develops metta in a person for others.

- **On the other hand …** it is very easy to become attached to a rupa and give it too much significance. A worshipper is then distracted into thinking that the rupa has special power.

Do Buddhist symbols only make sense if someone explains them?
Points to consider:

- **On the one hand ...** the point of a symbol is that a person doesn't need it explaining but just thinks about it and lets their mind draw its own conclusions. A Buddhist will apply Buddhist ideas naturally to the symbol.

- **On the other hand ...** not all symbols have obvious Buddhist meaning. It is not very clear that a vajra means having spiritual energy; this and other symbols need to be explained by a Buddhist teacher if they are to make sense.

Mudras, chanting and mantras

Knowing about mudras, chanting and mantras

Mudras

- Mudras are **special hand gestures** used in puja and meditation.

- They are also found in **Buddhist art**.

- The Buddha used the mudra of **touching the Earth** when defeating Mara.

- Other mudras include mudras of **argument**, **understanding**, **respect** and **meditation**.

Chanting

- Chanting is used to help **mental concentration** and devotion.

- Chanting helps **remember dharma**.

- Some use a **string of beads** to count off each time the **chant is repeated**.

- A chant is halfway between a **song** and singing on a **single note**.

- A well-known chant is: Honour to the Lord, Arahat, perfectly and completely Enlightened One!

Mantras

- Mantras are short **repeated phrases**.

- The words **do not need to mean anything**.

- Each bodhisattva has a **mantra**.

- The most famous mantra is: **Om mani padme hum**.

Understanding mudras, chanting and mantras

- Chanting, like any form of singing, involves a **different emotional** side of oneself which is necessary for worship and meditation.

- Mantras act like a **tuning fork** helping the mind to resonate at a **spiritual level**.

- **Om mani padme hum** has six syllables representing the **six realms** of existence and rebirth.

- Reciting this mantra enables the mind to enter and **experience each of the six realms**.

Evaluating mudras, chanting and mantras
Is the mudra of respect the most significant mudra?
Points to consider:

- **On the one hand ...** respect is fundamentally important in Buddhism. Metta and karuna for all sentient beings and for oneself is at the heart of the Buddhist life, so it must therefore be the most significant mudra.

- **On the other hand ...** Buddhism also requires one to learn, teach, understand and witness the dharma, so having different mudras means a person can think about these actions and use them to focus the mind. So, they are all equally significant.

Does it matter if a mantra's words are completely meaningless?
Points to consider:

- **On the one hand ...** if the words are completely meaningless then it follows that what is being chanted is meaningless. Even mantras such as Om mani padme hum, where the meaning is not obvious, have some meaning to reflect on.

- **On the other hand ...** it is not the meaning of the words that matter but the sounds and rhythms of the words and their syllables. If the words are tuning the mind to a higher level of thoughts, the actual meaning of the words is irrelevant.

2.3 Festivals and ceremonies

Buddhist festivals are times when people can show compassion to each other. They bring together lay and ordained members of the sangha. There are very few festivals in Buddhism (especially compared to other world religions).

Wesak

Knowing about Wesak

- Wesak is celebrated at the **full moon** in **May**.

- It commemorates the **birth** of the **Buddha** and is known also as **Buddha Day**.

- It also celebrates the **Buddha's** other 'birth', his **enlightenment**.

- There are **joyful processions** and people visit temples and make offerings.

- Bhikkhus and bhikkhunis **teach** lay people the **dharma** from the **Buddhist scriptures**.

- **Lay people** give special **gifts** (dana) to the ordained (monks and nuns).

- Some lay people practise the extra **pansil** rules which are intended for ordained Buddhists.

- Many **bathe statues** (rupas) of the Buddha.

- People **decorate** their **local shrines** and **homes**.

- Parents read stories from the **Jataka Tales** to their children.

Understanding Wesak

- Wesak is an important time for encouraging **lay** and **ordained** Buddhists to show respect and **metta** for each other.

- It is the most widely celebrated Buddhist festival because it focuses on the Three Refuges (also called the Three Jewels): the **Buddha**, the **dharma** and the **sangha**.

- Bathing rupas is an outward sign of people **purifying** themselves from the three poisons.

- Remembering the Buddha's former lives in the Jataka Tales helps children see the many **struggles** the Buddha had as various animals before he was reborn as a human.

Evaluating Wesak

If Buddhists try to follow the dharma all the time, is Wesak necessary?
Points to consider:

- **On the one hand ...** even if Buddhists try to follow the dharma all the time, they may forget that the dharma is only one of the Three Refuges which are all equally important. The festival of Wesak is a good way in which to celebrate all three of the refuges.

- **On the other hand ...** Wesak may be a fun occasion but all the things that happen can and should be done all the time. Wesak might give the wrong impression that the dharma need only be followed on special occasions.

Should Buddhism have more festivals?
Points to consider:

- **On the one hand ...** other religions have many more festivals because it is good to focus on a particular teaching or event in a religion and use the time to celebrate it and reflect on it more. For example, Buddhism could have a metta festival, a karuna festival or 'four sights' festival and so on.

- **On the other hand ...** Buddhism doesn't have to be like other religions. There is a danger that festivals draw attention away from thinking that the Buddha, dharma and sangha are equally significant all the time.

Going for refuge ceremony

Knowing about the going for refuge ceremony

- When a person feels that they wish **to commit to Buddhism** they attend a 'going for refuge' ceremony.

- The ceremony takes place at a **shrine**.

- The person makes offerings of **candles**, **flowers** and **incense**.

- They **recite** the **Three Refuges** three times.

- **Everyone present** also recites the Three Refuges three times.

Understanding the going for refuge ceremony

- **Refuge** means finding ultimate **security** in the Buddha, dharma and sangha, **not ordinary human** refuges such as friends, hobbies or sports – because all these can cause **dukkha**.

- Becoming a Buddhist depends **primarily** on the **intention** to live and carry out the dharma and the pansils; this is far more important than the ceremony.

- The going for refuge ceremony tells others that a person intends to **live a Buddhist life**.

- The ceremony helps a **person realise** the **significance** of being committed to the Buddha, dharma and sangha.

- Being part of the sangha also means belonging to the **worldwide community** of all Buddhists.

- The ceremony reminds the person that they must now live by and apply the **five moral precepts** to **everyday life**.

Evaluating the going for refuge ceremony
Can someone be Buddhist without knowing it?
Points to consider:

- **On the one hand ...** one can be a Buddhist without knowing it if one shows metta and karuna for all sentient beings, practises the pansils and lives a mindful life.

- **On the other hand ...** without making a conscious decision to live according to the dharma and follow the example of the Buddha, then it is unlikely that one is actually fulfilling the explicit requirements of Buddhism.

Is the sangha the least important refuge?
Points to consider:

- **On the one hand ...** it is the least important refuge because the example of the Buddha and his teaching of the dharma are the means of pursuing the truth. Following the Four Noble Truths, for example, is at the heart of overcoming dukkha (suffering), but it doesn't require the sangha to do so.

- **On the other hand ...** the sangha is an essential refuge along with the other two refuges because the sangha supports, encourages and guides a person in following the dharma. Without the sangha, a person could become very self-centred.

Practise answering questions with *Theology, Philosophy and Religion 13+ Exam Practice Questions and Answers* pages 8–9 and 54–58.

Test yourself

1 Name two kinds of meditation.

2 What is satori?

3 What is a koan?

4 What might be found in a shrine room?

5 What is the purpose of a stupa?

6 What happens at puja?

7 Describe three Buddhist symbols.

8 Give two mudra examples.

9 Write out a famous mantra.

10 What does Wesak celebrate?

11 What happens at a going for refuge ceremony?

Glossary

anatta No self or no soul; the second of the three marks of existence

anicca Impermanence; the first of the three marks of existence

ascetic Giving up all physical pleasures, eating almost nothing and practising some extreme spiritual exercises

Asita A wise man who announced that Siddhartha would grow to be either a ruler or great religious teacher

Avalokiteshvara A popular bodhisattva usually depicted with a thousand arms

bhavana Cultivating or developing a life of loving kindness

Bodhi tree The fig tree under which Siddhartha achieved enlightenment. Bodhi means enlightenment.

bodhisattva An enlightened being who has vowed to practise Buddhism out of compassion for the world

breath-control Used in samatha meditation to focus the mind

Buddha nature The belief that everyone has the capacity to become enlightened

chanting Halfway between singing a tune and singing a single note. This is done as a means of remembering the Buddha's teaching.

dana Generosity; lay people give gifts or dana to the ordained

dharma Truth; the teaching of the Buddha

dukkha Suffering; the third of the three marks of existence

Five Precepts The five basic Buddhist moral principles (see pansils)

Four Noble Truths The four guiding principles the Buddha taught for living a happy life

karma Action with intention; the law of nature that every action has a consequence

karuna Compassion

koans Short perplexing stories designed to make one think

lay people Members of the Buddhist community who are not ordained as monks or nuns

Lumbini The place where Siddhartha was born

magga The way or path; the middle ground between a life of extremes (see Noble Eightfold Path)

mantra A short phrase which is repeated over and over in meditation

Mara The god of illusion who tried to tempt Siddhartha at his enlightenment

metta Loving kindness

mudra Hand gestures used in meditation

nirodha Cessation of suffering; the third of the Four Noble Truths

nirvana Extinguish; describes the state when all desires are gone and a person achieves a state of bliss

Noble Eightfold Path The eight ways of living the Buddhist life and training the mind (see magga)

pansils The Five Precepts (see Five Precepts)

parinirvana The final state of nirvana after death; also describes the Buddha's death

pilgrim A person who makes a spiritual journey, often to a special place

puja Worship at home or in a temple

rupa A statue or picture of the Buddha or a bodhisattva, used in puja and meditation

samsara Reincarnation or the process of birth and rebirth over many lifetimes

samudaya The cause of suffering or dukkha; the second of the Four Noble Truths

sangha The worldwide Buddhist community which includes the ordained (monks and nuns) and lay people (non-ordained men and women)

satori Used in Zen Buddhism to refer to the moment of spiritual awakening

stupa A monument used to commemorate the Buddha or any great Buddhist teacher

tanha Craving or desire (see three poisons)

Three Great Knowledges The knowledge gained by Buddha during his enlightenment in his previous lives, karma and the Four Noble Truths

Three Refuges The three central beliefs of the Buddha, the dharma and the sangha

vihara Buddhist monastery or temple

three poisons The poisons or cravings of greed, hatred and ignorance (see tanha)

Wheel of Life The wheel of samsara showing the six different realms of existence

B: Christianity

1 Christian beliefs and teachings

Read *Religion for Common Entrance 13+* pages 30–41.

1.1 The nature of God

God's nature is revealed in the Bible, in the Creation and in His relationship with people through prayer and worship. Christians believe there is nothing greater than God; God is not created and nothing has caused God. The word omni meaning 'all' or 'total' is used with several special words to describe God's nature.

Knowing about the nature of God

● Omnipotence – God is all powerful because:

- He **created** the universe and everything in it **from nothing**.

- He **designed** and ordered everything in the Creation.

- He **sustains** and maintains all matter.

- He is the **alpha and omega**, the beginning and end of everything.

- He is **transcendent** or beyond all matter.

● Omnibenevolence – God is all good because:

- Everything He creates is **good** and beautiful.

- Everything is **purposeful** and creative.

- God is love; He **reveals His love** in the giving of His Son, Jesus Christ to the world.

- He keeps His **promises** with humans.

● Omniscience – God is all knowing because:

- He knows all that has happened and what will happen.

- **Psalm 139** says God knows our thoughts before we think them.

● Omnipresence – God is everywhere because:

- As creator, He is **continuously present** in all that He has created.

- God's presence is experienced in **special places**, **prayer** and **worship** but also in ordinary moments of life.

- As **Spirit**, He is present or **immanent** in every aspect of the world.

Understanding the nature of God

- God is **not an abstract principle** of the universe but has a **living** involvement with it.

- As God is transcendent or **infinitely** beyond anything Christians can imagine, they can only know about who God is in a very **limited way**.

- But because God is also **immanent** or closely involved with His creation, Christians can become aware of His presence in **worship** and prayer.

- As God is all knowing, Christians can **trust** Him absolutely.

- **Suffering** and evil in the world of God are a **major challenge** to the Christian belief that God is love.

- Many argue that out of love, God gives humans **free will**, so suffering and evil is not His fault but the fault of humans.

- Many argue that if God is all powerful then He could remove suffering, but He allows it to exist so humans can **learn** from their mistakes.

- God always desires the **best for the world**, even if this is not always clear to humans.

Evaluating the nature of God

Can God really be omnipotent and omnibenevolent if there is evil in the world?
Points to consider:

- **On the one hand ...** if God were really all powerful and all loving He would not want any of His creation to suffer and He would have the ability to remove all such suffering. The conclusion therefore is that He is either not all loving or He is not all powerful. If that is the case, then He can't be the kind of God one would want to worship.

- **On the other hand ...** it is because God is all loving that he allows humans to make their own decisions. This means that evil is the result of human sin and selfishness and although God could remove it, He could only do so with the loss of free will.

Can God know how to ride a bicycle?
Points to consider:

- **On the one hand ...** although God knows in theory how to ride a bicycle He cannot know how to ride it as a human being knows how to do so. If this is so, it implies that God is not omniscient, as there are limits to His knowledge.

- **On the other hand ...** God does know how to ride a bicycle and if He so willed He could also make the bicycle move. We see how God does similar unusual things in the world; we call some of these events miracles.

1.2 Creation and stewardship

Knowing about the Creation and stewardship

- In Genesis 1 God creates the world by saying, '**Let there be ...**'

- His words give order and **purpose** to everything in the world.

- In the **Gospel of John**, God's Word or **logos** (in Greek) is also revealed in the person of **Jesus**.

- In Genesis 1 God is also described as the **Spirit**, hovering over the water that separates light from darkness.

- In Genesis 2 the Spirit is described as God's **breath** which gives **life** to Adam.
- **Ruach** (in Hebrew) means **breath** and **spirit**.
- God's **Spirit** continues to **inspire** His prophets and **guide** people.
- **Humans** are God's supreme creation and made in His **image and likeness.**
- In Genesis 1 God commands humans to rule over Creation.
- In Genesis 2, Adam is placed in the garden to **look after it and care for** it; this is called stewardship.
- Being a good steward means Christians must behave **responsibly** to each other and the environment.

Understanding the Creation and stewardship

- The world came into existence for a reason **not by accident.**
- The purpose of the Creation can be seen in its beauty and order.
- God is the only creator, He is the first cause of the universe because He created it **from nothing.**
- Creation from nothing means there are **no other gods.**
- Jesus is the **Word** because as *logos* he shares in God's creative power as seen in his teaching and miracles.
- Christians continue to learn about God and the Word because they are led and inspired by the **Holy Spirit.**
- **Stewardship** refers to a wide range of activities such as supporting one's family, friends and society and caring about green issues.
- **St Francis of Assisi** taught that Christians have a duty to care **for animals** as well as the environment.

Evaluating the Creation and stewardship
Do humans need to look after the environment if God is omnipotent?
Points to consider:

- **On the one hand ...** as God is all powerful and omnipresent in the world, then He is in a much better position to maintain the environment than humans are. God is unlikely to let humans destroy His creation.
- **On the other hand ...** God has created a world where every aspect of it is dependent on another. Humans have a particularly significant part to play because they are created in the image of God, and that means they are given power by God to act on His behalf by looking after the environment.

Should Jews and Christians treat animals as equals with humans?
Points to consider:

- **On the one hand ...** in Genesis 2 humans and animals lived with each other in harmony and as equals. Humans respected animals by not eating them and caring for them; that is the ideal Christians should live up to.
- **On the other hand ...** although humans should treat animals with respect, it doesn't means animals are equal with humans. In the God-given order humans are given plants and animals to eat; many animals also eat other animals and that is not considered to be wrong.

1.3 The Trinity

The **main** Christian **doctrines** or **beliefs** are contained in the **Creed** (meaning 'belief'). The Creed is often said at a church service and is what defines a person as a Christian. The main points referred to in the **Apostle's Creed** are that though God is one, He exists as a **Trinity** of **three persons** – the Father, the Son and the Holy Spirit.

Knowing the Trinity
The first person of the Trinity is **God the Father**.

- As **Father**, God is the **creator** of all things visible and invisible.
- Because God is Father, Christians believe they have a special relationship to Him, especially in prayer.
- Jesus called God, father or **abba** (in Hebrew).

The **second person** of the Trinity is God the **Son**.

- As **Son**, God is also the eternal **Word**.
- The Son or Word became incarnate in the person of **Jesus Christ**.
- The Son or Word reveals God's love for His creation.
- At the end of time **Christ will come again** to judge the living and the dead on the Day of Judgement.

The **third person** of the Trinity is the **Holy Spirit**.

- As **Holy Spirit**, God is the **source of inspiration**.
- The Holy Spirit lives or **dwells** on Earth in the **hearts of people** and in the **Church**.
- The Holy Spirit:
  - is **invisible**
  - gives **comfort**
  - inspires **prayer**
  - is the source of **truth**
  - was given to the apostles at Pentecost
  - is **symbolised** by **wind**, **fire**, **water** and **dove**
  - inspired people to write the **Bible**.

Understanding the Trinity

- The Trinity explains what makes Christian belief in God **different** from other religions.
- It is not possible **fully to understand** the Trinity; it is essentially a **mystery**.
- The Trinity supports **monotheism** as God is one and **cannot be divided**.
- The Trinity explains how God is always **active** in every aspect of the universe.
- Christians often remember the significance of the Trinity at the end of **prayers** and **blessings**, when they say, 'In the name of the Father, the Son and the Holy Spirit'.
- The Trinity is a **symbol** of what the Christian Church should be: one Church but many **different people** within it, worshipping in **unity**.

Evaluating the Trinity

Why can't God be four or five persons not just three?
Points to consider:

- **On the one hand ...** if the Trinity is just a symbol of the way God reveals Himself to humans then there is no reason why He should be thought of as three persons. In Islam, for example, God has 99 names as each of these describes one of His qualities.

- **On the other hand ...** for Christians, God has revealed Himself in three specific events: as Father when He created the universe, as Son when He appeared as Jesus Christ in the Incarnation and as the Holy Spirit when He spoke through the prophets and inspired the apostles at Pentecost.

Is the Holy Spirit the most significant person of the Trinity?
Points to consider:

- **On the one hand ...** the Holy Spirit is the most significant person of the Trinity because it is the Spirit which separates light from dark in the Creation, inspires Jesus at his baptism and continues to work in the Church today. Without the Spirit, God would not be known to humans.

- **On the other hand ...** the point of the Trinity is that Father, Son and Holy Spirit are equally significant. Whatever is said of one person is said equally of the other two. If the Spirit were more important, God would not be one.

1.4 Beliefs and teachings relating to Jesus Christ

Jesus Christ is the central figure in Christianity. Although Christians consider that he lived a mortal life, they also believe that he was divine and through his death and resurrection he brought people back into full relationship with God by overcoming sin.

The Incarnation

Knowing about the Incarnation

- Incarnation comes from the Latin for 'becoming flesh' or '**becoming a human being**' and therefore means God becoming human in the person of Jesus Christ.

- The incarnation refers also to Jesus' **earthly life from** birth to death.

- Jesus was born in **Bethlehem** around **4 B.C.E.** to Mary and Joseph.

- Mary was a **virgin** but the angel Gabriel announced to her that the Holy Spirit would cause her to become pregnant.

- Jesus' miracles and parables **prepared** people for the **Kingdom of God** – God's reign on Earth and in the world to come.

Understanding the Incarnation

- The Incarnation explains how, out of love, God is closely involved in **human history**.

- Without the Incarnation, Christians would not know directly about the **Son**, the second person of the Trinity.

- The Incarnation reveals how in the person of Jesus, **God experiences** everything humans do.

- Some Christians don't think Jesus' **virgin birth** was a miracle but that the story illustrates how Jesus came from very **humble** origins.

- Some Christians believe the virgin birth was a **miracle** and proves Jesus was God's **Son**.

Evaluating the Incarnation

Is Jesus' virgin birth a miracle or just a story?
Points to consider:

- **On the one hand ...** Jesus' birth or conception is not a miracle but a powerful story about how God chose Mary who was from a very poor background to act as His servant and bring up Jesus faithfully. Only two of the four Gospels refer to Jesus' virgin birth, so it is not a vital part of Christian belief.

- **On the other hand ...** Jesus' conception was a miracle because in Isaiah God promises that a young girl will give birth to Immanuel (God with us) and because the Incarnation shows how Jesus is uniquely God's son.

Was Jesus just an inspired teacher?
Points to consider:

- **On the one hand ...** Jesus was not only a teacher but also God's son whose life, death and resurrection brings humans into a different relationship with God. The Resurrection in particular shows how Jesus overcame death, so he cannot be just a teacher.

- **On the other hand ...** Jesus' teaching and his parables continue to influence people today. His miracles and his resurrection are very difficult to prove, so it is best to treat him as an inspired teacher.

The Crucifixion

Knowing about the Crucifixion

- Jesus' teaching often **upset** the **Jewish** and **Roman authorities**.

- He challenged traditional Jewish teaching on working on the Sabbath.

- He was **betrayed by Judas**, one of his disciples, **to the Jewish authorities** at Gethsemane.

- He was tried by the high priest, **Caiaphas**, on the charge of claiming to be God's son.

- The **Jewish** court accused Jesus of **blasphemy** and handed him to the Roman court.

- The Roman Governor, **Pontius Pilate**, charged Jesus with **treason** and sentenced him to **death**.

- Jesus was mocked by the Roman soldiers, then crucified at **Golgotha** in 29 C.E.

- Jesus' last words on the cross were, 'Into your hands I commend my spirit.'

- The **centurion** at the cross said, 'Surely this man was the Son of God.'

Understanding the Crucifixion

- Jesus' crucifixion presents him as the **suffering servant** which the prophet **Isaiah** described in the Old Testament.

- Isaiah's suffering servant dies because the people kill him out of hatred.

- His death makes the people feel **guilty** and aware of their sins.

- Jesus' death is also a sacrifice for sin and **guilt**.

- The Jews accuse Jesus of **blasphemy** because he claimed God's authority.

- Under Roman law, Jewish courts were not allowed to use the death penalty.

- Jesus faced the Roman charge of **treason** because they thought Jesus, as 'King of the Jews', **challenged their authority**.

- Jesus' cry from the cross showed his complete **trust** in God as his Father.

- The centurion believed in Jesus' relationship with God, because of Jesus' complete trust even when **suffering extreme pain** on the cross.

Evaluating the Crucifixion
Was it necessary for Jesus to die?
Points to consider:

- **On the one hand ...** it was necessary for Jesus to die because his death showed how unjust and cruel human beings can be. For Christians, Jesus' death was his sacrifice for the sins of the world and his obedience to God's will.

- **On the other hand ...** it was not necessary for Jesus to die as he could then have spent longer teaching and setting an example. Other great religious teachers such as the Buddha and Muhammad lived long lives and died naturally.

Does Christianity focus too much on suffering?
Points to consider:

- **On the one hand ...** Christianity does focus too much on suffering. Jesus warned his disciples that they would be persecuted for their faith and many died as martyrs. Religion should be about appreciating and enjoying the world and finding ways of overcoming suffering.

- **On the other hand ...** suffering is a part of ordinary life and Christianity simply reflects this. Its focus on suffering is also to make sure that Christians don't forget that many people suffer hardships and it is their Christian duty to help them.

The Resurrection

Knowing about the Resurrection

- Jesus was buried in a tomb given by **Joseph of Arimathea.**

- When the women arrived at the tomb three days after the burial, they found the **body had gone.**

- The **risen Jesus** appeared to many **hundreds of people.**

- He appeared to his **disciples** in a **locked room** and had a meal with them.

- **Thomas,** one of his disciples, said he would **not believe** unless he **touched Jesus.**

- Jesus appeared to Thomas and allowed him to touch his **hands** and **side.**

- Thomas believed and **worshipped** the risen Jesus as **God.**

Understanding the Resurrection

- The Resurrection means that Jesus' life did not **end in failure.**

- The Resurrection gives **hope to Christians** that there is **life after death.**

- The Resurrection shows that sin and **evil** can be **overcome.**

- The risen Jesus exists in a new kind of **spiritual body**; it is very difficult to know exactly what this was like.

- Thomas is told by Jesus that belief in the Resurrection should be based on belief and faith **not physical proof.**

Evaluating the Resurrection
Did the resurrected Jesus have a physical body?
Points to consider:

- **On the one hand ...** the resurrected Jesus did have a physical body. He didn't appear to Mary and Thomas as a ghost but as a real human being. He even invited Thomas to touch him. This is what makes the Resurrection a miracle and a sign of Jesus' divinity.

- **On the other hand ...** Jesus did not have a physical body as he was able to appear and disappear suddenly and he could pass through walls. What he had must have been some kind of spiritual body.

Is the Resurrection just a story about hope?
Points to consider:

- **On the one hand ...** the Resurrection is a story about hope over despair – this is what Christians remember at Easter. Resurrection is based on the experience the first disciples had after his death; Jesus' teaching continued to inspire them and they felt somehow he was with them.

- **On the other hand ...** the Resurrection is more than just a story of hope because it reveals that there is life after death. It also shows Jesus' victory over sin and suffering.

The Ascension

Knowing about the Ascension

- **Forty days** after his resurrection Jesus met his 11 disciples in a village outside Jerusalem on the Mount of Olives.

- He told them to wait for the coming of the **Holy Spirit**.

- He blessed his disciples and then **ascended** into **heaven** to be with God.

- Peter gave a speech and told the crowd not to stand looking into heaven but to **focus on this world**.

- A little later, at the **festival of Pentecost** the Holy Spirit came as **Jesus had promised**.

Understanding the Ascension

- The Ascension completes the Resurrection; the risen Jesus is no longer on Earth.

- In the Old Testament some of the prophets, such as **Enoch** and **Elijah**, were taken up into heaven as a sign of their **special relationship** with God.

- Jesus' ascension is a **symbol** that he, as God's Son, **rules with God in heaven**.

- The coming of the **Holy Spirit** explains how Jesus' role as teacher and healer is continued on Earth.

- The Holy Spirit continues to **guide** the **Church** and **Christian communities**.

Evaluating the Ascension
Is the significance of the Ascension what happened afterwards?
Points to consider:

- **On the one hand ...** the Ascension was less significant than the coming of the Holy Spirit and the creation of the Church. Ascension merely marks the end of Jesus' resurrection; the real focus is on the world and the life of the first Christians.

- **On the other hand ...** without the Ascension, the coming of the Holy Spirit would not have been possible. The Ascension completes Jesus' role with his return to God the Father and makes it possible for the Christian community to be led by the Holy Spirit.

Is the Ascension the climax of Jesus' life?
Points to consider:

- **On the one hand ...** the Ascension is the climax of Jesus' life as it marks the end of the Resurrection process when he finally leaves the world and is united with God as the second person of the Trinity. It also symbolises his victory over death and completion of his ministry.

- **On the other hand ...** the Ascension is not the climax of Jesus' life as that took place at the first Easter when the disciples encountered the risen Jesus. It is only then that they realise how his life has overcome death and turned despair into hope. The Ascension doesn't add anything significantly new to the Resurrection.

The atonement

Knowing about the atonement

- **Atonement** means literally '**being at one with God**' by making amends with God.
- Atonement enables humans to be in a **right relationship** with God.
- Jesus taught that as God's Son he would suffer on behalf of humans to **pay off the punishment for their sins**.
- He described his suffering and death as a **ransom** for human sins.
- Christians believe that because Jesus was a ransom for sin they can now be **reconciled** or reunited with God.

Understanding the atonement

- The story of the **Fall of Adam and Eve** is a way of saying that there is a **rift** or gap between humans and God.
- Atonement explains how this rift has been **mended**.
- There are many ways that Christians have attempted to explain the **mystery** of the atonement.
- Some think that Jesus' **selfless death** is an **example** which **inspires** us to repent of our sins and think what we can do to live better lives.
- Some describe Jesus' death as a **ransom** for sin. A ransom means that Jesus pays off God's punishment for human sin.
- The result of Jesus' sacrifice is that **everyone** is now able to go to heaven.

Evaluating the atonement
Does sin actually exist?
Points to consider:

- **On the one hand ...** sin does actually exist because people do bad things and their actions affect others. Some families and some societies are deeply corrupt, unjust and selfish. Sin exists wherever humans put themselves above others. This is what is meant by original sin.

- **On the other hand ...** sin does not exist as such but is a word used to describe the way humans fail to be good and fail to live up to God's values. It is not sin which exists but human actions and lack of positive moral values.

Can Jesus' death really take away the sins of the world?
Points to consider:

- **On the one hand ...** it could be argued that Jesus' death does take away the sins of the world because God accepted Jesus' suffering as a sacrifice on behalf of humans who are incapable of being truly good. This doesn't mean that people do not continue to sin, but that God accepts their efforts to repent.

- **On the other hand ...** it could be argued that Jesus' death doesn't actually remove all the sins of the world in any literal sense. His death makes people aware of their failings and so prompts them to live better lives.

Practise answering questions with *Theology, Philosophy and Religion 13+ Exam Practice Questions and Answers* pages 10–11 and 59–62.

Test yourself

1 Give two examples of God's omnipotence.

2 Give two examples of God's omnipresence.

3 What is Christian stewardship?

4 What does creed mean?

5 What is the role of God the Father in the Trinity?

6 Describe three roles of the Holy Spirit.

7 What does incarnation mean?

8 What is the virgin birth?

9 Who condemned Jesus to death?

10 To whom did the resurrected Jesus appear?

11 What happened at Jesus' ascension?

12 What does atonement mean?

2 Christian practices and ceremonies

Read *Religion for Common Entrance 13+* pages 42–60.

2.1 Different forms of worship

Christian **worship** is about showing respect, commitment, thanks and love to God and asking for His forgiveness both for oneself and for others.

Eucharist or Holy Communion

Holy Communion remembers **Jesus' last supper** with his disciples. For many Christians, this is the **most important** act of worship each week and is the moment when they feel that, through the symbols, they come into the presence of Christ. **Eucharist** or **Holy Communion** is called **Mass** and **the Lord's Supper** in different Christian traditions.

Knowing about the Eucharist or Holy Communion

- **Hymns**/songs are sung at the start and throughout the service.

- There are **prayers** of **intercession** and **repentance**.

- **Readings** follow from the **Bible**; usually one from the **Old Testament** and one or two from the **New Testament**.

- One New Testament reading must be from the **Gospels**.

- The minister gives a **sermon**.

- This part of the service concludes when the minister says the **peace**: 'The peace of the Lord be always with you.' The congregation respond, 'And also with you.'

- Many congregations then **exchange the peace** by shaking hands.

- The minister then **consecrates** the bread and wine by saying Jesus' words at his last supper.

- The minister says to each person when they receive the bread and wine: 'The **body of Christ**, given for you' and then, 'The **blood of Christ**, shed for you'.

- **Roman Catholics** and **Anglicans** come to the **altar rail** to receive communion.

- In the **Free Churches**, the congregations stay where they are **sitting**. They drink non-alcoholic wine in **small glasses** and **bread** is **passed round** from person to person.

- **After taking communion**, there are final **prayers of thanksgiving** and the final **blessing** is given by the **minister**.

Understanding the Eucharist or Holy Communion

- Because Jesus' last supper was a **Passover** meal many of the words and symbols of Holy Communion remember how God at the first Passover in Egypt rescued His people from slavery and death. For Christians, it is now Jesus, as God's son, who rescues humanity from the **slavery of sin** and death.

- **Consecrating** the bread and wine means they become special or holy. The **bread** represents Jesus' **body** and the **wine** his **blood**.

- Some Christians believe that although the **outward appearance** of the bread and wine remain the same, **inwardly** and **mysteriously** they become Jesus' body and blood.

- Other Christians believe that the bread and wine powerfully and mysteriously **represent** Jesus' presence.

- **Bread and wine** together represent Jesus' person and the **sacrifice** he made as a human being in body and soul when he gave up his life in **obedience** to God for the **sins of the world**.

- Communion for Christians is a reminder of the new covenant of love which Jesus established.

- Communion reminds Christians that they should **live in love** and **fellowship** with each other and in the wider community.

Evaluating the Eucharist or Holy Communion
Can the bread and wine at the Eucharist be anything more than bread and wine?
Points to consider:

- **On the one hand ...** bread and wine at the Eucharist are more than just bread and wine because the words the minister says at the consecration mean that in the minds of the worshippers the bread and wine have holy significance. In a mysterious way, Jesus is actually present during Holy Communion.

- **On the other hand ...** the bread and wine at the Eucharist are just bread and wine and remind worshippers of Jesus' Last Supper and his teaching about the new covenant of love and fellowship.

Would Jesus approve of the way the Eucharist is celebrated today?
Points to consider:

- **On the one hand ...** Jesus would not approve of the Eucharist today because when he celebrated the last supper with his disciples, he was not wearing special clothes and eating the meal in a special building with rituals and music.

- **On the other hand ...** the last supper was a Passover meal in which many special rituals are performed and songs are sung. Jesus would probably approve of modern Eucharistic worship where there are rituals and ceremonies, as long as the meaning of these is clear.

Liturgical, informal and individual worship

Knowing about liturgical, informal and individual worship

Liturgical worship

- Liturgical worship is **public worship** which has developed over many hundreds of years.

- Liturgical worship follows a **set pattern**.

- It is usually **led by a minister** or trained prayer leader.

- Ministers and the choir may wear **robes**.

- The pattern will include **formal or set prayers**, repeated words, **responses** to the minister's words, and **rituals** such as those found in the Holy Communion, and marriage, baptism and confirmation services.

- People may **sit formally** in rows.

- **Hymns** or songs are sung.

Informal worship

- Informal worship has **less structure** and is more **spontaneous**.

- People may not sit formally in rows.

- The minister does not lead worship but **assists**.

- Talks and prayers may be given by **members of the congregation**.

- Worship may be led by a band or **music group**.

- Popular Christian **songs** may be sung.

Individual worship

- In most liturgical and informal worship, there is time given to individual worship and prayer.

- Many Christians worship at home by saying **daily prayers**, such as **grace before meals** and prayers before going to bed.

- Some meditate by saying the **Jesus Prayer**; some use **Ignatius Loyola's spiritual exercises**.

- Some use specially designed **Bible study courses** at home.

Understanding liturgical, informal and individual worship

- Many churches **combine liturgical** and **informal** worship and mix formality and informality.

- Many **prefer liturgical** worship because it gives **respect to the** sacraments. The sacraments, such as baptism and Holy Communion, are serious moments when the **outward signs** represent the **inward and mysterious presence of God's love** or grace.

- Many prefer **informal** worship because it is closer to their **everyday lifestyle** and they find they can connect more easily with less formal language.

- Many find **Ignatius Loyola's spiritual exercises** useful as a way of carrying out individual daily prayer at home because they find prayer needs discipline and dedication.

- Many use the **Jesus Prayer** in their individual worship. The prayer repeats the phrase, 'Lord Jesus Christ, Son of God, have mercy on me, a sinner' which helps focus the mind on **repentance** and the hope of forgiveness.

Evaluating liturgical, informal and individual worship
Should all ritual be removed from worship?
Points to consider:

- **On the one hand ...** ritual has very little to do with worship. If worship means giving thanks to God and coming into His presence then rituals can get in the way and cause a distraction. In some cases, rituals are more about making ministers and choirs feel important rather than focusing on worship.

- **On the other hand ...** rituals can help give shape and purpose to worship. Many people use set patterns of doing things in their daily lives so in worship, rituals give purpose to prayer, especially when the rituals become familiar and their meaning is explained.

Is individual worship better than worship in church?
Points to consider:

- **On the one hand ...** it requires a lot of discipline to worship individually as it is easier not to pray. Individual worship is also better because people are not distracted by others in church and can focus on what suits them.

- **On the other hand ...** worshipping in church develops and sustains the Christian community. It means the individual doesn't become too self-centred and has to pray and think about things they might not have thought about themselves.

Places of worship

The most typical place of Christian worship is a church. Traditionally churches are found at the centre of a community. A large church, where a bishop resides, is called a **cathedral.** Many schools, colleges and hospitals have their own much smaller space for worship which is called a chapel. Churches and chapels often have several rooms attached to them for meetings, for the choir and clergy to robe (called vestries) and for entertainment and socialising.

Knowing about places of worship

A typical Anglican or Roman Catholic church or chapel

- There is an **altar** at the **east end** of the church.

- The east end of the church is called the **chancel.**

- There is a **crucifix** (a cross with Jesus' body on it) or **cross** (a cross without Jesus' body on it) on the altar to symbolise Jesus' **death and sacrifice.**

- The **pews** or seats are in the **nave** of the church for the **congregation.**

- The **pulpit** is a raised reading desk in the **nave** for **sermons.**

- The **lectern** is a reading desk used for **reading the Bible.**

- The **font** is usually at the **west** end of the church and is used for **baptisms.**

- The glass in the **windows** often depicts **stories** from the Bible.

- An **organ** may be used for music.

- There may be a **side chapel** dedicated to a particular **saint.**

- There may be statues or paintings of Jesus and specific saints associated with that church.

- There may be pictures of the **stations of the cross** on the wall depicting the key moments of Jesus' passion.

A typical Orthodox church or chapel

- There are many **icons** or special paintings of Christ and the saints.

- The main feature is an **iconostasis**, a screen containing the icons.

- The church is lit with many **candles.**

- The **font** is usually at the **west** end of the church and is used for **baptisms.**

- Often there are **no pews** or seats – people stand.

A **typical non-conformist church or chapel** may contain:

- a **table** for the Lord's Supper, called the Lord's Table

- a central pulpit or reading desk

- a baptistery

- plain windows with no decoration
- an organ or piano for music
- very little decoration or pictures.

Understanding places of worship

- Pictures on the wall or windows help **teach** people about Bible stories.
- **Statues**, art and icons create an atmosphere of worship and **spiritual awareness**.
- Some churches **avoid art** and statues as they consider these lead to **idolatry** (treating the object as if it is divine). Idolatry is forbidden in the Ten Commandments.
- The layout of the church can assist in **liturgical worship**. At Holy Communion, for example, a person moves from the **nave**, representing ordinary life, up to the **chancel** and the altar, representing God's and Jesus' presence.
- Many modern churches **don't have chancels** and place the altar or Lord's Table with the people to symbolise that God is present in worship and not contained in a separate place.
- In many **non-conformist** churches, reading the Bible and preaching God's Word is more important for **regular worship** than the Lord's Supper, so the pulpit and lectern are placed centrally.

Evaluating places of worship

Should churches be as simple as possible and money be spent on those who need it?
Points to consider:

- **On the one hand ...** far too much time and money is spent looking after church buildings when it is a Christian duty to look after the poor and the weak. It is also wrong to decorate buildings as this can distract from the real purpose of worship.
- **On the other hand ...** church buildings are places to honour and praise God through beautiful art, music, song and architecture. Spending money on making special places of worship is in addition to helping the poor and needy.

Should churches only be used by Christians?
Points to consider:

- **On the one hand ...** churches are often the most significant building in the community. The word 'church' means a gathering of people, so it is appropriate for the church building to be used by all kinds of people, provided it is treated with respect.
- **On the other hand ...** churches are built for Christian worship. It is wrong to use a church for non-Christian worship. Only Christians know how to treat the building appropriately, so only they should be allowed to use it.

2.2 Rites of passage

A rite of passage is a significant moment in a person's life, usually marked by a special ceremony. For Christians, rites of passage are part of their spiritual journey in life, sometimes compared to a pilgrimage where every stage marks a moment on the road to the Kingdom of God.

Baptism

Knowing about baptism

Infant baptism

- An **infant** is baptised using a **font** filled with **water**.
- **Parents** and **godparents** make **promises** to bring up the child in a Christian way.
- The child may be given a **Christian name**.
- The sign of the cross is made on the child's forehead.
- **Water** is poured over the child's **head three times** in the name of the Father, Son and Holy Spirit.
- The **priest** prays that the child will be **protected from evil**.
- The **sign of the cross** is made. Sometimes this is done with oil and called **christmation**.
- A **lighted candle** is given to **parents** and **godparents** or sponsors to remind them of their **duties** to the child.

Believer's baptism

- This usually happens for people who are aged **12 and older**.
- They must **ask** for it to happen.
- They must **repent** of their sins.
- They often give a testimony or a witness speech to the congregation explaining why they wish to be a Christian.
- The **minister** holds their **head** and **hand**.
- They are **plunged** backwards fully into **water**.

Understanding baptism

- Baptism is the moment when a **person becomes a Christian**.
- Jesus used **water baptism** to symbolise the **end** of one's **old life** and the **beginning** of a **new** one.
- **Water** is a symbol of **life** and of **washing away sins**.
- **Oil** is a symbol of God's **Spirit**.
- The **candle** is a symbol of the **presence of Christ** who is the 'light of the world'.
- The **candle** also symbolises how a person passes from **darkness** (their old life) **to light** (new life in Christ).

Evaluating baptism

Should only adults be baptised?
Points to consider:

- **On the one hand ...** only adults should be baptised as the promises made at baptism are life changing and children are not in a position to understand what these promises involve. Baptism of babies is therefore contrary to the purpose of baptism.

- **On the other hand ...** babies are baptised as it is the first stage in the Christian journey and if later they wish to confirm or reject the promises made on their behalf, they may do so. Older children may also be baptised as it is perfectly possible for them to understand the difference between right and wrong.

Is baptism the most important moment in a Christian's life?
Points to consider:

- **On the one hand ...** Jesus' baptism by John the Baptist marked the start of his public ministry and so baptism also marks the formal start of a person's Christian life. Baptism is the most important moment in a Christian's life as it marks the end of their old life and the start of a new one.

- **On the other hand ...** baptism is just the start of a Christian life and without all that follows it – prayer, worship, carrying out Christian morals – it would be meaningless. So, although it is an important moment, it is not the most important.

Confirmation

Knowing about confirmation

- Confirmation takes place when a person is old enough to **publicly** confirm the baptismal promises made on their behalf when they were a baby.

- Confirmation **preparation** will depend on what a person already knows about Christianity but it can take from two months to a year.

- Confirmation is carried out by a **bishop**.

- A **confirmand** is someone who is preparing for confirmation.

- A confirmand who **has not been baptised** as a child is baptised shortly before the confirmation service.

- In the service, the bishop asks confirmands if they are baptised.

- He then asks them to confirm their baptismal promises.

- He places his **hands** on each **confirmand's head**.

- He says to each confirmand, 'Confirm O God, your servant [their name] with Your Holy Spirit'.

Understanding confirmation

- It is carried out by a bishop because **only the bishop** can lay his hands on the confirmands and call on the Holy Spirit to enter their life.

- The coming of the **Holy Spirit** means that baptism is **complete** and the person is now a full member of the Christian Church.

- The signing of the **cross with oil** (or chrism) is a symbol of anointing with the Holy Spirit. The Holy Spirit leads and guides a person throughout their life.

- As in baptism, the person's old life '**dies**' in Jesus' death and is '**resurrected**' in his resurrection; this symbolises the person's new life as a Christian.

- The promises of turning away from the '**devil**' means resisting temptations and living in accordance with Jesus' example and teaching.

Evaluation confirmation
If a person is baptised is there any need for confirmation?
Points to consider:

- **On the one hand ...** if baptism should only take place when a person is old enough to understand the promises they are making, there should be no child baptisms and that would make confirmation irrelevant.

- **On the other hand ...** if baptism is a two-stage process of making promises and then confirming that one understands the nature of these promises, then there is a need for confirmation. Child baptism is important as it reminds parents and godparents of their Christian duties to the child.

Does the devil actually exist?
Points to consider:

- **On the one hand ...** although one might refer to the devil, he does not actually exist but represents the side of human nature that is destructive, selfish and disobeys God's will. There is only one supreme power and that is God.

- **On the other hand ...** if there can be a supreme power of good, there can also be a power of evil. The existence of the devil explains why some people are tempted to do terrible things; it is not enough simply to say they have failed to do good things.

Marriage

For many Christians marriage is a **sacrament**, a holy bond, which cannot be undone through divorce. All Christians regard it as a sign of the **life-long bond of love** between a man and a woman.

Knowing about marriage

- The minister explains the **purpose of marriage**.

- Marriage is to **one person** for the **whole of this life**.

- Marriage is for **children** to **grow up securely**.

- Marriage is for two people to **grow** in **love** and **companionship**.

- The bride and groom both make **three promises** to the **congregation**.

  - They promise to **love** and be **faithful** only to each other for life.

  - They promise to **honour** each other for life.

  - They promise to **protect** and look after each other for the rest of their lives.

- The **minister pronounces** them to be **husband and wife**.

Understanding marriage

- The **outward symbols** used in the marriage ceremony symbolise the special relationship which husband and wife share with each other.

- **Rings** symbolise eternal love; the **exchange of rings** symbolises the promise of binding love which husband and wife make to each other.

- Marriage is a **covenant**, a two-way promise. It is a reminder of **God's** covenant with Israel in the Old Testament and through **Christ** in the New Testament. God's covenant is also a promise of His commitment and love for the world.

Evaluating marriage

Is a marriage ceremony necessary to get married?
Points to consider:

- **On the one hand ...** a marriage ceremony ensures the vows the couple make to each other in front of their family and friends are serious and important. The marriage ceremony lasts in the mind of the couple and reminds them of their promises.

- **On the other hand ...** what matters is that two people are committed to each other. Marriage ceremonies and rituals add nothing to the intention of the couple to remain faithful and committed to each other.

Should marriage be life long?
Points to consider:

- **On the one hand ...** marriage is a sacrament in which two people become one in body and in mind. For Christians, this means that God has joined the couple and therefore they should intend to live together for the rest of their lives.

- **On the other hand ...** if one is not a Christian, then although it may be desirable to stay with one person for the rest of one's life many things can change in life and so the couple may choose to end their relationship by divorcing and marrying someone else.

2.3 Prayer

There are many reasons why people pray. It is not always to ask God for something but often to reflect on what God is and what He wants. Christians believe prayer is offered through Jesus Christ and is guided by the Holy Spirit.

Knowing about prayer
Christians might:

- go to **church** to pray and worship

- use **icons** or a picture of a saint, Jesus or the Holy Family to focus on

- light a **candle**

- **kneel** as a sign of **humbleness** before God

- make the **sign of the cross**

- pray to their own particular **saint**.

Christians pray using the **Lord's Prayer**:

- It is the prayer Jesus taught his disciples.

- It begins by **honouring God's name**.

- It asks that God's **Kingdom** will **arrive**.

- It asks that God will carry out His **will** or **promises** on Earth.

- It asks that people receive **daily bread** or sustenance.

- It asks **God to forgive** Christians their sins and for them to forgive each other their sins.

- It asks God not to bring us to a time of great **testing** or temptation.

Christians use set prayers such as intercessions:

- Set prayers are **written** and **formal**.

- Intercessions ask God to **act on behalf** of humans.

- Intercessory prayer is also known as **petitionary** prayer.

- Intercessory prayer may **name events** in the world, the Church, local issues and particular people who need help and encouragement.

- At each stage of the prayer, the person leading the prayer in church may say, '**Lord in your mercy**' and the congregation reply, '**Hear our prayer.**'

Christians use **informal prayer**:

- Informal prayer may be a prayer said in a **person's own words**.

- Informal prayer may be **extemporary** prayer in a church or at a prayer meeting when people use words they feel the Holy Spirit is giving them or helping them to say.

Understanding prayer

- Prayers serve many different purposes: they may **praise** and **thank** God for what He has done.

- Prayers may ask for **forgiveness** and spiritual strength to repent and change one's ways.

- They may seek inner help or guidance for **the person who is praying**.

- They may form part of **meditation** or reflection by **focusing the mind** and helping a person to come into the presence of God.

- **Set prayers or** formal prayers have the advantage of being **carefully composed** with rhythms which help express the prayer clearly.

- **Intercessory prayer** is the most difficult to understand because God's ways are not the ways of humans, so Christians believe that God acts according to what **He thinks is just and fair**.

- **Informal prayer** has the advantage of **spontaneity** and conveys more **personal** emotions and thoughts.

Evaluating prayer
Would it be enough for Christians just to pray using the Lord's Prayer?
Points to consider:

- **On the one hand ...** it might be enough to pray just using the Lord's Prayer as it is the prayer Jesus taught his disciples. It also covers all the main types of prayer: intercession, thanksgiving, confession and praise.

- **On the other hand ...** although the Lord's Prayer is the prayer Jesus taught, he did not say it was the only one. Informal prayer is important for Christians as it helps to develop a personal relationship with God and different occasions require different kinds of prayer.

Are set prayers more meaningful than informal prayers?
Points to consider:

- **On the one hand ...** set prayers have been carefully composed, tried and tested over many years. This means they are more precise and express ideas clearly. Informal prayers often lack structure and focus and when used in the presence of others are too personal to mean a great deal.

- **On the other hand ...** set prayers can be too formal and don't allow a more personal engagement with God. Informal prayers can be from the heart and convey more emotion and meaning than set prayers.

2.4 Pilgrimage

Pilgrimage is the act of making a journey to a place which has special religious significance. People who make them are known as **pilgrims**.

The syllabus states that you should know at least **two contrasting examples** of pilgrimages, such as Canterbury, Walsingham, Rome and the Vatican, Lourdes, the Holy Land and Santiago de Compostela.

Knowing about pilgrimages

Canterbury

- **Canterbury** is **home** to the senior bishop or **archbishop** in the **Church of England**.
- **The Archbishop of Canterbury** is also the senior bishop of the Anglican Church.
- **St Thomas à Becket** was martyred (killed for his beliefs) in Canterbury Cathedral on 29 December **1170 C.E.**
- **Becket** is remembered as a **saintly man** who **refused** to carry out the **orders** of **King Henry II**.
- **Miracles** were recorded at **his tomb**.
- **Canterbury** has been a very popular **pilgrimage** centre ever since.
- For example, **Chaucer's** *Canterbury Tales* contains the kind of **stories pilgrims told** on their way to Canterbury.

Walsingham

- Lady **Richeldis** had a vision of **Mary** in **1061 C.E.**
- In the **vision** she saw a **spring of water** which could **heal**.
- The spring was **discovered** and a special **house** was **built** over it.
- The shrine was **destroyed** in **1538 C.E.** but **rebuilt** in the **twentieth century**.
- People **today** go there to seek **healing** and **peace**.
- In addition to the **Anglican** church in Walsingham there are **Roman Catholic** and **Orthodox** churches.

Rome and the Vatican

- The **Vatican** is **home** of the **Pope**.
- The Pope is the **successor** of **St Peter**.
- **St Peter** is **buried** beneath **St Peter's Church** in the Vatican.
- **Pilgrims** often attend large **audiences** there given by the **Pope**.
- Pilgrims also **visit** other churches in Rome such as the **Basilica of St Paul**.
- They also go to the **catacombs** outside Rome where **early Christians worshipped** and were **buried**.

The Holy Land

- The Holy Land is modern-day Israel.
- Pilgrims visit the **Church of the Nativity** in **Bethlehem** where **Jesus** was **born**.
- They travel to **Galilee** and visit **Capernaum** where **Jesus taught**.
- Pilgrims go to the **Mount of Beatitudes** where Jesus gave the **Sermon on the Mount**.
- In **Jerusalem** they follow the **route** Jesus took to his **crucifixion**; this is called the **Via Dolorosa**.
- Pilgrims visit **Jesus' tomb** and **pray** at the **Church of the Holy Sepulchre**.

Lourdes

- In **1858**, near Lourdes in France, a young Roman Catholic girl **Bernadette** had visions of **Mary**.

- In her visions Mary pointed to a **spring of water** which could **heal**.

- A **spring** later appeared in a cave.

- Thousands come each year for the **healing gift** of the water.

Santiago de Compostela

- Santiago is Spanish for **St James**. St James was one of **Jesus' disciples**.

- Santiago de Compostela is a town in north-western **Spain**.

- In the ninth century C.E. a monk called **Pelagius** saw a bright light shining from **the tomb of St James**.

- News spread of Pelagius' experience and the town became a **major pilgrimage** destination.

- Pilgrims visit the **statue of St James** and **kiss or embrace** it and then descend to the **Crypt of the Apostles** where St James' remains are kept in a silver casket.

- The **scallop shell** is a traditional sign or token that one has been on pilgrimage to Santiago de Compostela.

Understanding pilgrimages

- Pilgrimage requires **physical**, **mental** and **spiritual** effort; the journey is as important as arriving at the destination.

- The journey **mirrors** a Christian's own **journey through life**.

- Meeting other pilgrims is a chance to **share** and **reflect** on their spiritual journey.

- Each pilgrimage **destination** offers a **special insight** and experience of one or more of the following: the life of Jesus, his disciples, early Christians, a Christian saint.

- It doesn't always matter whether the sites are **historically very accurate**; what matters is that thousands of Christians have been **inspired** and found answers to their prayers by going to these special places.

Evaluating pilgrimages
Should Christians go on pilgrimage at least once in their life?
Points to consider:

- **On the one hand ...** making the effort of going on a journey to a holy place gives a Christian time to reflect and think about their faith; most people are too busy to think about such things in ordinary life. For the Christian, pilgrimage is essential preparation for the journey beyond this world.

- **On the other hand ...** pilgrimage may not suit everyone and a person can still gain spiritual insight from reading the Bible, prayer and worship at home. Pilgrimage is useful but it is not essential.

Is the pilgrimage journey more important than the destination?
Points to consider:

- **On the one hand ...** the destination is what makes sense of the pilgrimage journey; otherwise any journey could be a pilgrimage. The destination is linked with a special Christian event or spiritual experience.

- **On the other hand ...** the Christian life is often described as a pilgrimage or journey. It is the experiences along the way which help shape a Christian's thoughts and relationship with God. The destination is important but not the sole purpose of pilgrimage.

2.5 Festivals and celebrations

Holy Week
Knowing about Holy Week

Palm Sunday

- On Palm Sunday Christians remember **Jesus' entry** into **Jerusalem**.
- **Palm branches** are placed in churches and some Christians wear palm crosses.
- There are church **processions** and special **services** in church.

Maundy Thursday

- On Maundy Thursday Christians remember **Jesus' Last Supper** with his disciples.
- Maundy means **commandment**. Jesus commanded his disciples to **love one another as equals**.
- As Jesus washed his disciples' feet, many **ministers wash** the **feet** of their **congregation**.
- There are special **services** of **Holy Communion**.
- Many churches hold **special prayer services**.
- In many churches the **altar** is **stripped** of its covering and the **candles are removed** at the **last service of the day**.

Good Friday

- On Good Friday Christians remember Jesus' **trial** and **death** by **crucifixion**.
- **Pictures** and **crosses** in the church are **covered** with **dark materials**.
- In church services the story of Jesus' passion is read.
- **Penitential psalms** or psalms remembering one's sins are read or sung.
- In Roman Catholic church services, people honour the cross by **kissing the feet** of the figure of Jesus on the cross.
- It is traditional to **eat spiced buns** (hot cross buns) which have decorative crosses on top.

Holy Saturday vigil

- On Holy Saturday Christians remember the moment when **Jesus** was **raised from the tomb**.
- Worshippers wait up **late** and **pray**.
- **Candles** and **bonfires** are lit.

Understanding Holy Week
Revise this topic by going over Christian teaching on atonement (see page 101).

- The week begins in **triumph** and hope on Palm Sunday when Jesus enters Jerusalem and the crowds (and congregations) shout out 'Hosanna' and welcome him as the messiah.
- The week ends in **despair** on Good Friday, when the crowds (and congregations) shout out 'Crucify him, crucify him!'
- Maundy Thursday reminds Christians that Jesus was not a great warrior messiah but **humble and peaceful**. Washing each other's feet is a symbol of **humility** and acting as a servant to each other and therefore to members of the **Christian community**.

- **Good Friday** presents Jesus as the **suffering servant** who dies for the sins of the world. It is the most solemn and **serious day** in the Christian year when personal sins are remembered.

- Good Friday is also a day of **hope** as Christians know that Jesus' crucifixion was a **sacrifice for the sins of the world** which makes it possible for humans to enter into a full relationship with God.

- On **Holy Saturday** the **lighting** of candles and bonfires symbolises the **light** of **hope over evil** which the Resurrection brings and that Jesus is the 'light of the world'.

Evaluating Holy Week

Does Holy Week focus too much on sin?
Points to consider:

- **On the one hand ...** as the Resurrection and Easter are about overcoming sin, then it is entirely appropriate in the week before to focus on sin and reflect on the way it affected Jesus and how it continues to control people today.

- **On the other hand ...** many parts of Holy Week do not focus on sin. Palm Sunday, for example, rejoices in Jesus' role as the bringer of peace and Maundy Thursday celebrates his commandment of love and fellowship.

Should the Holy Saturday vigil be part of Holy Week?
Points to consider:

- **On the one hand ...** Holy Saturday should not be part of Holy Week because in anticipating the Resurrection and the first Easter it detracts (takes away) from the joy of Easter Day.

- **On the other hand ...** the whole of Holy Week is preparation for the Resurrection and Easter Day. The vigil builds up the hope and joy which Jesus' women followers and disciples must have experienced when they first came to the tomb and encountered the risen Jesus.

Easter Day

Knowing about Easter Day

- On Easter Sunday Christians remember the moment when the **women** came to the **empty tomb** and then met the risen Jesus.

- People attend church for special **services**.

- The **readings** in church recall when **Mary Magdalene** and the other disciples **met** the **risen Jesus**.

- There are **joyful hymns** celebrating Jesus' **resurrection**.

- In the service the minister greets the people by saying, **'He is risen!'**

- People reply with **'He is risen indeed, hallelujah!'**

- The church is filled with **flowers**, and **eggs** are given to children.

Understanding Easter Day

- The **symbols** of Easter, such as **flowers** and **eggs**, represent **hope**, **new life** and **eternal life**.

- The altar is covered in a **white** or **silver** cloth to symbolise **purity, holiness** and **Jesus' resurrection**. The minister also wears a **white scarf** or stole as Easter is one of the great holy days in the Christian year.

- For those who have kept Holy Week, Easter Day has special **spiritual significance** after a week of thinking about sin and death.

Evaluating Easter Day

Is Easter Day the most important day in the Christian year?
Points to consider:

- **On the one hand ...** it must be the most important day in the Christian year, as Jesus' resurrection showed how his death was not the end and how punishment for sin had been overcome.

- **On the other hand ...** Easter Day is not the most important day in the Christian year because Christmas celebrates the Incarnation when God humbles himself and, by becoming human, lives among people. Without Christmas, Easter would have very little meaning.

Is the Resurrection just a symbol of new life?
Points to consider:

- **On the one hand ...** the Resurrection is just a symbol of new life. It seems very unlikely that Jesus was actually brought back to life but whatever the disciples experienced transformed their lives. Resurrection is like baptism, the death of the old way of life and birth of a new way of living.

- **On the other hand ...** if the Resurrection did not actually happen, then there would be no reason to believe Jesus' message of eternal life and the forgiveness of sins. Resurrection is more than just a symbol of new life, it actually is new life.

Christmas

Knowing about Christmas

- Christmas is preceded by the four weeks of **Advent**.

- On **Christmas day** Christians remember Jesus' **birth** and his **Incarnation** as the Son of God.

- People **attend church** and listen to **readings** about Jesus' special **birth** in **Bethlehem** and the visit of the **shepherds**.

- There may be a **nativity scene** in the church. Many people set up one at home.

- **Prayers** remember the **poor**, the **sick** and **children in need**.

- **Christmas carols** are sung in church and often round the parish.

- It is a time of **giving to charities**.

- At home **presents** are exchanged.

Understanding Christmas

Revise also the topic on the Incarnation on page 97.

- **Light** is an important Christmas symbol as it represents **hope** over **ignorance**, **creation** over **disorder**.

- Jesus is the **light of the world**. His birth is a sign that God enters into the human world of **sin or darkness**.

- As Jesus' birth is a sign of **God's generosity** and gift of his son to the world, Christians are encouraged to make a special effort to give to **charities**, especially to the poor and homeless as Jesus was **born in a humble stable**.

- Christmas is a family time as the festival celebrates the **Holy Family** of Mary, Joseph and Jesus. Christians are also encouraged to invite those who **are lonely** or have **no family** to share in their family Christmas meal.

Evaluating Christmas

Should Christians give presents at Christmas?
Points to consider:

- **On the one hand …** giving presents is expensive and people often spend far too much on gifts which are unwanted and unnecessary. Christmas should be about being generous in other ways: reaching out to the lonely, giving to charities and spending time with family and friends.

- **On the other hand …** the wise men brought gifts to the baby Jesus and Christmas is about God's gift of Jesus to the world. By exchanging presents with one another, people experience something of what lies at the heart of Christmas.

Has Christmas lost its meaning today?
Points to consider:

- **On the one hand …** Christmas has become a national holiday in many countries and so for many people it is a time to enjoy themselves regardless of religious belief. It has become very commercialised but there is still a spirit of generosity.

- **On the other hand …** Christmas has lost its meaning, especially when shops start advertising Christmas gifts several months before Christmas itself. Local councils sometimes put up Christmas decorations even before Advent. The Christmas spirit has been lost by making Christmas commercial.

> Practise answering questions with *Theology, Philosophy and Religion 13+ Exam Practice Questions and Answers* pages 11–12 and 63–66.

Test yourself

1. What event in Jesus' life does the Eucharist remember?
2. What words does the minister say to those receiving bread and wine at the Eucharist?
3. What is liturgical worship?
4. Give two examples of individual worship.
5. What is the purpose of the altar or Lord's Table in a church or chapel?
6. What is an iconostasis?
7. What is chrismation?
8. What happens at a believer's baptism?
9. Who conducts a confirmation service?
10. Outline the promises a man and woman make at a marriage service.
11. What is intercessory prayer?
12. Give two reasons for Christian pilgrimage.
13. What happens at a Good Friday service?
14. What event does Christmas remember and celebrate?

Glossary

atonement The belief that Jesus' death is a sacrifice for the sins of the world, and brings people back into a full relationship with God

ascension The belief that Jesus went back into heaven after his resurrection

baptism Ceremony using water to welcome a person into the church family

chapel A room attached to a building and used as a place of worship for some Christian groups, such as Methodists and Baptists

confirmation Ceremony marking a person's full membership of the Church

covenant The agreement between God and his people

crucifixion Method of Roman execution used to kill Jesus

doctrine Teaching about a belief

Eucharist The service sharing bread and wine, celebrating the Last Supper

Incarnation God in human form

intercessions Prayers for others and the world

liturgical worship A formal type of public worship with set prayers and readings which has developed over many hundreds of years

Maundy Commandment; Jesus' new commandment is that Christians should 'love one another' as equals

new covenant The new agreement between God and his people made through Jesus

omnibenevolence Unlimited goodness

omnipotence Unlimited power

omnipresence The state of being always present everywhere

omniscience Unlimited knowledge

pilgrimage A special journey usually made for religious reasons

resurrection The belief that Jesus rose from the dead

Sabbath The Jewish day of rest when no work is to be done

sacrament An outward sign of God's blessing/grace

sacrifice Offering something of value to God

sin Wrongdoing

stewardship Taking care of the world for God

testimony A person's story about what God means to them or how they came to faith

Trinity The doctrine that God is three in one and one in three: Father, Son and Holy Spirit

worship Offering praise to God

C: Hinduism

1 Hindu beliefs and teachings

Read *Religion for Common Entrance 13+* pages 61–72.

1.1 Key beliefs and concepts

Brahman, atman, samsara and karma

Knowing about Brahman, atman, samsara and karma

Brahman

- Brahman is the **Spirit** or life force of the universe and the origin of everything.
- Brahman is in **everything** but **cannot be seen**.
- Brahman is **ultimate reality** or absolute truth.
- Brahman is **one**.
- **Brahman** is both **impersonal** and **personal**.
- Brahman is referred to as **God** when He is experienced in a more personal way.
- Aum, or Om, represents the **deepest vibration** of the universe which is Brahman.
- As God, Brahman manifests Himself in **many forms**.
- These **forms** are the Hindu **deities** such as **Brahma**, **Vishnu**, **Shiva** and Devi.
- The **worship of Brahman** is called bhakti.

Atman

- Atman is the **eternal self** or **soul** of every living creature.
- It is distinct from the material body.
- Atman is also **part of Brahman**, the Spirit of the universe.
- When the atman occupies an individual person, it is called jivatman.
- At death, the atman is **reincarnated** (samsara) into another body unless it achieves moksha (liberation from samsara).

Samsara

- Samsara means **passage**.
- Samsara describes the **changes we go through in life** as our bodies change.
- A person's **character** may change but deep down they are the **same person** or **atman**.
- The passage of life to a new life after death is called **reincarnation**.
- Samsara **comes to end** at moksha.

Karma

- Karma is the **law of cause and effect**.

- Karma describes the laws of **moral action** and **reaction**.

- Karma affects **samsara** and what kind of life a person lives when **reincarnated**.

- A **good life** now means the **next life** will be **happier or better**.

- A **bad life** now means the **next life** will be **unhappier or unlucky**.

- **Bad karma** could even result in being reincarnated as a **lower life form**.

Understanding Brahman, atman, samsara and karma

- Brahman illustrates the important idea that although there are **many religions** and many gods, they are **all paths to the same God** or reality.

- The parable of the **blind men and the elephant** illustrates that one religion cannot completely claim to know God.

- The great twentieth-century Hindu guru **Vivekananda** made it his mission to teach how all religions point to the one God or Brahman.

- Because all living creatures have atman, it means each has an **aspect of God within** them.

- It is not easy to know atman, so meditation is often used to become more aware of it.

- When **jivatman and the mind** are in harmony, then a person has achieved true happiness.

- Some people claim to **remember previous lives** when hypnotised as proof of reincarnation or samsara.

- **Karma** means that those who think they can get away with being morally bad will be **punished** in their next life.

- Karma is **not fate** as humans have **free will** and can control their life.

Evaluating Brahman, atman, samsara and karma

Is there any proof that Brahman exists?
Points to consider:

- **On the one hand ...** there is no proof that Brahman exists because He is not a thing and He is not physical but spiritual. It is just a question of personal belief as to whether he exists.

- **On the other hand ...** the proof of Brahman's existence is that many people find a deep connection between their own spirit and the spirit of nature and its beauty and purpose. The proof is that so many religions believe in an absolute spirit. They can't all be wrong.

Does belief in samsara make any difference to how one behaves in life?
Points to consider:

- **On the one hand ...** belief in samsara does make a difference because it can give hope that if one is suffering now, then by being good and accumulating good karma the next life will be better.

- **On the other hand ...** if one believes that samsara or reincarnation is inevitable then it will make no difference how one behaves. This is because whether someone lives a morally good or a morally bad life they will still be reborn.

Dharma

Knowing about dharma

- Dharma refers to the **laws of life** and the universe.

- Dharma is eternal and referred to as **eternal truth**.

- The **two levels of dharma** are laws of **reality** and laws of **morality**.

- Carrying out **dharma** means being obedient to these laws, carrying out one's **duty** and doing what is **morally right**.

- **Dharma** is known through **conscience** and the sacred Hindu **scriptures**.

- Dharma informs how a person should behave according to their **caste** or varna and **stage of life** or ashrama. This is called varnashrama dharma.

- There are **four castes** or **varnas**:

  - Brahmins are **priests** and **teachers**.

  - Kshatriyas are **rulers** and **fighters**.

  - Vaishyas are **farmers**, **traders** and **skilled workers**.

  - Shudras are **unskilled workers**.

- Each caste has specific **duties** or **dharma** it has to carry out.

- There are **four stages of life** or **ashrama**:

  - **student**

  - **householder**

  - **forest dweller**

  - **wandering holy person**.

Understanding dharma

- The law or **dharma of reality** teaches that **although everything changes**, the **universe continues to exist** because there is the eternal law of dharma sustaining it.

- The law or **dharma of morality** teaches that life is a constant **battle** between **good and evil**.

- The popular Hindu epic story, **The Ramayana**, telling of **Sita's** rescue by **Rama** from the evil **Ravana**, reminds humans that they need to constantly **struggle against evil**.

- Carrying out one's caste duties affects one's **karma** and therefore one's **place in society in the next life**.

- Only a **few people** opt to go beyond the ashrama **householder stage** because duties to family have to come first.

- It is **illegal in India today** to **discriminate** against someone because of their **caste**.

- Many scholars today teach a **more spiritual version** of the varnas. The varnas describe different types of **spiritual people** and their **lifestyles**.

Evaluating dharma

Is it selfish to choose the ashrama of a forest dweller?
Points to consider:

- **On the one hand ...** it is not selfish as by the time a person reaches this stage of life, their family has probably grown up and they are ready to explore the next stage of their spiritual journey.

- **On the other hand ...** it is selfish as there will almost always be friends and family to whom a person has responsibilities. The path of karma yoga teaches that one should do good things for other people.

Are there really eternal laws of the universe?
Points to consider:

- **On the one hand ...** if, as many scientists claim, the universe is here by chance then there can't have been any eternal laws existing before the creation of the universe. There are no eternal laws; just the laws of physics.

- **On the other hand ...** without the existence of eternal laws there would be no laws which enable the universe to continue existing. The laws which science describe give a glimpse of these eternal laws.

Moksha

Knowing about moksha

- **Moksha** means **release** from **samsara** – the **cycle of rebirths**. Every living thing has a **goal or purpose** to reach during its lifetime.

- When the soul or **atman** is **pure** and **free from delusion and desire**, it is **released** to become **one with Brahman** where it experiences perpetual **bliss**.

- There are traditionally **four paths to moksha** for humans:

  - **Karma yoga** path of **action** or good works

  - Jnana yoga path of **knowledge** of God

  - Bhakti yoga path of **devotion** to God

  - Raja yoga or royal yoga path of meditation over bodily/mental control.

Understanding moksha

- Moksha may take many **lifetimes** or reincarnations to achieve because all **negative karma** has to be overcome and removed.

- When moksha is achieved the atman experiences **pure happiness** or **bliss** in its relationship with Brahman.

- Some teach that atman **becomes totally one** with Brahman and **ceases to exist** as an individual.

- **Selfish desires** and **ignorance** hold the atman back from achieving moksha.

Evaluating moksha

Is moksha less desirable than reincarnation?
Points to consider:

- **On the one hand ...** moksha is not desirable because once released from the cycle of birth and rebirth there would be no challenges in life. It would be boring with nothing to do.

- **On the other hand ...** moksha is much more desirable than reincarnation as it is a state of great happiness, love and bliss. It would not be boring as being in the presence of Brahman or God would be constantly creative.

Is jnana yoga the best path to moksha?
Points to consider:

- **On the one hand ...** it is the best path as meditating enables one to have a much better knowledge and understanding of Brahman which will guide the soul towards Him and achieve spiritual freedom.

- **On the other hand ...** it is not the best path as it only suits the few people who can meditate. Worship or bhakti comes much more easily to most people, so that is the better path to moksha.

1.2 Manifestations of the divine

- Many Hindus believe in only **one God** who is **Brahman.**
- God/Brahman has **many aspects** and this means He can appear and be worshipped in **many different forms** or **gods.**
- The gods are presented in **male** and **female** forms.

The tri-murti and the male gods

Knowing about the tri-murti and the male gods

- Traditionally God is depicted as the tri-murti or 'three forms': **Brahma**, **Vishnu** and **Shiva.**
- The three forms of God illustrate His **cosmic roles** as **creator** (Brahma), **preserver** (Vishnu) and **transformer** (Shiva).
- Hindus are usually a **devotee** or worshipper of **one** of the tri-murti gods as their **supreme God.**

Brahma

- Brahma is the **first** aspect of the tri-murti and represents **God the creator.**
- He is depicted in art as having **four hands** representing the **four corners of the cosmos.**
- He has **four faces** representing the **four Vedas** (the Hindu scriptures).
- He holds a **book** as a symbol of **knowledge.**
- His **crown** depicts his supreme **authority.**

Vishnu

- Vishnu is the **second** aspect of the tri-murti and represents **God the preserver** of the **cosmos.**
- He is depicted in two forms – as a **standing figure** and as a **seated figure.**
- As a **standing figure**, he has **four arms** symbolising **power.**
- His **conch** shell symbolises Aum.
- His **discus** symbolises mind.
- His **mace** symbolises **strength** and power.
- As a **seated figure**, Vishnu lies on **Sesha**, a cobra, symbolising his power over the waters of chaos.
- He descends to Earth in **ten forms** or avatars.
- **Four avatars** are **animal forms**, **six** are **human forms.**
- The avatars include **a boar**, **Rama** and **Krishna.**
- As **Krishna** he is depicted playing a **flute**, with a **feather in his hair** and as a **cow herder.**
- There are many **popular stories** about Krishna such as 'Krishna's trick on the village girls'.

Shiva

- Shiva is the **third** aspect of the tri-murti and represents **God the transformer** of the **cosmos**.

- Shiva transforms the universe by **creating**, **preserving** and **destroying**.

- He is depicted in two forms: as a **dancing figure** and as a **meditating figure**.

- As **Nataraja** or the **dancing figure**, he is presented creating, preserving and destroying.

- The **ring of fire** which surrounds him symbolises his **power to create and destroy**.

- He holds a **drum** which symbolises the **rhythm of life**.

- His foot stands on the **demon** of **ignorance**.

- As **Maha-Yogi** or the **meditating figure**, he is presented with his mind **focused on God**.

- His eyes are **half closed**.

- His third or **middle ey**e is his spiritual eye which connects **atman with Brahman**.

Understanding the tri-murti and the male gods

- The different forms of God illustrate that **God is active** in the world and that He **loves** His creation and **defends** it against evil.

- Some Hindus prefer to think of the tri-murti as an **internal representation** of human **spiritual potentials** (atman) and not as a supreme external being.

- The **symbols** of each of the tri-murti are used in meditation to **focus the mind** on the different aspects and characteristics of God.

- Some devotees worship **Krishna in his own right** as the supreme form of God as he is also a manifestation of Vishnu.

- Many of the **stories about Krishna** present him teasing people; this is because he wants them to look **beyond the world of appearances** and see the great power and beauty of the universe and then God/Brahman Himself.

Evaluating the tri-murti and the male gods
Should all three of the tri-murti be worshipped equally?
Points to consider:

- **On the one hand ...** if each of the tri-murti is a different aspect of Brahman, then to worship God fully they should all be worshipped equally.

- **On the other hand ...** each of the tri-murti shares characteristics of the others, especially Vishnu and Shiva. Therefore as each of the deities can represent Brahman, each can be worshipped alone as the supreme God.

Do the symbols of the tri-murti lead to a false view of God?
Points to consider:

- **On the one hand ...** it is possible that the symbols of each of the gods in the tri-murti could be treated at face value rather than as representations of God. This could lead people to thinking falsely of God in human terms.

- **On the other hand ...** the symbols of the tri-murti are not treated literally by worshippers. The symbols help people visualise what God is like and when the symbols are used in the stories about the deities to show how God is actively part of the world.

The female deities

Knowing about the female deities

Devi, the Mother Goddess (or shakti)

- Many Hindus are devotees of **Devi**, the **Mother Goddess** or **shakti** (meaning power).

- She shares many of the **same roles as Shiva.**

- She is a representation of the **supreme form of God.**

- In one story the male deities use their powers to create **Devi** to destroy the evil Mahisha.

- Devi slays **Mahisha**, the **buffalo demon.**

- Devi appears in various forms such as **Durga** and **Kali.**

Durga

- As Durga she has **eight** or **ten hands** which symbolise how she **protects** her devotees.

- She holds **many weapons** symbolising her energy and role as **remover of miseries.**

- She has **three eyes** representing **desire**, **action** and **knowledge.**

Kali

- As Kali she has a black or **blue body** and **red tongue.**

- She wears a **necklace of skulls** and holds a severed head.

- In her other hand, she holds **many weapons.**

- All her symbols represent her resistance to **evil, ignorance and death.**

Understanding the female deities

- Although female deities are worshipped by men and women, they offer **women worshippers** encouragement to be **resourceful** and **independent.**

- Female deities **share many 'male'** characteristics, so both female and male deities are **not male/female in the human sense.**

- **Durga** gives her devotees hope that **obstacles to life can be overcome** with spiritual and physical effort.

- **Kali** means **time**, as time destroys all things. Kali reminds humans that eventually **all things will come to an end.**

- Kali's frightening features remind people what **evil looks** like, so as to make them turn away from it and **seek moksha.**

Evaluating the female deities
Is Kali too violent?
Points to consider:

- **On the one hand ...** Kali is too violent as her symbols and her behaviour as told in stories about her are extreme. It is hard to reconcile her violence with love for God.

- **On the other hand ...** In an evil world where people do terrible things, then Kali inspires her devotees not to do nothing but to fight against injustice. Kali is not too violent in a literal sense.

Does evil really exist in the world?
Points to consider:

- **On the one hand ...** evil doesn't really exist as a power or force in the world but as a metaphor of extremely bad acts which are destructive and show no respect for life.

- **On the other hand ...** evil really does exist in the world as a force which can take over people's lives and make them do terrible things. The battle between good (God) and evil is not a metaphor, it is real.

Murtis

Knowing about murtis

- A murti is an **image** of a deity in the form of a **picture**, **carving** or **statue**.

- Murtis may be **cheap** or **expensive**.

- Murtis represent **Brahman** and therefore must be given **great respect**.

- In **worship** (puja) at home, the murti is treated as an **honoured guest**.

- As an honoured guest at **puja** the murti is woken up, washed, fed and offered incense and flowers.

Understanding murtis

- A murti's symbols represent the deity's **characteristics** and **powers**.

- Murti means **embodiment** so it is **more than a picture** or statue, it is a **channel** of God's **love**.

- The **channel** of love is a form of **communication** between God and the worshipper.

- A murti is not **actually worshipped** as that would be idol worship but is treated with great **reverence** and respect.

Evaluating murtis
Can a statue really be a channel of God's presence?
Points to consider:

- **On the one hand ...** a statue cannot be a channel of God's presence because it is made by a human being and only has the meaning given to it by the person who made it. As God is infinitely greater than anything, then a statue remains simply an object.

- **On the other hand ...** a statue can be a channel of God's loving presence when the worshipper treats it with respect. The symbols of the statue may communicate God's presence in the same way in which God can be experienced through nature.

Can any object be used as a murti in worship?
Points to consider:

- **On the one hand ...** if the object helps the worshipper communicate with God and brings them into His presence then it can be used. A murti gains its power because it represents something significant about God to the worshipper.

- **On the other hand ...** not any object can be a murti because its symbols and form must be ones which are recognised as belonging to a deity. The symbols gain meaning as part of the stories told about the deity and that gives them power and significance.

Practise answering questions with *Theology, Philosophy and Religion 13+ Exam Practice Questions and Answers* pages 13–14 and 67–71.

Test yourself

1 What is Aum?

2 What is atman?

3 What is karma?

4 Describe two forms of dharma.

5 Name any two of the varnas (castes).

6 What is the aim of moksha?

7 Name the three gods of the tri-murti.

8 Describe two of Vishnu's symbols.

9 Describe two different ways in which Shiva is represented.

10 Outline the story of how Devi gained her power.

11 Describe Kali.

12 Why should a murti be given respect?

2 Hindu practices and ceremonies

Read *Religion for Common Entrance 13+* pages 73–84.

2.1 Forms of worship and meditation

The third of the paths to moksha is called **bhakti yoga** (see page 123). Bhakti is love of God through worship, meditation and living a spiritual life.

The fourth of the moksha paths is called **raja yoga** or the royal pathway. Raja yoga uses many meditation techniques to **settle the mind** and become aware of Brahman.

Havan, arti and puja

Knowing about havan, arti and puja
Fire plays an important symbolic role in Hindu worship. It is an ancient symbol of power and the presence of God.

Havan

- Havan means **to offer**.
- Havan ceremonies use **fire** as a symbol of **cleansing**.
- A fire is **blessed by a priest** and people make offerings.
- Offerings can be **mental** as well as **physical**.
- Havan ceremonies may be carried out **publicly** or **privately**.

Arti

- Arti means **complete love**.
- In an arti ceremony a **lighted candle** or lamp is **waved clockwise** in front of the murti.
- Worshippers put their **hands near the lamp** to receive God's **blessings**.
- In **temple worship** the priest performs arti **five times a day**.

Puja

- Puja means **to worship** and **to honour**.
- Puja is practised differently according to religious and family traditions.
- Puja is carried out:
  - in **daily** worship at home
  - at **festivals**
  - at the **naming** of a child
  - at **weddings**
  - at **funerals**.
- A **priest** usually carries out puja in the **temple**.

- Puja at home and in the temple often consists of:
  - **welcoming** the deity by **sprinkling water** on the **murti**
  - making **offerings** of flowers, incense and food
  - sounding a **bell** and performing **arti**
  - **meditating** and reciting **mantras**
  - taking the **blessed food** or prashad and sharing it with others at home or at the temple.
- At **night time** puja is performed again and the **murti** is then **put away**.

Understanding havan, arti and puja

- Fire and light are used in **many religions** as symbols of God's presence, creativeness and goodness.
- Fire symbolises **constructive** as well **destructive** powers.
- Fire as a **destructive symbol** represents **overcoming negative desires** such as hatred, jealousy and envy.
- Fire and light as **constructive symbols** represent the **presence**, **love** and **knowledge** of God.
- **Puja** at home or in the temple develops the **mind of the worshipper** to be generous, respectful, welcoming and loving.
- Carrying out daily worship at home requires **discipline** and **devotion**, **qualities** which lie at the heart of **bhakti yoga**.

Evaluating havan, arti and puja
Can puja be performed by anyone?
Points to consider:

- **On the one hand ...** anyone can perform puja if they show reverence to the murti and are old enough to understand the meaning and purpose of the rituals.
- **On the other hand ...** temple puja can't be carried out by anyone as it is the role of the priest to perform the rituals according to traditional Hindu religious laws. It would also be wrong for a non-Hindu to perform puja as their intentions would not be right.

Does devotion to God require rituals and ceremonies?
Points to consider:

- **On the one hand ...** if God is supreme He does not need human rituals and ceremonies in order to be worshipped. Rituals and ceremonies can easily get in the way and become more important than devotion to God.
- **On the other hand ...** rituals and ceremonies, especially when they are well-known, are useful ways of focusing the mind on God. Rituals and ceremonies give structure to worship and enhance devotion to God.

Bhajans and kirtans
Knowing about bhajans and kirtans

- Bhajans are songs used in **worship**.
- The songs are usually led by a **music group**.
- The songs are based on **stories** of the gods and **teachings of holy people**.

- They may be performed at **home** or in the **temple**.

- Kirtans are **repeated chants** based on mantras.

- Kirtans may include **dancing** and **music**.

Understanding bhajans and kirtans

- **Music** uses a different aspect of **human consciousness** to meditate and to worship God.

- **Telling stories** through music develops the **spiritual imagination** of worshippers.

- Stories of the deities appeal to old and young alike and is a means of **passing on important Hindu teaching** and values.

- Performing a kirtan helps **quieten the mind** and prepare it to become more **aware of God**.

Evaluating bhajans and kirtan

Is music essential to worship?
Points to consider:

- **On the one hand ...** music is essential to worship as it can express ideas and emotions about God that go beyond words. If God is beyond all words, then music is an essential part of worship.

- **On the other hand ...** music is not essential as some worship and meditation is best done in silence and by lifting the mind to a higher level without interruption.

Should all puja use at least one kirtan?
Points to consider:

- **On the one hand ...** if the purpose of worship is to lift the mind and soul to a higher level to become aware of God, then the use of a kirtan is essential as this is what it is designed to do.

- **On the other hand ...** a mantra or silent meditation could achieve the same end as a kirtan.

Mantras and japas
Knowing about mantras and japas

- A **mantra** is a **short, repeated phrase**.

- The words do not need to mean anything.

- A japa is mantra chanted to a **special rhythm**.

- A widely used mantra is the Gayatri mantra.

- It is dedicated to the **power of the sun**.

- **Aum** or Om is said before reciting the mantra.

Understanding mantras and japas

- The words of the mantra are like a **tuning fork of the mind**.

- Sometimes the **sounds** of the words in a mantra are **more important than their meaning**. **Sounds** of words resonate with the mind.

- In the **Gayatri mantra** the power of the **sun** refers to the **source of spiritual understanding**.

- **Aum** resonates with the **deepest vibration** of the universe which is Brahman or God.

- The rhythms used in japas are to **quieten** the mind and focus thoughts on a **higher level of awareness**.

Evaluating mantras and japas
Can any repeated phrase be a mantra?
Points to consider:

- **On the one hand ...** although the words of a mantra may not have immediate meaning, the words at very least have to connect the person saying them to their deity or to Brahman. Reciting a shopping list cannot do this.

- **On the other hand ...** all words make sounds and sounds can connect the person saying them with Brahman, who is beyond all words, in the way the word Aum does. So repeating even a meaningless phrase can be a mantra.

Are mantras just a form of hypnotism?
Points to consider:

- **On the one hand ...** even though the worshipper repeats a phrase many times, mantras are not a form of hypnotism but a way of getting the mind to let go of earthly thoughts and focus on higher spiritual matters.

- **On the other hand ...** all that mantras do is to put someone into a kind of trance or hypnotic state. This may be very pleasant and psychologically relaxing but they don't do any more than this.

Murtis, darshan and shrines
Also read page 127 on murtis.

Knowing about murtis, darshan and shrines

- A **murti** is a **statute** or picture of a deity.

- A murti is **not an idol** but an **icon**.

- Darshan means **viewing** or seeing a deity.

- A **holy person** (guru) or **object** (such as a murti) can be a source of darshan.

- Darshan gives the deity or guru **honour** and in return brings **blessings** on the worshipper.

- A shrine is a special place at **home** or in the **temple** where a murti is looked after and treated with great respect.

Understanding murtis, darshan and shrines

- An **icon** (or murti) acts like a **window into another world**. When a person worships an icon, it is not the statue or picture itself that is being worshipped, but the world that the icon points to.

- **Darshan** is a **two-way process** in which the worshipper or devotee practises **bhakti** or devotion to and love for the deity or guru.

- As in any **loving relationship**, in showing love for the deity, the worshipper experiences the deity's love for them. This is what is meant by a blessing.

- A famous example of darshan, mutual love and blessing is between **Arjuna** and **Krishna**.

- **Blessings** may be both **spiritual** and **material** and develop **good karma**.

- Looking after a shrine is a religious and spiritual duty and blessing.

- A **home shrine** acts as the **spiritual centre** of the home. It reminds the family of their moral and religious duties.

Evaluating murtis, darshan and shrines

Can a person really be a source of darshan?
Points to consider:

- **On the one hand ...** if a person has been a very inspirational teacher or led a moral and spiritually noble life, then coming into their presence transmits something of these qualities to the student or devotee.

- **On the other hand ...** however good or noble a person is, they will never be holy enough to be a source of darshan. It is also dangerous to treat any human being in this way as it can lead to false hero worship.

Should every home have a shrine?
Points to consider:

- **On the one hand ...** every home should have a shrine perhaps to remember family or friends and to be a special place for quiet and reflection. It need not be explicitly religious to have a spiritual effect.

- **On the other hand ...** although some homes might benefit from having a shrine, a shrine could become psychologically unhealthy if it appears to give certain objects supernatural powers.

Priests and gurus

Most religions have religious leaders and teachers. Hinduism is no exception; for thousands of years it has been led by priests and guided by its great teachers or gurus.

Knowing about priests and gurus

- Priests belong to the **brahmin** caste. Only **brahmins** may carry out certain Hindu ceremonies and rituals.

- Brahmins today are respected for their **wisdom** and knowledge of Hinduism.

- A **guru** is a Hindu **teacher of wisdom**.

- A guru has spent many years **studying** and **teaching**.

- He may have a group of students who follow him and his teaching.

- A guru may be given the title **swami** by his students.

Understanding priests and gurus

- Many Hindus consider it a blessing to have a ceremony such as marriage or naming ceremony carried out by a **brahmin** because of his knowledge of the ancient rituals.

- Particular gurus are also given great reverence and considered to be a source of **darshan**.

- Many Hindus keep the festival of **Guru Purnima** or Reverence for Gurus and Teachers. Worshipping a guru or teacher does not mean treating them as a god but wanting to **live by their teachings** and pass on these teachings to others.

Evaluating priests and gurus

Is Hinduism sexist if only men can be priests?
Points to consider:

- **On the one hand ...** Hinduism is not sexist, it is just keeping to the ancient traditions set down in the Vedas, the Hindu holy scriptures, which state that only men from the brahmin varna may carry out the rituals. Women may have other equally significant spiritual roles.

- **On the other hand ...** some modern Hindu movements think that it is sexist for only men to be brahmins and have allowed women to be priests. However, this is not widespread and so at the moment Hinduism is sexist.

Should all teachers be respected?
Points to consider:

- **On the one hand ...** even if the teacher is not a good teacher, he must be given some respect for trying to convey knowledge and wisdom which is necessary for students to progress in life.

- **On the other hand ...** a teacher who does not care what he is teaching or has little concern for his students does not deserve to be respected as he is not imparting wisdom.

2.2 Places of worship

Knowing about places of worship

Home shrines
For worship or puja at home read pages 129–130.

- A home shrine contains a **murti** of the family's chosen deity.

- The shrine may be a **special room** in the house, a **corner of a room** or a **shelf**.

- The shrine has **candles**, **lights** and **decorations**.

- The shrine is used for **daily worship** (puja) at home.

Temples or mandir

- The temple is called a mandir.

- It is **dedicated** to a particular **god or goddess**.

- It is the **home** of the deity's **image** or **murti**.

- The **spire** is called a shikhara.

- The shikhara contains **carvings** from the **animal**, **human** and **divine worlds**.

- The **porch** contains the '**vehicle**' of the deity.

- The **main hall** or mandapa often has **pillars** and is used for **religious dancing** and music.

- The **inner shrine**, or sanctuary, contains the **image** (murti) of the deity or deities and **altar**.

Worship in the temple

- **Worship** in the temple is similar to **puja at home**.

- People take their **shoes off** before entering the **mandapa**.

- Each person **rings a bell** to **tell** the **deity** that they have **arrived**.

- Some **pray** by **themselves** or in **family groups**.

- Some people **meditate quietly**, others **sing hymns or prayers**.

- **Hindu scriptures** are read at various times.

- The **priest** blows a **conch shell** and sounds the **puja bell**.

- He offers the murti **incense**, **fire**, **flowers** and **water**.

- He circles the **arti lamp** in front of the **image** and then offers it to the **worshippers** who place their hands near it.

- The **worshippers offer gifts** of **money**, **food** and **flowers**.

- The **priest** offers worshippers **prashad** (blessed food) in return.

- The **priest** carries out a **final arti ceremony** and prepares the **murti** for the **night**.

Understanding places of worship

- The **temple** is **built** to symbolise the meeting of **heaven and Earth**.

- The **shikhara** is usually very **tall** like a **mountain range** (the God realm) and symbolises the **journey of the soul to moksha**.

- The **vehicle** of the deity represents their spiritual powers.

- Whereas at **home** the murti is treated as an **honoured guest**, in the **temple** worshippers are the guests as it is the murti's **home**.

- At home only **the family** carry out puja; in the temple it is the **priest's** role to **look after** the **murti**. Every day he **prepares** the **murti** ready **for worshippers**.

- Temple worship offers the Hindu community the opportunity to **worship together** by participating in **bhajans and kirtans** which would be less common at home.

Evaluating places of worship

Is the shikhara the most significant feature of a mandir?
Points to consider:

- **On the one hand ...** the shikhara is the most significant feature of the mandir as it is placed above the shrine room and signifies the relationship between this world and God. This is the primary purpose of the mandir.

- **On the other hand ...** the shikhara is not the most significant feature as not all mandirs have a shikhara but they must have the shrine where the murti of the deity is kept and honoured.

Would it be wrong for a Hindu only to worship at their home shrine?
Points to consider:

- **On the one hand ...** it would be wrong only to worship at home because worshipping in the mandir brings the Hindu community together in fellowship and support of each other.

- **On the other hand ...** it would not be wrong because there are many different paths to Brahman which include very different forms of worship. Furthermore, worship at the home shrine has fewer distractions than at the mandir.

2.3 Festivals

There are many Hindu festivals which celebrate the deities, Hindu stories and gurus. The festivals of Divali and Holi are particularly popular. Festivals are a time of fun, learning and community spirit.

Knowing about festivals

Divali

- Divali takes place in late **autumn**.

- It lasts **between two** and **five days**.

- Divali means **row of lights**.

- People light **oil lamps** or divas.

- The **lamps** are placed on **window ledges or by doors**.

- The **light** commemorates how **Rama** was **welcomed home** after he **defeated** the wicked demon king **Ravana**.

- On his return home, there was no moon so people placed **lanterns** to welcome Rama and his wife Sita home.

- The **lights** are also to welcome **Lakshmi** into people's homes.
- **Gifts and sweets** are exchanged.
- People wear **new clothes**.
- People set off **fireworks**.

Holi

- Holi is a **spring festival**.
- It is named after the evil **Princess Holika**.
- Holika tried to **kill** her **nephew Prahlad**, a devotee of Vishnu.
- **Vishnu descended to Earth** and saved him.
- **Holika was burned** in the fire instead.
- Large **bonfires** are lit on the **eve** of the festival.
- Food is **roasted on the fires** and given as **prashad**.
- The **morning after** is a time for **practical jokes**.
- **Coloured water** and powder is thrown over people.
- **Children** are allowed to be **cheeky to adults**.

Understanding festivals

- At Divali the **story is recited**; its main theme is that evil can be destroyed by good.
- The light of the divas lamps symbolises goodness and wisdom.
- **Lakshmi** is the goddess of **good fortune**, **wealth** and **prosperity**. Divali is a festival of good fortune which is why it is a time when people give to **charities**.
- **Holi** teaches that good will triumph over evil and that **evil will be punished**.
- **Krishna** is remembered at Holi because he is an **avatar of Vishnu**.
- Krishna's sense of **fun** is a way of making people aware of life and their **spiritual journey**.
- It also breaks **down barriers** between old and young people.
- Throwing coloured water and powder recalls the time when **Krishna threw coloured water** over his **sister because she had fair skin** and his skin was **dark**. The story **teaches** about who and what we are.

Evaluating festivals
Does good fortune really exist?
Points to consider:

- **On the one hand ...** good fortune does not exist. Although things may happen by chance to a person's advantage, good fortune is created by people choosing the right thing to do.
- **On the other hand ...** it is in the gift of the deities to reward those whom they wish. Good fortune does not happen by chance but because a person deserves it for reasons which only God can know.

Is the festival of Holi just about having fun?
Points to consider:

- **On the one hand ...** Holi is meant to be a festival of having fun, enjoying life and mixing with people old and young. Krishna enjoyed life in this way, so should everyone else.

- **On the other hand ...** although Holi is about having fun, there is more to it than that. It is about valuing the good things in life and resisting evil; it is about respecting and mixing with all kinds of people.

2.4 Pilgrimage

Pilgrimage is the act of making a journey to a place which has special religious significance. People who make these journeys are known as **pilgrims**. The syllabus states that you should know about at least **two places** of pilgrimage, such as Badrinath, Varanasi (Benares) and the Ganges River.

Knowing about pilgrimage

- Most pilgrimages **end** with a visit to a **temple**.
- There are **many temples** but the important ones are **Badrinath**, **Rameshwaram**, **Puri** and **Dwarka**.
- Some pilgrims visit **special places** like the **Ganges River** and the holy city of **Varanasi**.
- Some pilgrims visit **Jagannath** because there is a huge **murti** or image of **Krishna** there.

Badrinath

- Badrinath is **3,000 metres** up in the **Himalayas**.
- Its temple is the most holy one dedicated to **Vishnu**.
- The temple contains many murti of deities and gurus.
- The chief murti is the **one-metre** high black **stone** of Lord **Vishnu**.
- A **golden canopy** covers the Vishnu murti.
- The Vishnu murti is flanked by **Nar and Narayan**, two avatars of Vishnu.

Varanasi (Benares)

- The city of Varanasi or Benares is the **most popular pilgrimage** destination for Hindus.
- It is the dwelling place on Earth of Lord **Shiva**.
- Pilgrims visit many **temples** and shrines there.
- It is an ancient place of **learning**.
- Two tributaries of the **Ganges River** converge at Varanasi.

The Ganges River

- The Ganges River is believed to have been created by Lord **Shiva**.
- It is the **most sacred river** in India.
- **Bathing** in the river and performing the rituals **washes away sins** or negative karma.

Understanding pilgrimage

- Pilgrimage is a sign of **religious dedication** as it costs time and money.
- Pilgrimage is **social** because pilgrims can meet other Hindus but it is **also** a time of **spiritual cleansing**.
- **Badrinath** is the place where **Vishnu descended** in many forms. It is therefore especially associated with his **darshan** (presence) along with the darshan of the great gurus who are represented there.

- Pilgrims at **Badrinath** also **cleanse** themselves in the **Alakananda River.**

- Some pilgrims believe that because the **Ganges River** is so holy, bathing in it can remove all **negative karma** and achieve **immediate moksha.**

- At **Varanasi** the presence of so many pilgrims gives the place a **special spiritual** atmosphere as everyone hopes to experience the darshan of God.

Evaluating pilgrimage

Can bathing in a river such as the Ganges or Alakananda really wash away sin?
Points to consider:

- **On the one hand ...** when a river is associated with a particular deity it is no longer just a river but a holy river which communicates the presence of God to the pilgrim. When the pilgrim's mind is focused on God, His love can overcome their negative karma and their sins are washed away.

- **On the other hand ...** a sacred river may have an emotional effect on the pilgrim, but it can't actually wash away sin. It is possible that the pilgrim may be moved to be a better person by seeing so many other pilgrims wanting to wash away their sins.

Is the pilgrimage journey more important than the destination?
Points to consider:

- **On the one hand ...** the destination is what makes sense of the pilgrimage journey, otherwise any journey could be a pilgrimage. The destination is linked with a special Hindu god or guru and it is because of this that the pilgrim will want to visit.

- **On the other hand ...** the samsara is often described as a pilgrimage or journey. It is the experiences along the way which help shape a Hindu's thoughts and relationship with God. The destination is important but not the sole purpose of pilgrimage.

2.5 Rites of passage

Hindus divide up a lifetime into stages, each of which corresponds with an **important life event.**

- Each of the **16 stages of life** is marked by a special **ceremony** or samskara.

- The **important samskaras** are birth/naming, starting education, sacred thread, marriage and death.

Knowing about rites of passage

Birth

- When a baby is born he or she is given a **secret name.**

- The baby is given his or her first taste of **ghee** (butter).

- Eleven days later the **priest** works out a **horoscope** to see how the planets will affect the baby's life.

- The horoscope tells the parents which **letter** their **child's name** should begin with.

- The name is **whispered** into the child's ear.

- Some parents **choose the names** of **gods or deities** such as **Lakshmi** for a girl or **Krishna** for a boy.

- The naming ceremony is called namakarana.

Initiation or the sacred thread ceremony

- The ceremony takes place for a **boy** sometime between his **eighth and eleventh birthday**.

- This is the **tenth samskara**.

- It is called upanayana.

- The ceremony is only for those boys who belong to the **first three castes** or varnas.

- The **thread** consists of **three strands** (white, red and yellow) which are reminders of the boy's **three duties**:

  - his **first** duty to **God**

  - his **second** duty to his **parents**

  - his **third** duty to his religious **teachers**.

- The **ceremony** is held at **home**.

- The **thread** is placed over the boy's **left shoulder** by his **priest or teacher**.

- The boy will **wear the thread all his life**.

- It is a **sign** that he is now an **adult**.

- The youngster is introduced to the **Gayatri** (the central mantra of Hinduism).

Understanding rites of passage

- Each **samsakara ceremony** marks an important moment of **samsara** in the cycle of life to death.

- The birth of a child is a **sacred moment** which is why **choosing a name** has to be done with care to give the child a **propitious life** – a life of good fortune and blessing.

- The **sacred thread** ceremony marks an important moment when traditionally a boy would be allowed to study the sacred Vedas, the holy books of Hinduism.

- Today **upanayana** is also used to mark the start of a boy's formal education. A growing number of people are using the ceremony for **girls** as well as boys but this is controversial.

Evaluating rites of passage
Should children be allowed to choose their own names?
Points to consider:

- **On the one hand ...** children should be allowed to choose their own names because there may be some names they dislike and some names that mean much more to them. Letting children choose their own name would be a way of giving them more respect.

- **On the other hand ...** choosing a name for a child is a special role for parents and helps them bond with their child. Parents know more about their family history and are in a better position to choose a name that respects an ancestor, for example.

Should girls also be allowed to go through the sacred thread ceremony?
Points to consider:

- **On the one hand ...** as there are depictions in Hindu art of the Mother Goddess wearing the sacred thread, then girls today should be able to go through the ceremony. Educating girls in Hinduism means they can pass on Hindu values to their children more effectively.

- **On the other hand ...** the sacred Vedas only permit men to study them, so the sacred thread ceremony is restricted to boys. Also, marriage is equivalent to upanayana for girls; their role is to be homemakers.

Practise answering questions with *Theology, Philosophy and Religion 13+ Exam Practice Questions and Answers* pages 14–15 and 71–75.

Test yourself ✓

1. What is bhakti yoga?
2. Name two ceremonies using fire.
3. What does 'puja' mean?
4. What is prashad?
5. What is the main difference between a bhajan and kirtan?
6. What is the purpose of a mantra?
7. What does 'darshan' mean?
8. Who might be given the title swami?
9. What is the mandapa?
10. When might a priest blow a conch shell?
11. Explain why Varanasi is a major pilgrimage centre.
12. What is a samskara?

Glossary

arti Complete love; performed by waving a lighted candle in front of the deity

ashrama The four stages of life from student to wandering holy man

atman Soul, spirit, true or unique self

Aum or **Om** A word that represents the deepest vibration or essence of the universe

avatars Descent; describes the ten forms in which Vishnu appears on Earth

Badrinath A city in India; the temple there is dedicated to Vishnu and is often visited by pilgrims

bhajans Songs and dances used in worship

bhakti The worship of Brahman

bhakti yoga The path to enlightenment through love and devotion to God

Brahman The ultimate reality of the universe, invisible Spirit and source of all matter

brahmin Teacher or priest

darshan Viewing; the blessing of God experienced through a murti or holy person

Divali A late autumn festival of light which celebrates defeat of the wicked demon king Ravana

Devi The Mother Goddess

dharma Refers to the 'moral code' in Hinduism, constituting the fundamental laws of life and the universe

divas Oil lamps lit at the festival of Divali

Ganges The most holy river in India; pilgrims bathe there and visit the city of Varanasi

Gayatri mantra An ancient and widely used mantra which meditates on the power of the sun

guru A greatly respected wise person and teacher

havan To offer; a fire ceremony is used to make the offerings

Holi A spring festival which celebrates the defeat of the wicked Princess Holika

japa A mantra that is recited many times to a special rhythm

jivatman The individual soul or spirit as distinct from the mind

jnana yoga The path to enlightenment by knowing God through mind and meditation

karma The law of cause and effect in nature

kirtan A chant based on a mantra used in worship

mandapa The main prayer hall in the mandir

mandir A Hindu temple

meditation A means of quietening the mind and body to become more aware of the self and of God

moksha Liberation; when all negative karma is overcome and the atman becomes one with Brahman

murti An image or statue of a god or deity

namakarana Naming ceremony of a child (fifth samskara)

prashad Blessed food prepared for the deity and distributed at puja to devotees

puja Worship that takes place at home or in a temple

raja yoga Royal yoga; meditating on God by stilling the mind

samsara Reincarnation or the process of birth and rebirth over many lifetimes

samskara Sixteen stages of life, each of which has a special ceremony

shikhara The spire outside a mandir (temple)

shrine The most holy part of a temple or home where the deities are worshipped

Tri-murti The three forms of God: Brahma, Vishnu and Shiva

upanayana Sacred thread ceremony that takes place when a boy enters the student stage of his life

Varanasi Holy city in the Himalayas visited by many pilgrims

varna Caste or social groups in society

varnashrama dharma The moral duties performed according to a person's place in society and stage of life

D: Islam

In traditional Islam, dates are given from the time of the migration (hijrah) from Makkah to Madinah as **A.H. (after the hijrah)**, but in this chapter, dates are given as **B.C.E.** or **C.E.**

Muslim beliefs and teachings

> Read *Religion for Common Entrance 13+* pages 85–97.

Iman is the **belief** in the **Six Articles of Faith**:

1 The oneness of God

2 God's angels

3 God's books

4 God's prophets

5 The Last Day

6 The divine plan

Iman must be accompanied by ihsan or **good works**.

1.1 The oneness of God

Knowing about the oneness of God
Muslims (followers of Islam) believe the following about God:

- God's oneness or unity is called tawhid.

- God is **one**; there are **no other gods**.

- **Only God** may be **worshipped**.

- God is omnipotent or **all powerful** and is the **creator** of everything.

- He is the **Absolute** and there is nothing greater than Him.

- God is also **beneficent** or **all good**, **generous** and **merciful**.

- As the beneficent, He is the **giver of life** and sends His **messengers** to guide humans.

- His greatest act of generosity was **sending the** Qur'an.

- **God** has **99 sublime** or **beautiful names**.

- All the names are **found** in the **Qur'an**.

- The names describe some of God's **many characteristics**.

- The names include: The **Merciful**, The **Creator** and The **All-Knowing**.

- **Prayer beads** (subha) are used in worship and prayer as a **reminder** of the **99 names**.

Understanding the oneness of God

- God is both transcendent, beyond time and space, but also immanent and closely involved with humans and the world.

- God's beneficence is experienced by humans on the **Day of Judgement** when He will **reward** the good and **punish** the wicked.

- Anything that undermines God's oneness is called shirk.

- Shirk includes **representing** God in **art** or believing **other gods** exist. This is why only **abstract art** is permitted in mosques.

- Anything that is considered to be more powerful or greater than God is called **shirk**; as God is the greatest then only He may be **worshipped**.

- Shirk is caused by human **pride** and ignorance and humans thinking they know more than God.

Evaluating the oneness of God
Is God really beneficent when there are evil people in the world?
Points to consider:

- **On the one hand ...** God is good because He allows people the freedom to choose to do good or evil. Life is therefore a test to see who will live according to His laws; everyone will be judged on the Last Day and the wicked will be punished.

- **On the other hand ...** God is not really beneficent, because if He were, then evil people would be punished now to allow good people to enjoy this world. It is too late to wait until the Last Day.

Is pride the greatest human sin?
Points to consider:

- **On the one hand ...** pride is not the greatest sin because it is good to be proud of what one does to make sure it is as good as it can be. Pride celebrates the gifts and talents which God has given to humans.

- **On the other hand ...** pride is the greatest sin because it makes people think only about themselves and not about the needs of others. Pride gives people a false sense of power and they think they are more important than God.

1.2 God's angels

Knowing about God's angels

- Angels are God's **servants** and communicate His will.

- They bring **God's message** to **humans** especially when they pray.

- They **cannot** usually **be seen**; they can only be sensed.

- They are **neither male nor female** but can take on **human form**.

- They look after humans and are **felt** as **love and peace**.

- **Jibril** (Gabriel) is the chief angel who **delivers messages** to the prophets.

- **Mikail** (Michael) looks after **heaven**.

- **Israfil** sounds the last trumpet at the **Last Judgement**.

Understanding God's angels

- Angels are **different from humans** because they **do not have free will**.

- They are also different because they were **created at the beginning of time**.

- Shaitan (Satan) is different from the other angels because he was **expelled from heaven**.

- Shaitan will be **judged on the Last Day** along with all humans.

- Angels have a **special relationship to humans**: recording angels record all human actions which will be read out on the Last Day.

- **Guardian angels** protect humans against Shaitan; life is a **constant battle against temptation** (acting against God's will).

Evaluating God's angels

Is there in any evidence for angels?
Points to consider:

- **On the one hand ...** many people say they have experienced the presence of a guardian angel. Furthermore, the Torah and the Bible make frequent references to angels, so Islam is not the only religion that acknowledges the existence of angels.

- **On the other hand ...** angels are just metaphors for explaining how prophets and religious people experience God's presence. They have roles in stories but don't actually exist.

Is belief in God more important than belief in angels?
Points to consider:

- **On the one hand ...** a Muslim who believes in iman must equally believe in God's angels. Angels explain how God communicates with people, therefore belief in angels and belief in God are equally important.

- **On the other hand ...** belief in the oneness of God is more important than belief in angels, because the Shahadah states a Muslim must bear witness to the one and only God. It does not require belief in angels.

1.3 God's books

Knowing about God's books
The Qur'an

- The Qur'an is the **central holy book** of Islam.

- Qur'an means **recitation**.

- The Qur'an was **revealed** to **Muhammad** by God **through** His angel **Gabriel**.

- The occasion of the first revelation in 610 C.E. on Mount Nur is called the Night of Power.

- The Qur'an was revealed gradually **over 22 years**.

- **Various people**, including many of the **companions** of Muhammad, wrote down the revelations.

- One of Muhammad's wives, **Hafsa**, kept many of the sayings in a **chest**.

- **Abu Bakr** ordered that a **standard copy** should be made.

- It was **checked** by those who had **heard** it **directly** from **Muhammad**.

- **Caliph Uthman** established the definitive Qur'an and ordered all other versions to be burnt.

- There are 114 surahs or chapters in the Qur'an.

- A verse is called an ayah.

- Every surah except Surah 1 begins with the bismillah.

- The bismillah is 'In the name of God, the Compassionate'.

- The Qur'an acknowledges that before Muhammad many prophets had brought special **books** to the world.

- **Moses** brought the **Law**.

- **David** brought the **Psalms**.

- **Jesus** brought the **Gospel**.

- The Qur'an is the full and **final revelation** of God.

The Hadith

- The Hadith refer to various **books** that tell of the **words and actions** of **Muhammad** himself.

- A **hadith** is a saying of Muhammad.

- The Hadith may be consulted by Muslims to see how **Muhammad acted in various situations**.

Understanding God's books

- The **Qur'an** is the **word of God**.

- Unlike other revelations through other holy books it has **not become distorted**.

- The Qur'an cannot be **translated** and should be **read in Arabic**.

- It is God's **final and complete revelation** to humans.

- Qur'an means **recitation** and so many **learn** the Qur'an **by heart**.

- These people are called hafiz and are treated with great respect.

- Surah 1 or the **Al Fatihah** (The Opening) sets out the main Muslim beliefs and therefore is often used in worship and prayer.

- Every copy of the Qur'an must be treated with **respect** because it is the word of God. This means there must be **no eating or drinking** when reading it.

- Before touching it, a person must **wash** and be in the **right state of mind**.

- When it is not being read the Qur'an must be covered and placed on a **high shelf**.

- The most important hadith is the **Hadith Gabriel** because unusually Jibril (Gabriel) **actually appeared** to Muhammad and gave him the **Six Articles of Faith**, **Five Pillars of Islam** and **ihsan** (how to live well).

Evaluating God's books
Is the Hadith just as significant for Muslims as the Qur'an?
Points to consider:

- **On the one hand ...** Muslims look to the example of Muhammad to guide them in their lives. So the Hadith provides them with Muhammad's personal understanding of the Qur'an and how to live by God's commands.

- **On the other hand ...** there are many hadiths and one Qur'an. The Qur'an is the word of God and so has much more authority and significance than the Hadith. It is significant but less so than the Qur'an.

Should Muslims be allowed to study the Bible?
Points to consider:

- **On the one hand ...** Muslims should be able to study the Bible as long as they know that only the Qur'an is God's word. The Bible provides interesting insights which may help a Muslim understand how Christians view the prophets, Jesus and Mary.

- **On the other hand ...** Muslims should not study the Bible as it is not the word of God. As the Bible has distorted God's revelation, many parts are shirk, so there is no point in studying it.

1.4 God's prophets

There any many prophets in Islam but the most significant of them is Muhammad, because it was to him that God revealed the Qur'an.

Knowing about God's prophets

- The Qur'an mentions **24 prophets by name**.

- The first prophet is **Adam** and the last is **Muhammad**.

- The prophets are all **examples** of how to live.

- All the prophets taught that there is only **one God**.

- **Muhammad** is the **last prophet**. His message **seals** the **earlier messages**.

- His message is contained in the **Qur'an**.

- Only the **Qu'ran** is a **perfect presentation** of God's word.

Muhammad's early life

- **Muhammad** was born in **570 C.E.** in **Makkah**.

- His **father died before** he was **born** and his **mother died** when he was **six**.

- After his grandfather's death he was **brought up** by an uncle, **Abu Talib**.

- Muhammad was very **honest** and his **uncle** let him go on **business journeys**.

- He **impressed** a merchant called Khadija and she let him **run her business**.

- In 595 C.E. he **married her** when he was **25**.

- They had children but Muhammad also looked after his **uncle's son Ali**.

Muhammad and the Night of Power

- **Muhammad** often went to **pray** in a **cave** called **Hira** on **Mount Nur outside Makkah**.

- In **610 C.E.** when Muhammad was **40** the **angel Jibril** (Gabriel) appeared to him.

- Jibril told him to **read** and recite God's message.

- Muhammad **refused three times**.

- The angel squeezed **him three times**.

- Then Muhammad **recited God's words**.

- He spent some time in **shock**.

- But he was **reassured by Khadija** that he had indeed **received God's word**.

- This first revelation of God to Muhammad is called the Night of Power or **Laylat al-Qadr**.

Muhammad's message in Makkah

- **Khadija, Ali, Zayd ibn Harith** and **Abu Bakr** become the **first Muslims.**
- To begin with the **message spread slowly.**
- Muhammad taught the people of **Makkah not** to **worship idols** and that there was only one God.
- This made the **Quraysh** merchants **angry** as they considered he was **putting off pilgrims** who also **brought their business** to Makkah.
- They accused Muhammad of being **mad** and a **liar.**
- Some of his **companions** were **tortured** and **killed.**

The migration or hijrah

- In 620 C.E. six men from the town of **Yathrib** asked Muhammad to come and **settle their disputes.**
- Muhammad said he would if they agreed to worship the one God.
- In **622 C.E.** Muhammad, his family and followers went to **Yathrib.**
- The event is called the **hijrah** or migration and is the **first year** in the Muslim calendar (1 After Hijrah).
- Yathrib was renamed **Madinah al-Nabi** or City of the Prophet.

Muhammad's life and teaching in Madinah

- Muhammad started his **first Muslim community** in Madinah.
- He built his first **mosque.**
- His new laws taught that under **God's rule all people** were to be treated as **equal.**
- Many people were **impressed** by life at **Madinah** and **converted** to Islam.

Return to Makkah and cleansing of the Ka'bah

- Muhammad **marched** with ten thousand men on **Makkah** in **630 C.E.**
- The Makkans **gave up without** a **fight.**
- Muhammad **removed** all the **idols** from the Ka'bah (the shrine in the centre of Makkah).
- The Makkans accepted Islam.
- Muhammad gave his **Farewell Sermon** from Mount Arafat and **died** in 632 C.E.

Understanding God's prophets

- **Muhammad is only mentioned a few times** in the Qur'an because the Qur'an is not about him but is God's words.
- Muhammad is the **'seal of the prophets'** because the Qur'an he receives is final and perfect.
- Some prophets are also **messengers** because they delivered **a book** of God's words.
- Isa (Jesus) is a **prophet and messenger** because he brought the Gospel.
- Although all the prophets are male, **Mary, the mother of Isa**, is very important because she was visited by Jibril and is an **example of perfect obedience.**
- **Muhammad's leadership** in Madinah **set an example** of how Islam as a spiritual and moral way of life should be practised everywhere.

- Madinah is an example of Muslim **umma** or community. Umma also refers to the **worldwide Muslim community** and fellowship.

Evaluating God's prophets
Could Mary be considered a prophet?
Points to consider:

- **On the one hand ...** Mary is not a prophet because her role is to be an example of someone who perfectly obeys God's will. Mary did not preach or deliver God's message to people.

- **On the other hand ...** Mary could be considered a prophet because she was visited by Jibril, as were all the other prophets, and she responded by living faithfully to God's Word. The Qur'an gives her great significance.

Could there be more prophets after Muhammad?
Points to consider:

- **On the one hand ...** there could not be any more prophets after Muhammad because he was the 'seal of prophecy' and the final prophet before the Last Day. He delivered the Qur'an so there is no need for more prophets.

- **On the other hand ...** no one can assume to know the mind of God. There were many prophets before Muhammad so it is possible that when the world is again in crisis God might send another prophet.

1.5 The Day of Judgement and afterlife

Knowing about the Day of Judgement and afterlife

- Akhirah means the Last Day and afterlife.

- When a person dies their soul is taken by the angel **Azra'il** to barzakh.

- Before the Last Day, a great **world battle** takes place.

- Then on the **Last Day** the **angel Israfil** will sound the last trumpet and everything will die.

- When he blows it again all human **souls and bodies** will be reunited and **resurrected**.

- Then **God will judge** each person according to the record kept by the recording **angels** of their **deeds** and **beliefs** on **Earth**.

- The **good** will be rewarded with **paradise** or **Jannah** – a life of **peace** and **purity**.

- **Unbelievers** or the **disobedient** will be sent to **hell** or **Jahanam** – a life of **torment**.

Understanding the Day of Judgement and afterlife

- No one truly knows what **heaven and hell** will actually be like; the Qur'an describes them using **various metaphors**.

- **Heaven** or paradise is described using the metaphor of a **beautiful garden** where there is a fountain of delicious drinks served by women.

- **Hell** is described using **metaphors** of **fire** and **perpetual pain** and suffering.

- Akhirah reminds people that **this life is a test** for the next.

- Judgement is a sign of **God's mercy and justice**, so that even if in this life a person is not rewarded, they will be in the next.

Evaluating the Day of Judgement and afterlife
Are heaven and hell actual places or symbols of the afterlife?
Points to consider:

- **On the one hand ...** the Qur'an uses metaphors to describe heaven and hell because they are not actual places but describe our relationship with God. For example, the metaphors used to describe hell are really expressions for what it would be like to be totally cut off from God's mercy.

- **On the other hand ...** the Qur'an may use metaphors to describe heaven and hell, but this doesn't mean that they don't exist. The metaphors use human experiences to describe what is almost impossible for us to understand while we live on Earth.

Is God really merciful if he sends wicked people to hell?
Points to consider:

- **On the one hand ...** if God were truly merciful He would want all people to be saved and enter paradise. Even wicked people have some good in them, and so a really merciful God would recognise this and not send them to hell.

- **On the other hand ...** it isn't God who sends wicked people to hell but they themselves. God is merciful as probably most people fall short of His laws, but he doesn't send them to hell. Wicked people ignore His commands, so deserve their punishment.

1.6 The divine plan

Knowing about the divine plan

- Al Qadr means the divine plan.

- The divine plan is the belief that as God **created** the **world** then everything is **controlled** by Him.

- God has **complete knowledge** of everything that happens.

- God is the **controller of destiny; nothing happens by chance**.

Understanding the divine plan

- There is much **debate** among Muslim scholars as to **whether humans have free will or not** if God knows how they will be rewarded at Judgement Day.

- Some argue that **free will is limited** by situation, which only God can fully know.

- Some argue that God allows each person to make **full use** of their **free will** by permitting them to do good or evil.

Evaluating the divine plan
Do humans only have limited free will?
Points to consider:

- **On the one hand ...** humans only have limited free will because there are many things we cannot control completely such as the personality we are born with. We have to learn to develop our character within these limits.

- **On the other hand ...** humans do not have limited free will because otherwise we would not be morally responsible for our actions and could blame our faults on factors outside our control.

Is there any point in being good if God knows everything?
Points to consider:

- **On the one hand ...** God may know everything but humans do not. So, we have to live as best we can and hope that this is what God wills.

- **On the other hand ...** there is no point in trying to be good if God knows what kind of fate awaits us at Judgement Day. As it makes little difference whether we live good or bad lives, we might as well live the kind of life that suits us best.

> Practise answering questions with *Theology, Philosophy and Religion 13+ Exam Practice Questions and Answers* pages 16–17 and 76–80.

Test yourself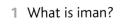

1 What is iman?

2 Name the Six Articles of Faith.

3 What does 'tawhid' mean?

4 Give two of God's 99 names.

5 Name two angels in Islam.

6 What is the role of angels?

7 Over how many years was the Qur'an revealed to Muhammad?

8 What is the Al Fatihah?

9 What is the Hadith?

10 What must a Muslim do before touching the Qur'an?

11 Why is Muhammad known as the seal of the prophets?

12 Name two prophets of Islam besides Muhammad.

13 What does the angel Israfil do on the Last Day?

14 What is Al Qadr?

2 Muslim practices and ceremonies

> Read *Religion for Common Entrance 13+* pages 98–111.

2.1 The Five Pillars of (Sunni) Islam and their significance in Islam

In addition to **iman** (belief in God), the Five Pillars of Islam are the five duties or amal (actions) that apply to every Muslim.

1 **Shahadah**, or witness to the **one God** and His messenger **Muhammad**

2 Salah or **prayer**

3 Zakah or **alms giving**

4 Sawm or **fasting**

5 Hajj or **pilgrimage** to **Makkah**

Shahadah

Knowing about the Shahadah

● Shahadah means **witness**.

● It is the declaration of faith in the **one God** and that **Muhammad is His messenger.**

● The Shahadah is contained in the adhan or the **call to prayer.**

● The **adhan** begins, 'Allah (God) is the greatest … I bear witness that there is no God but Allah.'

Understanding the Shahadah

● The Shahadah is recited by every Muslim to indicate a **promise to carry out God's will.**

● To **become a Muslim** a person says the Shahadah in front of **two witnesses.**

● Shahadah also involves ibadah, the desire to **worship God** and carry out the other **four pillars.**

● The **adhan** is recited five times a day when calling Muslims to prayer; it is a constant reminder of the significance of the Shahadah.

Evaluating the Shahadah
Should a person's religious beliefs remain private?
Points to consider:

● **On the one hand …** religion is a personal matter and people should keep their religious views to themselves. In today's society people have many different beliefs – some religious, some not – and so all of them have to be treated the same by not allowing views to be expressed publicly.

- **On the other hand ...** if religion means anything it has to change the way a person lives and treats others. Religious beliefs cannot remain private as that would contradict what it means to be a religious person.

Should one always tell the truth?
Points to consider:

- **On the one hand ...** one should always tell the truth because not to do so would, in the end, cause confusion and mistrust. Telling the truth may be difficult and painful, but in the end people always respect those who are truthful.

- **On the other hand ...** always telling the truth may cause more harm than good. Sometimes not telling the whole truth may be kinder to someone and a greater good may come from it.

Salah

Salah or **prayer** is the **second Pillar of Islam**. There are **five compulsory** prayer times a day as well as du'a, personal prayer.

Knowing about salah

- Salah means **prayer**.

- Prayers are **directed** towards the **Ka'bah** in Makkah.

- Prayer can take place in **any clean place**.

- **Before** prayer a Muslim must perform wudu or **washing** of the hands, mouth, nose, face, arms, neck, behind the ears and feet.

- **Compulsory prayers** must be said **each day**:

  - between **dawn and sunrise** (fajr)

  - at **noon** (dhuhr)

  - in mid **afternoon** (asr)

  - at **sunset** (maghrib)

  - before **midnight** (isha'a).

Prayer at home

- Prayer at **home** may be held in any clean room where a point indicates the **direction of Makkah**.

- **Women** usually stand **behind men**.

- Prayer starts with a series of **prayer movements** called rakat.

Friday prayers in the mosque

- Jummah or **Friday prayers** are held in the **mosque**.

- **Men** are encouraged to pray in a **mosque**; **women** pray at **home** or in a separate area from men.

- Prayers are led by an imam or prayer leader.

- The muezzin calls the people to prayer.

- Worshippers carry out their own prayers and rakat.

- The muezzin recites the iqama or 'set up' prayer which summons worshippers to **form up** for formal prayers.

- The **imam** then gives the **sermon** or khutba.

- The congregation then carry out **rakat shoulder to shoulder**.

- At the end of formal worship some mosques sing **hymns** and **religious songs**.
- **Personal prayer** or **du'a** may take place at any time.

Understanding salah

- Prayer must come **from the heart**.
- Praying together is a sign of Muslim **unity** and **brotherhood**.
- Prayer is a **reminder** of **God's greatness** and **obedience** to Him.
- **Wudu** is to develop the right **frame of mind** and intention or niyah to worship God.
- Water symbolises cleanliness but only when niyah is to submit to the will of God.
- The rakat symbolise **submission to God** and loyalty and solidarity with other Muslim worshippers, especially congregational rakat at Friday prayers.
- The **rakat end** by wishing the person to the left and right **'salaam' – peace**.
- **Du'a** prayers may be said at anytime and are useful when wishing to give **thanks** or to seek **forgiveness** of God or to **meditate** on God outside the compulsory prayer times.

Evaluating salah

Is private prayer the best form of prayer?
Points to consider:

- **On the one hand ...** private prayer is better because it requires more effort and discipline to pray or meditate by oneself. Prayer is a personal relationship with God and so public prayer or worship can be distracting.
- **On the other hand ...** private prayer is good but it is not necessarily the best form of prayer. Sometimes public prayer is better because it expresses the feelings of the congregation or community which can be very powerful and different from private prayer.

Should prayer in any religion be compulsory?
Points to consider:

- **On the one hand ...** it is good to have compulsory prayer as it teaches people how to pray and through time they become better at it. It is also a good spiritual discipline to pray at certain times and make sure one always remains aware of God.
- **On the other hand ...** it is not possible to make prayer compulsory as it is personal. Making someone say the words of a prayer does not mean they are actually praying. It could also make people resent prayer and put them off religion.

Zakah

Zakah or alms giving is the **third Pillar of Faith**.

Knowing about zakah

- Zakah means **giving to charity**.
- It is an act of **worship** and a **duty**.
- It is a **test** to ensure that one is **not selfish**.
- Zakah is to be **paid once a year**.
- Zakah should be **2.5 per cent** of a Muslim's **overall wealth**.
- Zakah money is given to the weak, the poor, schools, hospitals and many other worthy social causes.
- Islam **forbids usury** or charging interest on loans.

Understanding zakah

- Zakah is a **reminder** that as everything **belongs to God**, material things are on **loan to humans**.

- It builds on two principles of Shahadah, witnessing to God in mind and action.

- It ensures the **weak and marginalised** in society are cared for.

- It is usual for a person to give zakah in **secret** so they **do not get false praise**.

- The Qur'an states that those who practise zakah will be **rewarded** on the Last Day; just as they have **shown mercy** to others, so **God will show mercy** to them.

- Usury is wrong because it **exploits the weak** and can create **debt** which **benefits the rich** at the expense of someone else's life.

Evaluating zakah

Is lending money for interest necessarily morally bad?
Points to consider:

- **On the one hand ...** lending money for interest is morally bad because helping someone should be freely done not as a way of looking for reward or gain. Lending money for interest may exploit those who are less well-off which is morally wrong.

- **On the other hand ...** lending money for interest is no different from many other business arrangements. Banks lend money and make a profit so as to stay in business, pay their employees and then loan money to others.

Is zakah really a form of worship?
Points to consider:

- **On the one hand ...** zakah is a form of worship as giving in charity is an act of generosity and mercy which honours God who is the Merciful. Giving zakah is also acting as a good steward and honouring God's creation.

- **On the other hand ...** worship means honouring God through prayer and attending mosque. Although it may be morally good to give zakah, it is not quite the same as saying prayers or carrying out the rakat.

Sawm

Sawm or fasting is the **fourth Pillar of Faith**.

Knowing about sawm

- Sawm means **fasting**.

- It occurs during the month of Ramadan.

- No food must be eaten from just **before dawn** until just **after sunset**.

- There must be no chewing of food, drinking or smoking.

- Those who are **excused sawm** include:
  - children under 12
  - pregnant women and those nursing young babies
  - the sick
  - those doing physically demanding work.

- Ramadan is also the **month when the Qur'an** was first revealed to Muhammad and so many Muslims try to read, reflect and meditate on the **whole of the Qur'an** during the last ten days of Ramadan.

Understanding sawm

- Fasting is an **act of worship** and **spiritual** development.

- As it involves **enduring hardship for the sake of God**, it is a sign of **obedience** and devotion.

- The Muslim scholar **al-Ghazali** sets out ten reasons why **fasting and hunger** are spiritually important. These include making one more **aware of oneself** and **God**, and **overcoming** selfish and **sinful desires**.

- Fasting helps Muslims to **appreciate the plight of the poor** and so become more generous.

- Other **good works** or **actions**, as well as fasting, are just as important.

- Ramadan helps develop spiritual **unity** or **umma** and **common purpose** with other **Muslims**.

Evaluating sawm

Is fasting the best way to worship God?
Points to consider:

- **On the one hand ...** by fasting a person becomes much more aware of all the good things in creation which they take for granted and forget that they are given by God. Fasting makes one give thanks to God.

- **On the other hand ...** fasting is one way to worship God but it is not the best way because the Pillars of Faith suggest worship can equally be through salah or hajj or zakah.

Should all people practise fasting?
Points to consider:

- **On the one hand ...** whether one is religious or not, fasting from time to time makes one more aware of the environment and its limited resources and how we use them. It might also make one more appreciative of those who labour to produce food.

- **On the other hand ...** not everyone should fast because small children, those who are sick and the old are not strong enough to do so. There is no guarantee that fasting will make someone more aware of their environment.

Hajj

Hajj or pilgrimage is the **fifth Pillar of Faith**.

Knowing about hajj

- Hajj means **visitation of holy places**.

- It takes place once a year for five days.

- It is expected that every **adult Muslim** will go on **hajj** or **pilgrimage** at least **once in his or her lifetime** if they are able (they have the financial means, are healthy and there is a safe route to Makkah).

- There are **seven key moments** of hajj:

1 Preparation

  - Men and women must be in a state of **spiritual purity** or ihram ready to enter Makkah.

  - Men wear two pieces of white cloth.

2 Makkah

- On the **first day** pilgrims **circle** the **Ka'bah seven times** (tawaf).

- Pilgrims then **run between** the **two hills** and the **Zamzam well** as a reminder of how **Hajar** ran to find water for her son Ishma'il (this ritual is called the sa'y).

3 Mina

- Pilgrims **travel** five miles to Mina for midday prayers.

- They pray until last prayers.

- **They camp overnight.**

4 Mount Arafat

- The next day at sunrise the pilgrims travel to Mount Arafat.

- They stand and confess their sins from noon to sunset. This is called **Wuquf Arafat.**

- Wuquf ends with a **sermon** as a reminder of **Muhammad's final sermon.**

- The following part of hajj is called **the unfurling** (stages 5–7).

5 Muzdalifah

- Pilgrims travel to **Muzdalifah.**

- They collect **small stones.**

6 Mina

- The following day pilgrims return to **Mina** and **throw stones** at the **three pillars** to drive out **Shaitan** (Satan).

- Pilgrims **sacrifice** a **sheep or cow** for the festival of Id-ul-Adha.

- It reminds them of **Ibrahim's** willingness to sacrifice **Ishmael.**

- **Men** often **shave their heads.**

- Pilgrims are **no longer** in a state of **ihram.**

7 Return to Makkah

- Pilgrims return to **Makkah** and perform one more **tawaf** and **sa'y.**

- Some visit **Madinah** to see the **tomb of Muhammad.**

- Someone who has been on a pilgrimage is called a hajji (man) or hajjah (woman).

Understanding hajj

- Hajj gives a unique sense of **umma** or Muslim unity as it is often attended by over **2 million pilgrims** from all over the world.

- Hajj follows the **example of Muhammad** when he led the **pilgrimage to Makkah** in 629 C.E. and he **circled the Ka'bah.**

- The ceremonies on Hajj remind pilgrims of:

  - the **oneness and majesty of God**

  - **human sin** and the **need for repentance**

  - the **faithfulness** of the prophets

  - **thanksgiving** to God and **sacrifice.**

- The rituals of Hajj remind Muslims that Islam is **not a new religion** because it recalls how **Ibrahim** (Abraham) was **tested by God to sacrifice Ishmael** and how **Hajar** (Hagar) trusted in God to provide water for her son, Ishma'il.

- Hajj also reminds pilgrims how despite their **sins in Eden**, **Adam and Eve** were **forgiven by God** and reunited after Adam had confessed his sins on **Mount Arafat**.

- Many pilgrims say that hajj reminds them that **life is a journey** and that hajj changes them **spiritually** to see life in relationship to God in a **dramatically new way**.

Evaluating hajj
Can one be a good Muslim and not go on hajj?
Points to consider:

- **On the one hand ...** it is a duty for all Muslims who are capable to go on hajj. This must be so because it is a test of one's true devotion to God and loyalty to Islam and the umma.

- **On the other hand ...** it is not actually going on hajj that indicates whether one is a good Muslim or not because what matters is niyah or intention. Just going on hajj is not enough if the intention is weak. A better Muslim way might be helping the sick and the poor.

Is going on pilgrimage selfish?
Points to consider:

- **On the one hand ...** going on pilgrimage to escape responsibilities at home or to friends might be considered selfish. It might be using up money or resources that could be given to worthy causes.

- **On the other hand ...** going on pilgrimage is not selfish because it requires effort and dedication. It is a time of learning more about oneself so that one becomes less selfish and more aware of God's will.

2.2 Festivals

Id or **Eid** in Arabic means festival. There are many festivals in Islam. Id-ul-Adha and Id-ul-Fitr are two of the most important ones.

Knowing about Id-ul-Adha

- The festival takes place **towards** the **end of the hajj**.

- It is also celebrated by **those not on hajj**.

- It celebrates the time when **Ibrahim** was ready to **sacrifice Ishmael**.

- The festival **begins** with **prayers** at the **mosque**.

- Everyone wears their **best clothes** and performs a **special rakat**.

- Muslims are encouraged to invite **non-Muslim** friends and work colleagues.

- A **sheep or goat** is **sacrificed** to commemorate Ibrahim's sacrifice of an animal.

- The **meat** is **shared** with family, relatives and the poor.

Understanding Id-ul-Adha

- The festival remembers Ibrahim because he was willing to obey God.

- Ibrahim was commanded by God in a dream to sacrifice Ishmael, but it was **Ishmael** who encouraged Ibrahim to obey because of **his faith in God**.

- In another story Ibrahim **was tempted by Shaitan not to sacrifice** Ishmael, but he had the wisdom to resist and carry out God's will.

- These stories teach **Muslims** to be **ready** to **sacrifice their lives** for God.
- Shaitan symbolises **human struggles** to overcome inner temptations.

Knowing about Id-ul-Fitr

- The festival was **started** by **Muhammad**.
- It marks the **end of Ramadan** and 30 days of fasting.
- It is also a time to **thank God** for the **Qur'an**.
- It is **obligatory** for the head of the family to give a **ul-Fitr zakah** gift on behalf of each person of his family.
- No one speaks until after the **ul-Fitr salah** in the mosque.
- People dress up and **children** are given **presents**.
- There is **no work or school**.
- A **special midday meal** is eaten.

Understanding Id-ul-Fitr

- Muslims **thank God** for helping them **get through Ramadan**.
- Muslims are encouraged to be **generous** to the poor, orphans and the weak just as **God has been generous** to them.
- It is a time for **community** and bringing family and friends together and being part of the Muslim **umma** (community and fellowship).

Evaluating festivals

Can religious festivals really make people more generous?
Points to consider:

- **On the one hand ...** festivals are a time of fun when people enjoy themselves and the community comes together. A religious festival might encourage some to be more generous if they really understand the teaching and meaning of the festival.
- **On the other hand ...** religious festivals don't necessarily make people more generous because that may not be the aim of the festival. A festival might aim to think about a particular prophet or an event in the history of the religion.

Is obedience the most important aspect of Id-ul-Adha?
Points to consider:

- **On the one hand ...** obedience is the most important aspect of Id-ul-Adha because the story of Ibrahim's obedience to God's command is central to the festival. Islam means submission to the will of God, so the festival reinforces this central teaching.
- **On the other hand ...** although obedience is important, the festival is also about renewing and building up family and community relationships. It is a time of celebration and rejoicing, in God's gifts to people not just human obedience.

2.3 Rites of passage

Knowing about birth

- When a baby is born, the **father whispers** the call to prayer or **adhan** into the baby's **right ear**.
- The tahnik **ceremony** is when a small amount of softened **date or honey** is **rubbed** on to the baby's **gums**.

- The aqiqah **ceremony** follows **seven days** later when the baby's **head is shaved** and the baby is given a **name**.

- Boys names often combine **Abd** (meaning servant) with **one of God's 99 names** such as Abdul Karim (meaning 'servant of the Generous One').

- Girls are often named after Muhammad's various wives such as **Khadija** and **Aishah**.

- Aqiqah is a time of family **celebration**.

Understanding birth

- A child born to Muslim parents is considered to be a **Muslim at birth**.

- The **tahnik** ceremony symbolises living a **sweet and fortunate life**.

- **Birth ceremonies** welcome a child into the **family** and **local community**.

- Giving a child a **Muslim name** helps a child to have a **Muslim identity**.

Knowing about marriage

Marriage or nikah is important because it is the basis of family life and **Muhammad himself was married**. Muhammad taught that husband and wife should have equal rights. **Divorce** is allowed but only as a **last resort**.

- Marriages are **often arranged**. Love follows – it is not a primary reason for marriage.

- **Parents find** a suitable **bride or groom** for their son or daughter.

- At the **wedding** people wear their **best clothes**.

- The wedding may take place at the **mosque** or at the **bride's house**.

- **Two witnesses** have to be present at the signing of the **wedding contract**.

- The contract is completed when the **husband** gives his **wife** a **dowry** or mahr (a sum of money).

- Passages from the **Qur'an** are **recited**.

- A **feast** is given for the relatives within three days **of the marriage**.

Understanding marriage

- **Muhammad did not believe** men and women should live **single lives**.

- The **Hadith** states that marriage is a **religious duty**.

- Marriage is a union of man and woman **spiritually** and **sexually**.

- The **wife** is **traditionally responsible** for the **home** and **family** but she retains her property rights and may have paid employment.

- The **husband** must set **high moral standards** for his family by, for example, not drinking alcohol or gambling.

- His conduct as husband and father will be judged on the Day of Judgement.

- The **mahr** remains the property of the **wife** and provides for her should she **divorce**.

Evaluating rites of passage

Is a naming ceremony really necessary when a child is born?
Points to consider:

- **On the one hand ...** a naming ceremony is not necessary for a new-born child because in many cultures and societies a name doesn't have a special meaning so a ceremony would be meaningless.

- **On the other hand ...** a naming ceremony is more than just giving a child his or her special name; it also celebrates new life and welcomes the child into the family and community.

Should a couple marry only if they are in love?
Points to consider:

- **On the one hand ...** marriage is about companionship and working together to help each other and to bring up a family. A couple need not be in love, but they do need to trust and respect each other.

- **On the other hand ...** if a couple are not in love they will not have that deep bond which will help them through the difficult times.

2.4 The mosque

Knowing about the mosque

The word 'mosque' comes from the Arabic word, masjid, meaning **place of prostration**. Besides being a place of worship, mosques are also community centres and places of study.

Layout and purpose of a typical mosque

- The main room is the prayer hall.

- One wall of the **prayer hall** must be orientated in the direction of the **Ka'bah** in Makkah.

- This wall is called the qiblah (direction) wall.

- The qiblah wall has a niche or alcove in it called the mihrab.

- Over the prayer hall there is often a **dome**.

- The **pulpit** or **minbar** is a raised platform in the prayer hall where the **imam** stands when **preaching**.

- The usual decorations are **abstract patterns** and elaborate **extracts** from the **Qur'an**.

- There must be **no figurative pictures**.

- Mosques have **cloakrooms** for **shoes**.

- There are **separate areas** for **men** and **women**.

- There are **washrooms** and/or a fountain for ritual **washing** or **wudu** before prayer.

Muezzin and minaret

- A feature of many mosques is a **tower** or minaret.

- The minaret is used by the **muezzin**.

- The **muezzin calls** people to **prayer five times a day**.

- The **call to prayer** is called the **adhan**.

- The muezzin faces in the direction of the **Ka'bah** in Makkah.

- The muezzin must be of **good character**; he assists in the **functioning of the mosque**.

Women in mosques

- Traditionally men and women **sit and pray separately**.

- **Women may sit behind men** in the prayer hall or pray in a **separate gallery**.

Understanding the mosque

- The prayer hall has no chairs so that **rakat** may be performed, allowing worshippers to pray in **unity** with one another **without distinction** of class and social position.

- The dome symbolises the heavens and the oneness of God.

- There is **no figurative art** because pictures might lead to **idolatry** – treating the art as if it were an actual aspect of God.

- The **hadiths** forbid any **pictures of Muhammad**.

- **Abstract art**, especially **calligraphy** (writing), expresses the deep mysteries of God and His creation.

- Traditionally **men and women pray separately** so they are not distracted by each other.

- Some Muslims today argue that men and women should have **mixed congregations** in the mosque and worship equally.

- Some Muslims today, such as the **Inclusive Mosque Initiative**, argue that as Muhammad allowed a woman to lead prayers in her home, women should **lead worship** in the mosque.

Evaluating the mosque

Should men and women pray together in the mosque?
Points to consider:

- **On the one hand ...** even though Muhammad allowed women to lead worship at home he did not intend women to lead public prayers in the mosque. This is because men and women have different but equally valuable roles in society and in the home.

- **On the other hand ...** if praying shoulder to shoulder in the mosque indicates that there are no distinctions in class and race in Islam, this should also mean there should be no difference between men and women. If women can lead prayers at home, then they can lead prayers anywhere.

Should pictures be allowed in a mosque if they help worship?
Points to consider:

- **On the one hand ...** worship is about focusing one's mind on God and being aware of His greatness and mercy. Pictures can distract and they might also give the wrong impression about God and reduce Him to a human level.

- **On the other hand ...** many religious traditions use pictures and objects to focus on in prayer and meditation. Because it is very hard to imagine God, pictures act as parables to guide the mind to a higher level of thought and worship.

Practise answering questions with *Theology, Philosophy and Religion 13+ Exam Practice Questions and Answers* pages 17–18 and 80–84.

Test yourself ✓

1 Name the Five Pillars of Islam.

2 What is ibadah?

3 In what direction should all Muslim prayer be directed?

4 What is wudu?

5 What is the role of the muezzin?

6 What is rakat?

7 How much of a Muslim's overall wealth should be given as zakah?

8 When does sawm take place?

9 What is the Wuquf Arafat?

10 What does the festival of Id-ul-Fitr celebrate?

11 What is the tahnik ceremony?

12 What is the significance of the mahr?

13 What is the purpose of the qiblah in a mosque?

14 What is the minbar in a mosque?

Glossary

adhan The call to prayer

akhirah The Last Day in the afterlife when God rewards the good and punishes the wicked

Al Qadr The divine plan; God knows who will choose good and who will choose evil

Allah Arabic word meaning God

amal Action; constitutes leading a moral Muslim life

aqiqah Naming ceremony of a child

ayah A verse from the Qur'an

barzakh The barrier; where souls wait to be judged by God in the afterlife

beneficence Goodness; refers to God's nature: He is all good and merciful

bismillah The preface to all except the first chapters of the Qur'an; 'to God the Compassionate the Merciful'

du'a Private prayer which is not one of the five compulsory daily prayers

Hadith The sayings of Muhammad and stories about him

hafiz Someone who can recite the whole of the Qur'an by heart

hajj Pilgrimage to Makkah; one of the Five Pillars of Islam

hajji/hajjah Man/woman who has been on hajj

hijrah The migration of Muhammad's first followers from Makkah to Madinah

ibadah Worship of God

Id/Eid Arabic word meaning festival

Id-ul-Adha The festival of sacrifice, which remembers Ibrahim's (Abraham's) near sacrifice of Ishmael

Id-ul-Fitr Festival that marks the end of the Ramadan fast

ihram State of religious purity required for pilgrims to carry out the hajj

ihsan Doing good works

imam Muslim prayer leader

iman Belief and trust in God

immanent Closely involved with humans and the world (refers to God)

iqama Set up; when the muezzin summons worshippers to form up for prayer in the mosque

Isa The Prophet Jesus

Jummah Arabic word for Friday. Prayers at the mosque on Friday are called Jummah prayers.

Ka'bah The sacred cube-shaped shrine in the centre of Makkah

Khadija Muhammad's first wife

khutba Formal sermon preached by the imam at Friday prayers

mahr Marriage dowry or gift given by the husband to his wife

masjid Place of prostration or mosque

mihrab Alcove in the qiblah wall of a mosque indicating the specific direction of worship towards Makkah

minaret Tower from which traditionally the muezzin makes the call to prayer

mosque Muslim place of worship

muezzin The person who makes sure worship takes place properly in the mosque and who makes the call to prayer

Night of Power Or Laylat al-Qadr; the night when God first revealed Himself to Muhammad

nikah Arabic word for marriage

niyah Intention

omnipotent All powerful; God the creator of the universe

prophet A person chosen by God to deliver His message to the world

qiblah Direction; the wall in the mosque which indicates the direction of Makkah

Qur'an The holy book of Islam; the pure Word of God revealed to Muhammad

rakat Bendings; the sequence of Muslim prayer postures

Ramadan The month of fasting

salah Prayer; one of the Five Pillars of Islam

sawm Fasting; one of the Five Pillars of Islam

sa'y The run the pilgrims make between two hills during hajj

Shahadah Witness; expresses the promise to be obedient to God's will and the example of the Prophet Muhammad

Shaitan Arabic for Satan

shirk Failing to respect the oneness of God by reducing Him to the human level

surah Chapter of the Qur'an

tahnik Ceremony that takes place at the birth of a child which involves rubbing honey on to the baby's gums

tawaf Circling of the Ka'bah during hajj

tawhid The unity or oneness of God

transcendent Existing beyond; refers to God who exists outside time and space

umma Muslim community

wudu Ritual washing or cleansing in preparation for prayer

wuquf Standing; the moment when pilgrims stand and confess their sins at Arafat on hajj

zakah One of the Five Pillars of Islam; the obligation to give a percentage of one's money to charity

E: Judaism

In traditional Judaism dates are given from the creation of the world, but in this chapter, dates are given as **B.C.E.** or **C.E.**

Jewish beliefs and teachings

> Read *Religion for Common Entrance 13+* pages 112–24.

1.1 Beliefs about God

The belief in one God is called **monotheism** and is the foundation of all Jewish beliefs and the Jewish way of life.

Knowing about beliefs about God

God is one: monotheism

- Jews believe that **God is one**; there are **no other gods**.
- In the **first** of the **Ten Commandments**, it is stated that there are no other gods, and God alone is to be worshipped.
- The Shema is the most **important** Jewish **prayer** and reminds Jews that God is one and **He alone** is to be **worshipped**.
- The Shema begins, '**Hear O Israel**, the Lord our **God is one** …'

Creator, law-giver and judge

- God alone **created** the **world**.
- The world and all matter depends on God for its existence.
- As creator, God gives everything **order** and **purpose**.
- **God** gave the Torah so **humans** could **worship Him** and **live life fully**.
- God gave the **Law to Moses** on Mount Sinai.
- The **heart of the Law** is contained in the **Ten Commandments** or **Decalogue**.
- As a giver of law, God is also **judge**.
- God is a **fair and merciful** judge and will allow people to repent of their sins.

Divine presence (Shekinah)

- Shekinah means the **presence of God**.
- The rabbis or Jewish teachers taught that it was God's Shekinah which guided the Israelites during the exodus from Egypt as a **pillar of cloud** by day and **fire** by night.
- **Elijah** experienced God's Shekinah as a **quiet voice**.
- In the ancient Jewish Temple, God's Shekinah was present in the **Holy of Holies** above the Ark **of the** Covenant – a box containing the Law.

Understanding beliefs about God

God is one: monotheism

- Even though God may be referred to in **different ways** – as king, as judge, as shepherd – He is one and **never changes**.

- Being one means that God is **unique**. There is **nothing else like Him**; there is **nothing greater than** Him.

Creator, law-giver and judge

- As creator, God is **omniscient** because He **knows all things** that happen in His Creation.

- **Genesis 1** describes how every part of the Creation is designed and because God is good, everything has a purpose.

- God **cannot be known fully** because He is greater than anything the human mind can comprehend, but the **beauty and order** of the world **reveal** enough of Him for humans to understand something of His divine nature.

- The Law shows God's **love** for His people as following His commandments helps them to **overcome their sinful natures** and live good lives.

- At the yearly festival of **Rosh Hashanah**, Jews remember that God will **judge** each person according to their sins and righteous actions.

Divine presence (Shekinah)

- The images of cloud, fire and voice which depict **God's Shekinah** are **not to be taken literally** but are intended to express how God's presence is **experienced spiritually**.

- The symbols of fire and light are the reasons why the Shabbat **candles** are lit each week to symbolise and **welcome God's presence** into the Jewish home.

Evaluating beliefs about God
Can we ever know God fully?
Points to consider:

- **On the one hand ...** God cannot be known fully as creator of the universe as He is greater than anything a human mind can imagine.

- **On the other hand ...** God has revealed Himself through His Creation and specifically to humans in the Law. The only limits to knowing Him are due to human sinfulness.

Can God's Shekinah be experienced in non-Jewish religions?
Points to consider:

- **On the one hand ...** God's Shekinah was only revealed to Moses and to His other prophets; this means that non-Jewish religions have no direct experience of His presence.

- **On the other hand ...** as creator of the universe, God's presence is revealed throughout His Creation to all people. The beauty and order of the Creation mean non-Jewish religions may experience God's Shekinah.

1.2 Covenant

Knowing about the covenant

The meaning and nature of the covenant

- A covenant is an **agreement**.

- God's covenant is a promise that if His **people are loyal** and keep His commandments, He will **bless** and protect them.

- God made and **renewed** his covenant through Adam, Noah, Abraham, Moses, King David and the prophet Jeremiah.
- In His covenant with **Abraham**, God promised that the **Jews** will be His special or **chosen people**.

The Ten Commandments

- The Ten Commandments are at the **heart of the covenant** God made with Moses at **Mount Sinai**.
- Moses received them on **two tablets** of stone.
- The Ten Commandments are in **two parts**:
  - Commandments 1–4: the relationship between **people and God**
  - Commandments 5–10: the relationship **between people**.
- The Commandments are:

  1 Do not worship other gods.

  2 Do not make any images of God.

  3 Do not misuse God's name.

  4 Observe the Sabbath day and keep it holy.

  5 Honour your mother and father.

  6 Do not murder.

  7 Do not commit adultery.

  8 Do not steal.

  9 Do not bear false witness.

  10 Do not covet or envy your neighbour's possessions.

Shema

- Shema means **hear** or **listen** and is found in the Torah in the Book of Deuteronomy.
- The Shema reminds Jews that there is only **one God** and that **He alone** must be **worshipped**.

Signs of the covenant: mezuzah

- The mezuzah is a **portion** of the **Shema** written on **parchment** and is usually placed in a **decorative box** to keep it clean and safe.
- The **mezuzah box** should be placed on the **right-hand** side of **every door** in the home (except bathrooms).
- It **shows** that the house is a **Jewish home**.
- It is a reminder to **obey the Commandments**.
- The **Shema commands** that its words should be bound on the **forehead**.
- The tefillin or **prayer boxes** contain the Shema and are placed on the **forehead and arm**.
- Tefillin are worn by Jewish men and used in **daily prayer**.
- Another sign of the covenant is the tallit or **prayer shawl**.
- The Shema commands that the tallit must have **tassels** or tzitzit.

Understanding the covenant

Covenant

- In the covenant with **Adam** God promises to provide all that humans need to flourish.

- In the covenant with **Noah** God promises not to destroy human life (after the flood) again.

- In the covenant with **Abraham** God promises to make Abraham's descendants a great nation.

- In the covenant with **Moses** God promises to protect His people if they keep his **Commandments** or mitzvot.

- In the covenant with **David** God promises David will rule Israel and that God will choose one of **David's descendants** to bring peace.

- In the covenant with **Jeremiah** God promises that the 'new covenant' will be one of love written on their hearts.

The Ten Commandments

- All the Commandments are about worshipping God and are of **equal value**.

- The Commandments show how Jews must **respect each other** and each **other's property**.

- The Commandments emphasise the **covenant values** of:

  - **love** of the one God

  - **respect** for life

  - **treating** everyone **fairly**

  - **control** of words and **motives**.

Shema and signs of the covenant

- The Shema instructs Jews to **teach the Shema to their children** and to recite it in the morning and evening; God's presence is **kept constantly in mind**.

- The second part of the Shema is a reminder of God's **covenant relationship** with His people and that He will **bless** them if they keep His commands.

- Mezuzah, tefillin and tallit are **outward signs** of the significance of the **covenant** around the **home**, in daily **prayer** and in the synagogue.

- They help a person **feel Jewish** and remind them of their covenant duties.

Evaluating the covenant

Does God's covenant need renewing today?
Points to consider:

- **On the one hand ...** it does need renewing as the world today is very different from the times of Moses and Jeremiah. The technological and global political situation requires a new covenant with new commandments.

- **On the other hand ...** the covenant does not need renewing as everything that is needed between God and people is contained in the ancient covenant. The covenant is everlasting and can be reinterpreted for each new generation.

Should the outward signs of a religion only be used at home?

- **On the one hand ...** religious symbols are only appropriate and meaningful at home or in a place of worship. In today's less religious society it only causes friction and misunderstanding if they are worn.

- **On the other hand ...** wearing outward signs of one's religion in public is even more important in a less religious society as they show a person's commitment to a religious and spiritual way of life.

1.3 Messiah

Knowing about the messiah

- Messiah means **anointed one**.
- Originally it referred to the anointing of the king.
- Anointing meant the king had to carry out God's commands.
- Later the covenant promise made to King David was understood to mean that God would send a messiah.
- Other prophets described the messiah as **God's messenger of peace**.
- When he arrives, **everyone** will **obey the Commandments**.
- Jews are still **waiting** for his **arrival**.

Understanding the messiah

- At various times in Jewish history **people have claimed to be the messiah**. In 132 C.E. **Simon Bar Kochba** tried to overcome the Romans and he was thought to be the messiah.
- But Bar Kochba **failed to overcome the Romans**; peace did not arrive, so he was **not the messiah**.
- **Maimonides**, the thirteenth-century Jewish scholar, included in his **13 Principles of Faith** the belief that the messiah would arrive **sometime in the future** and establish a new **messianic age** of peace and justice.
- **Maimonides' teaching** has become the **standard view** among many Jews today.
- **Other** Jews think the messiah is **not an actual person** but a **peaceful state of** mind; the **messianic age** is just a time when the world will have achieved peace.

Evaluating the messiah

Is the messiah an idea of peace and not a person?
Points to consider:

- **On the one hand ...** the messiah is a person because the biblical prophets spoke of a person as did Maimonides. A messianic idea is very vague; it needs an actual person to lead others to make it happen.
- **On the other hand ...** a messianic idea is much more powerful and life changing than having an actual messiah. The idea can begin to grow in people's minds and hearts; it doesn't have to be a sudden event.

Is God the only one who can achieve world peace?
Points to consider:

- **On the one hand ...** given how sinful and selfish people are, then no one person can bring about world peace, however much people desire it. Only God has the power to make it happen.
- **On the other hand ...** believing that only God will establish world peace just means that humans give up and don't try hard enough to make it happen.

1.4 The world to come

Knowing about the world to come

- The world to come is called in Hebrew the Olam Ha'Ba.

- It is a future **eternal state of the world** which will **last forever**.

- It is **not clear** exactly what this will be like.

- The **prophet Daniel** wrote in the Hebrew Scriptures that after death God will resurrect some people to everlasting bliss and others to everlasting shame.

- God's **judgement** will depend on how **well a person has kept the Commandments**.

Understanding the world to come

- **Some** think the Olam Ha'Ba will be an **afterlife** in **heaven**.

- **Others** think Olam Ha'Ba will be **life in this world** but a transformed world which is **perfect** and **free from suffering**.

- **The** Mishnah (the oral teaching of the rabbis) describes this world and life like a lobby or **waiting room** in which we prepare for the **banquet hall**, the Olam Ha'Ba.

- Judgement does **not have to be directly from God** because those who do not keep God's Commandments **cut themselves off** from Him and the Jewish community.

Evaluating the world to come

Is heaven a place or a state of mind?
Points to consider:

- **On the one hand ...** heaven in the Torah does not have to be a place but can be one's relationship with God, carrying out daily life by 'walking with God' and through prayer and worship.

- **On the other hand ...** heaven is a place of perfection in which humans and God live in harmony. It is what God set up the world to be in the first place.

Is the world to come an important Jewish teaching?
Points to consider:

- **On the one hand ...** it is a very important Jewish teaching as the world to come is the time when God will reward those who have kept the mitzvot and punish those who have not.

- **On the other hand ...** it is not important because keeping to the mitzvot on a daily basis is all the reward one needs. The world to come as a reward after death is unimportant.

1.5 Mitzvot

Knowing about the mitzvot

Free will and the 613 mitzvot

- A **single commandment** from God is called in Hebrew a **mitzvah**.

- **Several commandments** are called **mitzvot**.

- In the **Torah** God commands **613 mitzvot**.

- The **ten central mitzvot** are called the **Decalogue** or Ten Commandments.

- There are **248 positive mitzvot** and **365 negative mitzvot**.

- God gave **humans free will** so they could choose to worship Him and keep His commandments.
- **Yetzer ha tov** means in Hebrew **desiring to do good**.
- **Yetzer ha ra** means in Hebrew **desiring to do wrong or evil**.

Mitzvot between people and God

- In the Ten Commandments, **commandments 1–4** summarise the **religious mitzvot** about how people should respond to God (read page 166).
- All other mitzvot rest on these **religious commandments**.
- Religious mitzvot include commandments about keeping religious signs such as the **mezuzah**, **tallit** and **tzitzit**.
- Mitzvot also include mitzvot which respect **God's world** such as **food laws** (kashrut) about what can and cannot be eaten.

Mitzvot between people

- In the Ten Commandments, **commandments 5–10** summarise the **social mitvzot** about how people should treat others (read page 166).
- These mitzvot may be summarised as **'Love the Lord your God and love your neighbour as yourself'**.
- **Social mitzvot** include visiting the sick, protecting others from injury and welcoming guests into one's home.

Understanding the mitzvot

- Carrying out a mitzvah to another person is **doubly good** because it **honours God** and honours and **respects the person**.
- Carrying out a **social mitzvah** builds up the Jewish community and sets an example for **Jews and non-Jews** on how to **behave well**.
- Mitzvot should be **applied to everyone** but **especially to fellow Jews**.
- It is especially important to carry out mitzvot to those who have **experienced misfortune** such as **widows** and **orphans**.

Evaluating the mitzvot
Is free will the most important gift God has given human beings?
Points to consider:

- **On the one hand ...** without free will, humans would not be able to love God. If God were to make people love Him, it would not be true love or devotion. Free will means being able to look after the world and make decisions about it on God's behalf.
- **On the other hand ...** desiring to do good and knowing God is the important gift. Having free will by itself could lead to terrible consequences in the world if humans are left to make decisions entirely based on their own selfish desires.

Are all the mitzvot religious commandments?
Points to consider:

- **On the one hand ...** not all mitzvot are religious. Some are purely social such as not committing adultery and not stealing. Dietary mitzvot, for example, are there for health reasons.
- **On the other hand ...** all mitzvot are religious because they all form part of the covenant between God and His people. So, carrying out social mitzvot is about developing God's will on Earth and so they are also religious.

Practise answering questions with *Theology, Philosophy and Religion 13+ Exam Practice Questions and Answers* pages 19–20 and 85–88.

Test yourself

1 What is the Shekinah?

2 How did Elijah experience the Shekinah?

3 Name three of God's covenants.

4 Name commandments 4 and 8 of the Ten Commandments.

5 How does the Shema prayer begin?

6 Where would one find a mezuzah?

7 What is a tallit?

8 What will happen in the world when the messiah arrives?

9 How does the Mishnah describe Olam Ha'Ba?

10 How many mitzvot are contained in the Torah?

11 How many negative mitzvot are there in the Torah?

12 What does 'Yetzer ha tov' mean?

2 Jewish practices and ceremonies

Read *Religion for Common Entrance 13+* pages 125–39.

2.1 Worship

The key act of worship every week is keeping the Shabbat. Shabbat worship begins on Friday evening and ends on Saturday evening at sunset. Shabbat worship is carried out at home and in the synagogue.

Worship on the Shabbat

Knowing about worship on the Shabbat

Synagogue worship on the Shabbat

- People must **dress modestly. Boys** and **men cover** their **heads**.
- Worship is set out in a **prayer book** called a siddur.
- Siddur means **order** and sets out the order of worship.
- The morning service may last up to **three hours**.
- In **Orthodox** synagogues, the service is **led** by a **man** or **rabbi**.
- In **Reform** synagogues, a **woman** or a **woman rabbi** may lead.
- There must be a **minyan** or a minimum of **ten adult men** for the service to take place.
- A cantor or **hazan** leads the **singing**.
- The service **begins** with the saying of **blessings** and **psalms**.
- The **amidah** or 'standing prayer' is first said in **silence** and then **out loud** by the whole congregation.
- Then the **Sefer Torah** or Torah scroll is **processed** from the ark to the bimah.
- The **Shema** is recited during the procession.
- **Portions** of the **Torah** are read from the bimah by various people.
- The Torah scroll is lifted up and displayed to the congregation.
- The Sefer Torah is then **processed back to the ark**.
- **Readings** follow from the **prophets** (the haftarah).
- The **rabbi** might give a **sermon** or address.
- The **aleynu** or thanksgiving prayer is recited.
- **Prayers** may be said for the **royal family**.
- The service **ends** with kiddush, a special **blessing** made over **wine**.

Home worship on the Shabbat

- On **Friday afternoon**, the mother and children (especially girls) **prepare the home** – all meals must be ready before dusk.

- Just before the Shabbat begins, the mother **lights the Shabbat candles**, **circles the candles** with her hands and says a **special blessing**.

- Then she places her **hands over her eyes** and meditates for a few moments.

- The **father** (and boys) return **from synagogue**.

- The **father blesses** his sons, 'God make you like Ephraim and Manasseh'.

- Then he **blesses his daughters**, 'God make you like Sarah, Rebekah, Rachel and Leah'.

- Then **he praises his wife**, 'An accomplished woman, who can find her? Far beyond pearls is her value.'

- The **kiddush** ceremony follows.

- The father says a special **blessing** over a **kiddush cup of wine** and then hands it round the family.

- On the table are **two loaves** of bread or hallot **loaves**. The loaves are sprinkled with **salt** and a **small portion is cut and offered to God**.

- A **blessing** is said, and each person eats a piece of hallah bread.

- After kiddush the husband ceremonially **washes his hands**.

- The family eat their **Shabbat meal**.

Havdalah ceremony

- Havdalah means **separation**.

- The havdalah ceremony marks the **end of the Shabbat**.

- A **plaited candle** with several wicks is lit.

- A **blessing** is said over a **cup of wine**.

- A **spice box** is passed round each member of the family.

- A **blessing** is said over the **candle**.

- Everyone wishes each other a good week, '**shavua tov**'.

- A small amount of wine is left to **extinguish the candle**.

Understanding worship on the Shabbat

- The Shabbat is commanded in the **fourth commandment** in the Decalogue. Because God rested on this day after creating the world, no work must be done.

- The Shabbat is a time of prayer, worship and relaxation with family and friends.

- **Kiddush** literally means **sanctification** or **making holy**. It is commanded by God in the Decalogue to make the **Shabbat holy**.

- **Orthodox Judaism** only permits men or male rabbis to lead worship because in ancient Judaism only men could be priests and after them only male rabbis could teach and instruct in Jewish law.

- **Reform Judaism** allows women and women rabbis to lead worship because it considers that women are equally capable of instructing and teaching the Jewish law.

- The Shabbat is treated like a **royal bride**, so the home must be **prepared** as for a very special person.

- The father acts as the **priest** of the family; his **blessings** recall the blessings given by **Aaron in the Torah**.

- **Wine** is a reminder of God's **creative powers** in the world.

- The **two hallot loaves** are a reminder of the **two portions of manna** God gave to Moses in the wilderness on the eve of the Shabbat (Exodus 16) as well as the **two tablets** of the Torah that Moses received at Sinai.

- The **havdalah** ceremony allows each person to experience all **five senses** which God has given humans. They:

  - **taste** the wine

  - **smell** the spices

  - **see** the flame of the candles

  - **feel** the heat of the candles

  - **hear** the blessings.

Evaluating worship on the Shabbat
Is worship at home more important than in the synagogue?
Points to consider:

- **On the one hand ...** the family is very important in Judaism and weekly worship on the Shabbat reinforces spiritual and moral values. When the father blesses his children and praises his wife, he is acting in a priestly way so being at the synagogue is not essential.

- **On the other hand ...** God's covenant is not aimed at individuals but is for the Jewish community. Worship in the synagogue brings the community together and also reminds Jews of their duties to each other. It is as important as worship at home.

Is it unfair that women cannot lead worship in Orthodox Judaism?
Points to consider:

- **On the one hand ...** it is unfair because women are allowed to study Torah and they have duties to perform which include educating children. In the past women were not considered capable of learning, which is clearly not true.

- **On the other hand ...** men and women are not better or worse than each other but have different roles to perform. From ancient times, Jewish men have led worship and maintaining the tradition gives Judaism its continuity.

Prayer and religious clothing

Knowing about prayer and religious clothing

Prayers

- A traditional Jew will say prayers **three times a day**.

- These may be said at home or in the synagogue.

- The **amidah** is an important prayer at home and in synagogue worship.

- It means **standing** and is said silently when praying alone.

- The **prayer book** is called a **siddur**; siddur means **order** as the book arranges the order in which prayers are said.

- The siddur orders **morning and evening prayers**, and prayers for the Shabbat and for many other occasions.

- The **Shema** is the most important Jewish prayer.

- The Shema is the summary of every Jew's belief in the **one God** and obedience to Him.

- It should be recited at least **twice a day**.

Religious clothing

- Men wear a **hat** or kippah as a sign of **respect** for God.

- In the synagogue men also wear a **prayer shawl** or **tallit** with **tassels** at each corner.

- Boys and girls (in Reform Judaism) begin to wear a tallit after their Bar or Bat Mitzvah.

- For **weekday prayers** men also wear two **special prayer boxes** or **tefillin** containing the **passages from the Torah**.

- **One box** is worn on the **head** between the eyes.

- The **other box** is attached to the **upper left arm** with straps which are **bound** round the hand, fingers and arm.

Understanding prayer and religious clothing

- Wearing a **tallit** is a **mitzvah** as it is commanded in the Torah. It symbolises **God's presence** (Shekinah) across the **four corners of the world**.

- Each of the tassels/fringes (tzitzit) is attached to the tallit with **five knots** symbolising the **five books of Moses**.

- The wearing of tefillin, one on the **arm** and one on the **forehead**, is a **mitzvah** as it is a sign of **binding** oneself to the Torah in **thought** (forehead) and **deed** (hand).

- In **Reform Judaism**, **women** may wear **tefillin**, **kippah** and **tallit** because they are equally capable of and responsible for carrying out the mitzvot of the Torah.

Evaluating prayer and religious clothing
Is praying together in the synagogue more meaningful than private prayer?
Points to consider:

- **On the one hand ...** worshipping together in the synagogue and listening to the same Torah readings can bring people together in a more meaningful and committed way than praying by oneself.

- **On the other hand ...** there are fewer distractions in private prayer than in the synagogue. Using the tefillin in private prayer enables Jewish men to focus their mind and heart on God.

Does religious clothing help prayer?
Points to consider:

- **On the one hand ...** the importance of prayer is saying the words and becoming more aware of God's presence. Using religious clothing adds little and can be a distraction.

- **On the other hand ...** prayer is often difficult so wearing special religious clothes can help a person to get into the right frame of mind.

2.2 The synagogue

Knowing about the synagogue
The synagogue is more than just a place of worship. It also serves as a place of learning and community centre. As it is a place of prayer, men and women must not only dress modestly but Orthodox men must also wear certain religious items (see previous section (2.1)).

- The **ark** is a **large cupboard** at the **front** of the synagogue which faces towards Jerusalem.

- The **ark** contains the **Torah Scroll** or **Sefer Torah** and other scrolls.

- A light called the ner tamid usually hangs above the ark.

- The ner tamid stays **alight** at all times.

- There is a menorah or **seven-branched candlestick**.
- In the **centre** of the synagogue there is a **bimah** or raised **reading platform**.
- The bimah often has a rail surrounding it.
- Men and women sit **separately** in **Orthodox synagogues**.
- Sometimes a **screen** or mechitzah is used.
- **Other rooms** include classrooms, libraries and meeting rooms.

Understanding the synagogue

- The synagogue or beth ha knesset, serves three functions:
  - beth tefillah – a house of **prayer**
  - beth ha midrash – a house of **study**
  - bet ha'am – a house of the **people**.
- The ark is a reminder of the **Ark of the Covenant** in ancient Israel. The Ark contained the **two tablets of the Law** which God had given Moses.
- In the **ancient Temple**, the Ark of the Covenant was placed in the **Holy of Holies** where God's **Shekinah** (presence) resided.
- The **ner tamid** is a reminder of the menorah which burnt in the ancient Temple.
- It symbolises God's **Shekinah**, and His **everlasting covenant** with His people.
- The **menorah** is another reminder of the Temple. It was used by Moses in the wilderness and then placed in the Temple.
- It symbolises **God's presence**, His **light** in Creation which overcame darkness, His **perfection** and **wisdom**.
- The **separation of men and women** dates back to the time of the **Temple** when there was a **separate court for women**.
- Separation of men and women means they **cannot be distracted** by each other when praying.
- **Reform Jews** do not have separation and **families sit together**.

Evaluating the synagogue
Is the ner tamid the most important feature of the synagogue?
Points to consider:

- **On the one hand ...** it is the most important feature as it represents the presence or Shekinah of God. Without God's Shekinah the synagogue would just be a room not a place of worship.
- **On the other hand ...** the ark is the most important feature because it contains the Sefer Torah and other sacred scrolls. As the central feature of worship in the synagogue is the reading from the Torah, the ark and its contents are more important than the ner tamid.

Is it right to have separate areas for men and women in the synagogue?
Points to consider:

- **On the one hand ...** many of the features of the synagogue are based on the ancient Jewish Temple and one of these is the separation of men and women. If this arrangement is removed, then a major link with the Temple would also be lost.
- **On the other hand ...** it is important today that families worship together in the synagogue. Mothers and fathers should sit together so men and women should not be separated in the synagogue.

2.3 Law

The terms **Tenakh**, **Torah** and **Talmud** refer to various Jewish holy books which are all closely related to each other. The Tenakh refers to the whole of the **Hebrew Bible** (which Christians refer to as the Old Testament), of which the **Written Torah** or **Law** is a significant part. The **Talmud** is a separate book (in fact many books) and contains the **Oral Torah**. For Orthodox Jews all these books can be referred to as **Torah**.

Knowing about the Law

Torah

- **Torah** means **teaching**.
- The heart of the Written Torah is contained in the **first five books** of the **Tenakh** or Hebrew Bible.
- The books of the Torah contain **commandments** and **stories**.
- The Torah is the **heart** of the **covenant** made with **Moses**.
- It contains **613 commandments** or **mitzvot**.
- The **Ten Commandments** are the ten central mitzvot.
- The Written Torah may also refer to the whole of the Tenakh.

Tenakh

- The **Tenakh** refers to the whole of the **Hebrew Bible**.
- The letters TNK of Tenakh refer to:
  - **Torah** or **Law** (the first five books of Moses: Genesis, Exodus, Leviticus, Numbers and Deuteronomy).
  - **Nevi'im** or the **Prophets**, such as **Elijah**, **Nathan**, **Isaiah**, **Ezekiel** and **Jeremiah**.
  - **Ketuvim** or **Writings**, such as **Psalms** and **Proverbs**.

Talmud

- The **Oral Torah** was passed on by word of mouth until it was written down in the **Mishnah**, meaning **repetition**, around 200 C.E.
- The rabbis continued to discuss the Mishnah; their debates were known as the Gemara, meaning **completion**.
- Around 500 C.E. the **Mishnah** and **Gemara** were combined to create the **Talmud**.
- **Talmud** means **study**.
- It contains **stories** and **teachings** of the **rabbis** on how to **keep Torah**.
- It also contains the **Oral Torah** given to **Moses**.
- It covers every **aspect of life** such as: the Shabbat, food laws, marriage, types of punishment, personal hygiene and festivals.

Torah in worship

- The Torah is **read** in the **synagogue**.
- The Torah scroll or **Sefer Torah** is made from **parchment** and is hand-written.
- It is treated with great **respect**.
- When stored or carried, the scroll is covered with a **mantle** which is removed before reading from it.

- When it is **processed** from the ark to the bimah in the synagogue people touch its case with the **fringes of their taillit.**

- In the synagogue, the Torah scroll is **read** using a **special pointer** called a **yad.**

Understanding the Law

Tenakh and Talmud

- The **interpretation** of the Written and Oral Torah depends on whether one belongs to **Orthodox** or **Reform** Judaism.

- The Reform movement started in the nineteenth century. It believed certain **laws needed to be revised** and adapted to the modern world.

- Reform Jews do **not believe** that **Moses was given the Written and Oral Torah** all at once.

- They believe that many people have contributed to the Torah over a long period of time.

- They argue that not all ancient customs of the Torah need to be kept today.

- For example, food laws (or kashrut) are not as significant to Reform Jews as they are for Orthodox Jews.

- **Orthodox** Jews believe the **whole of the Torah** is **inspired and given by God**, but that it takes time, debate and prayer to understand its meaning and application to life.

Torah in worship

- The **mantle** or outer case of the Sefer Torah is a reminder of the **clothes** which the **priests** used to wear in the ancient Jerusalem Temple.

- Another symbol are the **bells** which the priests wore on their garments which are now hung at the top of the Sefer Torah.

- When a Torah scroll is torn or **damaged**, in the same way as one respects a **person's body** when they die, it is **buried.**

Evaluating the Law

Has Reformed Judaism reduced the significance of the Torah?
Points to consider:

- **On the one hand ...** Reformed Judaism has not reduced the significance of the Torah but increased it by allowing its principles to be adapted to modern ways of living. This means some laws no longer apply.

- **On the other hand ...** it has reduced the significance of the Torah because it does not consider it was given by God and rather that much of it was created by people. The significance of the Oral Law shows how God's laws continue to provide ways of living faithfully today.

Are the Nevi'im and Ketuvim less important than the Torah?
Points to consider:

- **On the one hand ...** the main covenant with Moses is at the heart of the Torah along with the 613 mitzvot, so from that point of view the Nevi'im and Ketuvim are less important. The reading of the Torah is the focus of worship in the synagogue.

- **On the other hand ...** the Nevi'im and Ketuvim provide further understanding of the Torah and from an Orthodox point of view are regarded as Torah.

2.4 Rites of passage

A rite of passage is a special moment in a person's life which is usually marked by a special ceremony or rite. Almost all religions have special ceremonies with symbols that convey key teachings about that religion.

Knowing about rites of passage

Birth ceremonies

- When a **girl is born** she has a special **naming ceremony** in the synagogue.
- On the **eighth day** after his birth a **boy** must be **circumcised**.
- The circumcision ceremony is called brit milah, and may take place at home or in hospital or in a synagogue.
- The **father** says a special prayer.
- Sitting on an **Elijah chair** a **sandek**, or 'companion' to the baby, holds the baby.
- Being a sandek is a great **honour**.
- A mohel carries out the circumcision operation.
- A mohel is a **pious Jew** who is specially **trained** to carry out circumcisions.
- After this, the child is given his **Hebrew name** and an ordinary name.
- A **kiddush** takes place with a blessing over a cup of **wine**.

Bar and Bat Mitzvah

- Bar Mitzvah, for **boys,** and Bat Mitzvah, for **girls**, are ceremonies that recognise them as adults under Jewish Law.
- They are then responsible for their own actions and must set an example by following the commandments prescribed for them in the Torah.
- **Bar Mitzvah** means **son of the commandment**.
- **Bat Mitzah** means **daughter of the commandment**.
- In the year before a **boy is 13** and a **girl is 12** they attend classes to prepare them for their **Jewish responsibilities** and **duties**.
- On the day of his Bar Mitzvah a **boy reads publicly from the Torah** for the first time in the synagogue.
- In **Reform synagogues girls** may read from the Torah.
- In **Orthodox synagogues** girls have a **Bat Chayil** ceremony and may read from the Torah but only in the **presence of other women**.
- **Boys** may now wear **tefillin** (prayer boxes) and the **tallit** (prayer shawl).
- **Relatives** attend the synagogue **service** and there is often a **party** afterwards.

Marriage

Marriage is an important part of traditional Jewish life. Ideally the couple should both be Jewish.

- Kiddushin or **engagement** takes place prior to marriage.
- **Nisuin** is the marriage ceremony itself.
- The bride and groom marry under a **canopy** or huppah.
- They are **led** to the **huppah** by their **families**.
- The **bride circles** the **groom seven times**.
- A special **blessing** is made over a cup of **wine**, from which the **couple sip**.
- The **rabbi** reads from the ketubah or **marriage contract** in front of **two witnesses**.
- The **groom** gives a **ring** to his **bride**.
- The **seven blessings** are said by all.

- The **groom crushes glass** (in a bag) with his foot.
- All those present shout **mozel tov – congratulations**.

Understanding rites of passage

Birth

- A **boy's birth ceremony** of circumcision represents the **covenant or brit** or solemn promise between God and the child.
- It commemorates the **covenant promise** made by God to **Abraham** (see page 167) when God instructed him to carry out **circumcision** as an outward sign of being a Jew and His blessing on all future Jewish generations.
- The brit milah is a time of **rejoicing** in God's continued **blessing** in the gift of a new **human life**.

Bar Mitzvah

- The important aspects of a Bar and a Bat Mitzvah is that boys and girls learn that they are now **morally and religiously responsible** for their actions according to the Torah.
- Each learns what their duties will be to the **Jewish community** and later, when they **become parents, how to** look after their own families.

Marriage

- The **huppah** in the marriage ceremony symbolises the couple's **future home**.
- It also symbolises God's **presence** in their life together.
- When the bride circles the man, it symbolises the **destruction of any barriers between them** – just as **Joshua circled Jericho** seven times and destroyed its walls.
- The **ketubah** sets out the **duties of husband and wife** to each other.
- It also specifies the **amount of money** the man has to give his wife if they **divorce**.
- The **crushing of the glass** is a **symbol** of the destruction of the Temple in 70 C.E. as a reminder of God's promises and blessings for the couple's future.

Evaluating rites of passage
Should every child have a naming ceremony?
Points to consider:

- **On the one hand ...** having a naming ceremony marks a moment when a child becomes a member of the family and community. The child will have that name for life and so it needs to be celebrated.
- **On the other hand ...** giving a name to a child is important but a ceremony doesn't make it any more significant. It would be different if the child were old enough to remember the occasion and understand what it meant.

Is the Jewish marriage ceremony a necessary part of getting married?
Points to consider:

- **On the one hand ...** the most important part of marriage is that two people are in love with each other and wish to be committed companions. The marriage ceremony is fun but not necessary.
- **On the other hand ...** being Jewish means being part of an ancient tradition, so the marriage ceremony is not an extra but necessary in order for the couple to know that they will live together and keep the Torah.

2.5 Festivals

Jewish festivals follow the seasons and commemorate Israel's long history. They play an important part in the Jewish year; each one has its own special customs and food. There are 26 major Jewish festivals but the following are some of the most important.

Rosh Hashanah and Yom Kippur

Knowing about Rosh Hashanah and Yom Kippur

- Rosh Hashanah celebrates the **new year.**
- It is the beginning of a **ten-day period.**
- During this time people **apologise** and seek **forgiveness** from each other.
- People wear their **best clothes.**
- The festival **begins** and **ends** when a ram's horn or shofar is **blown.**
- The shofar is blown each day **100 times** in the synagogue.
- **Sweet foods**, such as apples dipped in honey, are eaten.
- **The** tashlikh ceremony is when **bread is thrown** into a river or stream.
- The **last day** is **Yom Kippur**, the **Day of** Atonement.
- Yom Kippur is a time to **fast**, to **attend synagogue** and to **repent** of one's **sins.**
- People wear **white** as a sign of repentance.
- The **Kol Nidrei** prayer is **sung** at the evening service in the synagogue.

Understanding Rosh Hashanah and Yom Kippur

- Rosh Hashanah **remembers** the **creation of the world** and God's goodness in giving it to humans to look after.
- It brings **healing** to family and community by **acknowledging faults** and sins and seeking forgiveness.
- In the '**ten days of returning**' sins are remembered through prayer and reflection.
- The wailing of the shofar sounds like people weeping for their sins.
- The tashlikh ceremony symbolises washing or casting away of sins.
- **Fasting focuses the mind** on the world and its needs, personal sin and desire for forgiveness from God.
- Yom Kippur or the **Day of Atonement** remembers how in **ancient Judaism** the high priest placed his **hands on a goat** which was then sent into the **wilderness.**
- The high priest then **prayed for God's forgiveness.**
- The ceremony of the '**scapegoat**' symbolised the sins of the people being taken away from them.

Evaluating Rosh Hashanah and Yom Kippur

Are we responsible for each other's sins?
Points to consider:

- **On the one hand ...** we are only responsible for our own actions as we each have free will and can only blame ourselves if we do bad or sinful things.
- **On the other hand ...** we live in communities and affect each other's behaviour by what we say and do. So, if a group or society can be sinful, we are also responsible for each other's sins.

Can only God forgive sins?
Points to consider:

- **On the one hand ...** ultimately only God can know our motives and whether we have repented of our sins and therefore only He is in a position to forgive.

- **On the other hand ...** we may forgive each other's sins because if we don't then there is no chance that we can overcome the things which divide us.

Pesach or Passover

Knowing about Pesach

- Pesach is a **spring festival**.

- It commemorates the time when **Moses** and the **Israelites** had to **escape** at night from **Egypt**.

- In **preparation**, the house is cleaned of all **yeast** or **hametz** products. It is forbidden to be in possession of hametz during Passover.

- A special seder meal is eaten **before the main meal**.

- The **seder begins** when the **youngest child** asks, '**Why is this night different from all others?**'

- The story of **Exodus** is **recited** from the **haggadah** or Passover storybook.

- At various parts of the story **four cups** of **wine** are drunk to remember **God's promises**.

- Everyone eats **unleavened bread** or **matzos**.

- The seder plate contains:

  - **maror** – bitter herbs such as horseradish

  - **haroset** – apple, nuts and honey mixture

  - **karpas** – green herbs such as parsley

  - **beitza** – roasted egg

  - **zeroa** – lamb shank bone.

- At various points in the telling of the Pesach story the foods are eaten, except the lamb shank bone.

- The karpas is dipped in **salt water**.

- Then the **main meal is eaten**.

- The toast of the **fourth cup** of wine is, '**Next year in Jerusalem!**'

- **Afterwards** everyone joins in traditional **table songs**.

Understanding Pesach

- As a spring festival Pesach teaches about **new life and hope** as symbolised by some of the food on the seder plate such as **karpas** and **egg**.

- Pesach teaches Jews about **liberation from oppressors** in the past and today. It reminds them that **God always sides with them** however difficult it might be to believe this.

- Pesach teaches about **looking forward to a better world**, and the **Olam Ha'Ba** (see page 169), when Jerusalem will be free, restored and renewed.

- The **bitter herbs** (maror) symbolise suffering in Egypt and at all other times when Jews have been persecuted.

- The **salt water** symbolises the 'tears of affliction' or suffering in Egypt and at all times of slavery and oppression.

- The **haroset** symbolises sweet times of freedom as well as the mortar used to build bricks for Pharaoh in Egypt when they were slaves.

- The **lamb shank bone** remembers the Passover lamb, the blood of which was smeared over the door posts so the angel of death would 'pass over' the Jews to allow them to escape from Egypt.

Evaluating Pesach

Is Pesach the most significant Jewish festival?
Points to consider:

- **On the one hand …** it is the most significant festival because it tells the story of how the Jews began to be a people and to have their own unique identity. The many symbols of the seder symbolise past as well as present Jewish experience.

- **On the other hand …** it is not the most significant festival because it doesn't focus as Yom Kippur does on sin and the personal relationship with God. Yom Kippur focuses on the most important aspect of Judaism, the covenant relationship.

Is freedom the main theme of Pesach?
Points to consider:

- **On the one hand …** freedom is the main theme of Pesach because it tells the story from the time of slavery in Egypt to the escape of the Jews and the four promises given to Moses.

- **On the other hand …** freedom is important but Pesach celebrates many more things such as new life, sadness, suffering and hope.

Hanukkah

Knowing about Hanukkah

- Hanukkah is a **winter festival**.

- It is a festival of **light**.

- It celebrates the time when the Jews won their **freedom** from the **Greeks** in **164 B.C.E.**

- Jews remember **Judas Maccabeus cleansing the Temple** and how when he lit the **menorah** with enough **oil for one day**, it burnt for **eight days**.

- Today a special **hanukkah lamp** is lit each **evening** for **eight days**.

- The lamp has **eight candleholders** – with a ninth holder in the middle from which to light the other candles.

- Oily foods are eaten such as **latkes** (made with shredded potato and egg) and **loukoumades** (doughnuts).

- The dreidel game is played; the dreidel is a **four-sided spinning top** which has various Hebrew letters on it representing, 'a great miracle happened here'.

- Hanukkah is a time to have **parties** and **exchange presents**.

Understanding Hanukkah

- Hanukkah teaches about Jewish history and connects Jews with their political struggle against oppressors then and now.

- As a winter festival of **light**, it brings **hope** and **joy** during the dark hours of the year.

- The dreidel commemorates the **miracle of the lamp and the oil**; it also commemorates all Jews who have been miraculously saved from oppression.

Evaluating Hanukkah

Is it good for Jewish festivals to think so much about the past?
Points to consider:

- **On the one hand ...** it is not good to think too much about past Jewish events as it is the present that matters. That is why Rosh Hashanah is better than Hanukkah or even Pesach because its focus is on repentance, forgiveness and renewal now.

- **On the other hand ...** knowing that one is part of an ancient tradition means one is much more conscious of one's identity and values. It is good that Jewish festivals help Jews to remember the past and to give God thanks for what He has done and will continue to do.

Does Hanukkah have much religious meaning?
Points to consider:

- **On the one hand ...** Hanukkah celebrates Judas Maccabeus as a hero. It is also a time of family and present giving. Compared to Yom Kippur it has very little religious meaning.

- **On the other hand ...** the religious meaning of Hanukkah is Judas Maccabeus' trust in God to help him win over the power of the Greeks; the miracle of the lamp and the dedication of the Temple.

2.6 Dietary and food laws

Food plays an important part in Jewish daily life, ceremonies and festivals. Keeping the food and dietary laws is a mitzvah, an obligation and a blessing.

Knowing about dietary and food laws

- Kosher means **suitable** or lawful.

- Trefa means **torn**, but more generally refers to food which it is **unlawful** to eat.

- **Kashrut** is the kosher/trefa food dietary laws laid down by Torah.

- **Kosher land mammals** are those that have **cloven** (split) **hooves** and **chew the cud**, such as **cows** and **sheep**.

- **Trefa** land animals include **pigs**.

- **Kosher water animals** must have **scales and fins** such as **trout** and **salmon**.

- **Trefa** water animals include **shellfish**, such as prawns and crabs, and eels.

- **Birds** that are trefa include **vultures** and **owls**.

- All **blood** must be **removed from meat** before eating it.

- **Shechitah** is the slaughter of animals in accordance with Jewish laws.

- **Meat and milk** products must be **kept and prepared separately** and **eaten separately** (not at the same meal).

- **Orthodox kitchens** have to have separate sinks, crockery and cutlery for meat and dairy.

- **Fruit and vegetables** are neither kosher nor trefa and may be eaten at any meal.

Understanding dietary and food laws

- The kashrut laws establish **Jewish identity** and make Jews conscious of their **religious duties** and loyalty to **God's covenant**.

- Kashrut helps Jews maintain **holiness** and **spiritual awareness** of God.

- Kashrut **respects animals** because it sets out how they are to be killed painlessly by a **shochet**, a Jewish person trained in slaughtering animals.

- **Blood** is a **symbol of life** which is why it must be fully drained from meat when slaughtered.
- Orthodox and Reform Judaism have different teachings about keeping kashrut:
  - **Orthodox Judaism** teaches that keeping kashrut is a sign of being a member of God's **covenant people** and in solidarity with all Jews **worldwide**.
  - **Reform Judaism** teaches that keeping kashrut is **good** if it helps one focus on **spiritual values**; others think that the dietary laws were developed at times so different from our own they have **no relevance today**.

Evaluating dietary and food laws
Is a Jewish person less Jewish if they don't keep kashrut?
Points to consider:

- **On the one hand ...** a person is not less Jewish but they would not be such a good Jew if they abandoned kashrut. Kashrut is a religious duty and discipline which is part of Jewish daily life.
- **On the other hand ...** Kashrut was developed in different times for hygiene reasons and to give Jews an identity. Many Reform Jews think they can be just as Jewish by carrying out moral laws rather than kashrut.

Are all Jewish dietary food laws equally important?
Points to consider:

- **On the one hand ...** for many, eating meat and dairy products separately is unnecessarily demanding and expensive as it means having to have a kitchen which keeps them separate. The intention of kashrut is to remember the covenant; not all food laws do so.
- **On the other hand ...** the food laws are not intended to be easy. They cannot be ranked from important to unimportant. By keeping all the food laws a Jew's mind is focused on the mitzvot.

> Practise answering questions with *Theology, Philosophy and Religion 13+ Exam Practice Questions and Answers* pages 20–21 and 89–92.

Test yourself

1 What is a minyan?
2 What happens to the Sefer Torah in Shabbat synagogue worship?
3 What is kiddush?
4 What is hallah bread?
5 What is the significance of the spice box at havdalah?
6 What is the amidah?
7 Name three features of the synagogue.
8 What do the letters TNK stand for in Tenakh?
9 What is the ceremony called when a girl comes of age at 12?
10 What is a ketubah?
11 When is shofar blown?
12 Name two symbolic foods on a seder plate.
13 Name two foods that are trefa.

Glossary

ark The box or cupboard in the synagogue in which the Torah scrolls are kept

atonement Making things right with God

Bar Mitzvah Ceremony for a 13-year-old boy (son of the commandment)

Bat Mitzvah Ceremony for a 12- or 13-year-old girl (daughter of the commandment)

bimah Platform in the synagogue from which the Torah is read

brit milah Ceremony of circumcision and naming of a baby boy

cantor Person (hazan in Hebrew) who leads the singing in Jewish worship

circumcision Cutting off the foreskin of the penis

covenant The agreement between God and his people

dreidel Game played at the festival of Hanukkah

Gemara Commentary on the Oral Torah; forms part of the Talmud

hallot (pl. hallah) Special loaves of bread used on Sabbaths and festivals

huppah The canopy under which a couple are married

kashrut Food laws

ketubah The marriage contract

kiddush Blessing said over wine

kiddushin The formal engagement of a couple to be married

kippah Cap worn by Jewish men and boys

kosher Lawful

mechitzah The screen dividing men and women in the synagogue

menorah A candlestick with seven branches

mezuzah Parchment scroll fixed to the right-hand doorpost usually in a decorative box

Mishnah The oral teaching of the rabbis

mitzvot (pl. mitzvot) A commandment

mohel The person who performs a circumcision

ner tamid The light in the synagogue that symbolises God's presence

Olam Ha'Ba The age to come, the perfect world, heaven or the afterlife

Pesach Festival of Passover

rabbi Spiritual leader and teacher of Torah

seder Order; the central Pesach ceremony

Shabbat The day each week commanded by God when no work is done

Shekinah The presence of God

Shema The 'hearing' prayer which remembers the oneness of God

shofar The ram's horn blown at Yom Kippur

siddur The Jewish prayer book

synagogue Jewish place of worship

tallit Prayer shawl

Talmud Many books which comprise the collection of the Oral Torah

tashlikh The act of throwing leftover crumbs from the Rosh Hashanah meal into running water symbolising the casting away of sins

tefillin Leather prayer boxes containing verses from the Hebrew scriptures, worn by Jewish men during weekday prayer

Tenakh Jewish scriptures (the Jewish or Hebrew Bible)

Torah The Jewish books of the law

trefa Unlawful to eat

tzitzit Tassels on a prayer shawl (tallit)

worship Offering praise to God

F: Sikhism

 Sikh beliefs and teachings

Read *Religion for Common Entrance 13+* pages 140–56.

Sikhism originated in the **Punjab** area of **northern Indian**, a fertile area which many foreign powers wanted to own and which was on the central trade routes to Europe, the Middle East, China and India.

- The traders brought with them different religions, notably **Hinduism** and **Islam**.
- Sikhism evolved principally by **combining the monotheism** of Islam and the Hindu belief in **reincarnation**.
- However, its teaching on the guru is distinctive and not part of Muslim or Hindu traditions.
- The word '**sikh**' means disciple or follower.
- Sikhs are those who **follow** the teaching of the **gurus**.

1.1 God's nature

The Mul Mantra

Knowing about the Mul Mantra
Beliefs about God are found in the **Mul Mantra prayer** written by **Guru Nanak**. It states that:

- There is **only one** God.
- God is **truth**.
- God is the **designer** and **creator** of everything.
- God is **timeless**.
- God's **Spirit** exists throughout the universe.
- God is **eternal** and is the **beginning and end** of everything.
- God is **self-existent**. He does not depend on anything else for His existence.
- God can be **known** through the **teaching of the gurus** (teachers).

Understanding the Mul Mantra

- The Mul Mantra is the **most important** prayer in Sikhism. It is found in the opening of the Guru Granth Sahib, the Sikh holy book.
- God may be known **personally** by thinking about His **name**.
- God's **name** should be **meditated upon** and **repeated** – this practice is called nam japna.

- One meditation practice is done by **repeating** the word Waheguru, or **wonderful Lord**; another is done by listening to hymns in the gurdwara.

- As creator, God allows the Creation to evolve and develop; He does not interfere with it or **limit human free will**.

- As truth, God exists **within us all**. He can be known by all people. This means different religions have access to Him in their different ways.

- Sikhism does **not claim** to have **exclusive knowledge** of God.

Evaluating the Mul Mantra

Can we know God just by repeating His name?
Points to consider:

- **On the one hand ...** repeating God's name is a form of meditation and helps focus the mind on His nature. Just as knowing a person's name is important for creating a relationship, so knowing and repeating God's name forms a closer relationship between the worshipper and God.

- **On the other hand ...** it is not enough just to repeat God's name to know Him. The worshipper needs also to study and reflect on what God demands and put His commands into action and test their truth.

Is there any point in being a Sikh if other religions also have access to God?
Points to consider:

- **On the one hand ...** if God is beyond all human comprehension, then all religions only offer partial insights in their different ways. Therefore, each religion will suit some people and not others. Some may choose Sikhism but Sikhism does not seek to convert them.

- **On the other hand ...** only Sikhism has the truth as revealed through the gurus and the Guru Granth Sahib. If the purpose of life is to achieve liberation from rebirths (mukti) and find peace in God, then there is every good reason for being a Sikh.

The gurmukh and the God-centred life

Knowing about the gurmukh and the God-centred life

- Gurmukh means **God-centred**.

- A **gurmukh** is someone who lives a God-centred life.

- Human life is an opportunity to **unite with God**.

- Sikhs become **God-centred** through:

  - **meditation**

  - **concentrating** on Sikh hymns (shabads)

  - **following** the **teaching of the gurus**.

- Haumai means **ego**, the selfish part of the self.

- Haumai stops a person living a God-centred life.

- A manmukh is someone who is selfish, greedy and angry.

Understanding the gurmukh and the God-centred life

- A gurkmukh is someone who has found the '**guru within themselves**' by living a good, clean, calm and ego-less life.

- A gurmukh follows the teaching of the gurus so **closely that they become at one with their words** and **not attached** to greed, envy and anger.

- They are said to have '**bathed in the pool of truth**'.
- Gurmukhs dedicate themselves to the **service** (sewa) of others.

Evaluating the gurmukh and the God-centred life

Are humans naturally generous?
Points to consider:

- **On the one hand ...** humans are not naturally generous but rather greedy and selfish. This is why society invents laws and rules so that people don't take what is not theirs or behave in ways that cause a nuisance to others.
- **On the other hand ...** although people can be selfish, if there is a crisis and someone needs help, most humans will respond generously even if it causes themselves harm.

Are religious people less likely to be selfish?
Points to consider:

- **On the one hand ...** all the great world religions focus on some reality or God greater than humans. Religious people therefore know that they have a duty to be obedient to God and not think of themselves.
- **On the other hand ...** a religious person could be more selfish because they just think about their relationship with God and their religious life and fail to consider other people.

Karma, rebirth and mukti

Knowing about karma, rebirth and mukti

Karma and rebirth

- Karma means **action with intention**.
- Karma is the law of nature that every **action has a consequence**.
- Karma affects **rebirth or reincarnation**.
- Those people who have been **selfish** and **ignored God's will** are reborn into a lower form of life.
- Rebirth is caused by being **envious** of others, by **greed** and by **lack of care** for others.

Mukti

- **Mukti** means **release from rebirth**.
- **Mukti** is **given by God's grace**.
- **Release** comes by **listening** to the gurbani and performing good karmic acts.
- Release may also come by **meditating** and **repeating** the **Name of God**.

Understanding karma, rebirth and mukti

- There are traditionally **five hindrances** to mukti which are the selfish aspects of ego: lust, anger, pride, greed and worldly attachment.
- Rebirth is caused when a person becomes psychologically **attached** to **maya**, the **material world of appearances** rather than the **reality** of the **eternal God**.
- The active life of **service** (sewa) to others and to God is central to the Sikh life and a key to **achieving mukti**.

Evaluating karma, rebirth and mukti

Does belief in rebirth (reincarnation) make any difference to how one behaves in life?
Points to consider:

- **On the one hand ...** belief in rebirth does make a difference because it can give hope that if one is suffering now, then by being good and accumulating good karma the next life will be better.

- **On the other hand ...** if one believes that reincarnation is inevitable then it will make no difference how one behaves. This is because whether someone lives a morally good or a morally bad life they will still be reborn.

Does karma explain why good people may suffer bad things?
Points to consider:

- **On the one hand ...** it does explain why good people suffer bad things because we cannot know exactly what their intentions were in the past, either in this life or a previous life. Sometimes appearances may deceive us and someone who may appear to be good is not truly so.

- **On the other hand ...** karma does not explain why good people suffer bad things. Their suffering could simply be bad luck or misfortune. It is hard to accept that a bad action in a previous life could specifically affect a person in a totally new life.

1.2 Service to others

Service to others and to God, or **sewa**, is central to the Sikh way of life and at the heart of being a member of the Khalsa, the Sikh community. The **ten gurus** are all **examples** of service; their teachings are contained in the Sikh holy book, the **Guru Granth Sahib**.

Guru Gobind Singh, the Khalsa and equality

Knowing about Guru Gobind Singh, the Khalsa and equality

Guru Gobind Singh

- **Guru Gobind Rai** (1666–1708 C.E.) was the **last** of the **ten gurus**.
- He was **later called Guru Gobind Singh**.
- He **became guru** in 1675 when he was nine.
- The **emperor** in India at this time did not allow anyone to believe in ideas which challenged his authority, and **so he persecuted Sikhs**.
- **Gobind Rai** was a **strong leader** and skilled **soldier**.
- He **trained Sikhs** to be **soldiers** to protect the rights and beliefs of others.
- He wrote **poetry** to give **spiritual strength** to others.

Formation of the Khalsa

- In **1699 C.E.** a large number of **Sikhs met** to **celebrate Vaisakhi** (the Sikh new year).
- **Gobind Rai** asked for **volunteers** who would **give** their **head** for him.
- **Gobind Rai** took the first volunteer into a tent and then **appeared** with a **sword dripping** with **blood**. This happened four more times.
- Then the **five men** appeared **unharmed**.
- These five men are called the **Panj Pyare** or 'five beloved ones'.
- They became the **basis** of the **Khalsa** or '**pure community**'.

- Gobind Rai mixed a **special food** called amrit which the five ate.
- This event inspired ordinary Sikhs to be **firm in their faith**.
- The **Sikhs** grew in **confidence** under his leadership.

The names Singh and Kaur

- In addition to their first name, **Khalsa** members take the **name** of Singh (men) or Kaur (women).
- **Singh** means **lion** and describes how **men** are to be strong, caring and fearless.
- **Kaur** means **princess** and describes how **women** should be treated as princesses.
- Male and female members of the Khalsa **wear five symbols**, the Five Ks or **Panj Kakke** (see page 205).

Equality

- The gurus rejected the **ancient Hindu caste system** which placed some people higher than others.
- The langar or kitchen also treats all **people as equals**.
- In the langar all people **sit together** and receive the **same food**.
- **No one who is hungry** is turned away from the langar because of their **religion**, class or **gender**.
- **Initiation** ceremonies are the **same for men and women**.

Understanding Guru Gobind Singh, the Khalsa and equality

- Khalsa refers to the Sikh community in **two ways**:
  - The **pure community**: those who have been through the Amritsanskar initiation ceremony and who make **promises** to uphold the special Sikh responsibilities. They should be willing to **die** for Guru and Sikhism.
  - The **Sikh community as a whole**: not all Sikhs are members of the Khalsa or have been through Amritsanskar.
- All **people are equal** because **God created them** and they are to worship only Him, no one else.
- **Men are women** are treated as **equals** by having the **same initiation ceremonies** and both may wear the Five Ks. Many women carry the kirpan (curved sword) as a sign of equality.
- Because all women have the name, **Kaur**, and all men the name, **Singh**, **there is no hierarchy** of women over women or men over men.

Evaluating Guru Gobind Singh, the Khalsa and equality
Was Guru Gobind Singh's test of the men at Vaisakhi fair?
Points to consider:

- **On the one hand ...** it was a fair test because he wanted to test how firm the five men's commitment was to God. Being prepared to die for a cause or belief is the ultimate test and was needed at the time to show just how sincere Sikhs were to God.
- **On the other hand ...** it was not a fair test because he was not actually killing the volunteers but only pretending and the use of violence gives the wrong impression about Sikh values.

Does giving people the same name really make them equal?
Points to consider:

- **On the one hand ...** people's names are part of their identity. Names are associated with particular families who have influence in society or who belong to political and religious groups. So, having the same surname makes people equal.

- **On the other hand ...** having the same surname makes little difference to how people are treated. Equality is an attitude and it is not affected by someone's name.

The gurus' lives as examples for Sikhs to follow

Knowing about the gurus' lives as examples for Sikhs to follow

Guru Nanak

- Guru Nanak was the first of the **ten gurus** (**religious teachers**).
- He was born near **Lahore** in **1469 C.E.** in the **Punjab** (now Pakistan).
- He was the **son** of **high-caste Hindu** parents.
- His **intelligence** and **wisdom impressed his teachers** at an early age.
- There are many stories told about his childhood and how he impressed both Hindu and Muslim religious teachers, and would therefore grow up to become a great religious teacher.
- One story tells how he used **money** given to him by his father to **help the poor**.
- Another story tells how a **deadly cobra shaded** him from the **sun**.
- He became an **accountant** for a **Muslim leader** and was well **known** for his **honesty**.
- One day when he came out of a **river**, he felt the strong **presence of God**.
- **Three days later** he set out to **teach** people how to **pray**, **live pure lives** and **give generously**.
- He went on **four great teaching journeys** accompanied by his **friend** and musician **Mardana**.
- He founded the **langar**, the free kitchen.
- In **1521 C.E.** he **founded** a new town, **Kartarpur** as the **first Sikh community**.
- He **died** in **1539 C.E.**

The gurus after Guru Nanak
A detailed knowledge of the other nine gurus is not needed.

- The **second** guru **Guru Angad** (1504–52) wrote down many of Guru Nanak's hymns and encouraged Sikhs to take part in sports.
- The **third** guru **Guru Amar Das** (1479–1574) developed the **langar** and made people sit together whatever their status in society.
- The **fourth** guru **Guru Ram Das** (1534–81) founded the city of **Amritsar** and wrote the **Lavan** hymn.
- The **fifth** guru **Guru Arjan** (1563–1606) built the Harmandir or **Golden Temple at Amritsar** – the most famous Sikh temple; he made the first **collection** of hymns and writings of the gurus.
- The **sixth** guru **Guru Hargobind** (1595–1644) used to carry two **curved swords** which were then symbolised on the **Sikh flag** (Nishan Sahib).
- The **seventh** guru **Guru Har Rai** developed medical treatment for the sick.

- The **eighth** guru was **Guru Har Krishen.**

- The **ninth** guru **Guru Tegh Bahadur** lived during the Mughal persecution and was martyred.

- The **tenth** guru **Guru Gobind Rai** (or Guru Gobind Singh) formed the **Khalsa** and declared he was the **last guru** and that the next guru would be a book, the **Guru Granth Sahib** – the Sikh holy book (see pages 193–194).

Understanding the gurus' lives as examples for Sikhs to follow

- A **guru** is a **religious leader**.

- **Gu** means darkness and **ru** means light.

- The ten gurus are all examples of different ways in which a guru serves God. Today a guru must be an **upright person** and **lead** people from **darkness into light**.

Evaluating the gurus' lives as examples for Sikhs to follow

Was Guru Gobind Singh right to decide that there should be no more human gurus after him?
Points to consider:

- **On the one hand ...** he was right because there is a danger that the gurus might become more interested in power and fame than teaching about God. Furthermore, as a book doesn't change, it can be studied as well as providing continuity.

- **On the other hand ...** the gurus provide a living example of how to live a good Sikh life. They dedicate themselves to God and to teaching His will. A book cannot easily change with the times.

Was Guru Nanak the greatest of the Sikh gurus?
Points to consider:

- **On the one hand ...** he was the greatest guru because he combined Muslim and Hindu teaching and created a religion which combined the best of both religions. His journeys spread Sikhism.

- **On the other hand ...** without Guru Gobind Singh, Sikhism would not have the Guru Granth Sahib and the Khalsa, and without these Sikhism would not be the religion it is today.

The Guru Granth Sahib

Knowing about the Guru Granth Sahib

- The **tenth Guru Gobind Singh** declared there would be **no more human gurus after his death**.

- The **scriptures** include some of the **teachings** of the ten **gurus** as well as **Hindu** and **Muslim hymns**.

- **Guru Arjan** was the first to make a **collection** of the **hymns** and **writings** of the gurus.

- The Guru Granth Sahib contains over **five thousand hymns or shabads**.

- The shabads are **arranged** according to their **tunes** or ragas.

- The **opening shabad** is the **Mul Mantra**.

- It is written in the **Gurmukhi script**.

- Its teachings are called **gurbani**.

- It is given the **place of honour** in the **gurdwara** and rests on a takht (throne) under a palki (canopy).

- It must be **present** at all **important ceremonies**.

- When **moved** at a ceremony, the Guru Granth Sahib must be **carried on a person's head** and everyone must stand.

- It must be **wrapped in clean decorated cloths**.

- It is **protected** by a person called a **granthi** waving a fan or chauri.

- **Another room** is set aside for the Guru Granth Sahib to be kept in at **night time**.

- A special ceremony takes place at **sunset each day** (sukhasan) when the Guru Granth Sahib is carried on the **head** of the **granthi** in a **clean cloth** to the special room.

- Many Sikhs have a separate room at **home** in which they read the Guru Granth Sahib.

- Many homes keep and read a **shortened version** called the **gutka**.

Understanding the Guru Granth Sahib

- The Guru Granth Sahib contains the teachings of the human gurus about **God's will**. Although it is considered to be the word of God, it is **respected** but **not worshipped**.

- Guru Arjan **compared** it to a **plate of food** which contains truth, contentment and meditation, three things that are needed to feed the soul and make it free from sorrow.

- Some **shabads** are **very short**, others **much longer**. They form the basis of worship at home and in the gurdwara.

- The Guru Granth Sahib's use of **different religious sources** such as Muslim and Hindu hymns shows that Sikhism respects the **wisdom and truth of different religions**.

Evaluating the Guru Granth Sahib

Do the ceremonies surrounding the Guru Granth Sahib encourage people to worship it?
Points to consider:

- **On the one hand ...** the ceremonies surrounding the Guru Granth Sahib such as placing it on a throne and moving it to a special room in the evening treat it as a god. This means people are encouraged to worship a book as if it were a being.

- **On the other hand ...** the ceremonies encourage respect but not worship of the Guru Granth Sahib. Sikhs know that God is beyond all human comprehension but that His words revealed through the gurus are very special.

May Sikhs follow other non-Sikh holy books?
Points to consider:

- **On the one hand ...** the Guru Granth Sahib contains teachings from Islam and Hinduism so in effect Sikhs are following non-Sikh holy books. Therefore, following the moral teaching of the Bible and what it reveals about God should not be a problem.

- **On the other hand ...** it might be acceptable to study non-Sikh holy books but not follow them. Some teachings may not be appropriate, such as Jesus Christ being the Incarnation of God.

Sewa

Knowing about sewa

- The Guru Granth Sahib teaches that worship must be accompanied by **good deeds**.

- Sewa means **serving the community** – Sikh and non-Sikh.

- There are **three forms of sewa:**

  - **mental or intellectual service** (maan) – service through words and thoughts such as meditating, worship and study

  - **physical or manual service** (taan) – service through doing practical things in the community

  - **material service** (dhan) – service to the world by giving money to charity and giving **one tenth of one's surplus wealth** to help others (daswandh).

Understanding sewa

- Sewa is one of **three Sikh duties** – the other two are: **remembering God** (nam japna) and **earning money honestly** (Kirat Karna).

- Sewa is fundamentally part of a Sikh's **worship of God**.

- Sikhs do not **try to convert others** but **live by example** and by the example of the gurus and should help anyone who needs it.

- **Taan** can be doing very **small tasks** for one's neighbour or taking part in a **community project** such a creating a community garden.

- An example of **dhan** is to give to **charities** such as **Sikh Relief** or **Khalsa Aid** who provide care and support for people locally and globally, regardless of their religious faith.

Evaluating sewa
If a non-Sikh carried out sewa could they achieve mukti?
Points to consider:

- **On the one hand ...** a person who helps his neighbours through taan and the community through dhan is carrying out God's will, accumulating good karma and so is on the path to mukti.

- **On the other hand ...** it is not enough just to be helpful to others. Sewa also requires one to remember God (nam japna) and worship Him. Nam japna ensures that karma is good and only then is mukti possible.

Is intellectual service better than manual service?
Points to consider:

- **On the one hand ...** intellectual service is better because by thinking about God and becoming more aware of His will, then a person's soul is purified and more capable of achieving mukti.

- **On the other hand ...** the gurus taught that service to the community through the langar was a sign of fulfilling God's will by showing respect to all people. Without manual service, intellectual service could become very selfish and suffer from haumai.

Community and worship

Belonging to the Khalsa means Sikhs have a strong sense of community.

Knowing about community and worship

- **Rahit** means **discipline**.
- The **Rahit Maryada** is a **code of conduct** for Sikhs.
- In the **first Khalsa** Guru Gobind Singh laid down clear rules.
- Over time some **new rules** were added which caused some **dispute**.
- In **1945**, the **rules** were made clear in the **Rahit Maryada**.
- The Rahit Maryada has been **translated** into **English**.
- It explains that a **Sikh** is anyone who:
  - believes in **one God**
  - follows the **ten gurus'** teaching
  - is guided by the **Guru Granth Sahib**
  - is **not a member of another religion**.
- It expects **Sikhs** to **meet together** and **think** about **gurbani**, the teaching of the Guru Granth Sahib.
- The Rahit Maryada teaches that every Sikh must:
  - **give money to help the poor**
  - **never gamble**
  - **never steal**
  - take part in **voluntary work**.

Understanding community and worship

- The **Rahit Maryada** says that a Sikh must **pray to God** before carrying out any task.
- The Rahit Maryada teaches that for **children** to grow up and worship God they must be **educated** and their **hair** should **not be cut** – uncut hair is a sign of belonging to nature and the world that God has created.
- **No Sikh** should take any **drugs, alcohol or tobacco** as these will cloud their minds and **stop them from thinking about God**.
- Out of respect for **their bodies**, women and men may not **pierce their bodies** for jewellery.
- Men may wear a **turban** and women a **headscarf** to contain and cover their hair and also as an outward sign of their Sikhism.
- The principle of **Kirat Karna** teaches that work must be honest and not exploit people because all people are equal; work should be for the good of the community.

Evaluating community and worship

Should everyone be expected to carry out voluntary work?
Points to consider:

- **On the one hand ...** the world would be a much better, happier and healthier place if everyone carried out voluntary work. There would be a real sense that everyone in the community cared for and respected everyone else.

- **On the other hand ...** it would be unrealistic for everyone to be expected to carry out voluntary work. Very young and old people may not be able to do so and some people may be unsuited to carrying out certain tasks.

Is gambling necessarily bad?
Points to consider:

- **On the one hand ...** gambling is not necessarily bad if it is a bit of fun and a person knows when to stop. Gambling as an addiction is bad, but that doesn't mean that all gambling is bad.

- **On the other hand ...** all gambling is bad because it is addictive. It may seem like just a bit of fun but it can quickly take over a person's life.

> Practise answering questions with *Theology, Philosophy and Religion 13+ Exam Practice Questions and Answers* pages 22–23 and 93–96.

Test yourself

1 What is the Mul Mantra?

2 What is nam japna?

3 What does Waheguru mean?

4 Who is a gurmukh?

5 What is haumai?

6 Give two ways of achieving mukti.

7 What is the Khalsa?

8 Name three gurus.

9 Describe how the Guru Granth Sahib is treated with honour in the gurdwara.

10 Outline three forms of sewa or service.

11 What is the Rahit Maryada?

12 Outline the principle of Kirat Karna.

2 Sikh practices and ceremonies

Read *Religion for Common Entrance 13+* pages 157–70.

2.1 Gurdwara

Knowing about the gurdwara

- A **Sikh temple** is called a **gurdwara**.
- **Gurdwara** means **door to the guru**.
- Outside the gurdwara there is usually a **Nishan Sahib** – a **saffron flag** with the symbol of the **Khalsa** on it.
- The **main hall** is called the diwan **hall** and contains many **pictures** of the **gurus**.
- The **Guru Granth Sahib** is usually placed on a **takht** (throne) or a raised platform under by a **palki** (canopy).
- The whole of this **area** is called the **takht** or **throne**.
- Other rooms may include meeting rooms, a library, classrooms, etc.

Worship or diwan in the gurdwara

- Worship is called **diwan**.
- A **granthi** leads the worship and **reads** from the Guru Granth Sahib.
- A granthi must be able to read **Gurmukhi** and may be a man or a woman.
- On entering the gurdwara everyone **removes their shoes** and **covers their head**.
- **Worshippers** approach the **takht** and make an **offering**.
- They **bow** to the **Guru Granth Sahib**.
- Everyone **sits** on the floor with **crossed legs**.
- Diwan begins when the **holy sweet** or Karah Parshad is placed **near** the **Guru Granth Sahib**.
- Karah Parshad is made from **sugar**, **butter** and **semolina**.
- **Kirtan** or hymns from the Guru Granth Sahib are led by a ragi or singer.
- Everyone **meditates** and **repeats** the **name of God**.
- There may be a **talk** or **sermon** on the **teachings** of Sikhism.
- Everyone sings the **Anand Sahib** followed by a portion the Japji.
- Everyone stands and **faces** the **Guru Granth Sahib** and the granthi says the **Ardas prayer**.
- Hukam (knowing the will of God) follows when the Guru Granth Sahib is opened at random and a passage is read.

- A **prayer** asks **God to accept** the **Karah Parshad** which is then touched with a **kirpan**.
- Everyone is **given** some of the **Karah Parshad**.

The langar or free kitchen

- The **langar** was first **established** by **Guru Nanak**.
- It is a sign of **equality**.
- The **food** is always the **same** for everyone.
- The food is usually **vegetarian**.
- It is a custom for **families** to **take it in turns** to buy and prepare the food.

Understanding the gurdwara

- The gurdwara serves an important role in the Sikh **community** for **worship** and **study**.
- The **Rahit Maryada** encourages people to attend the gurdwara as often as possible to **study** and **understand Sikh teaching**.
- The gurdwara is a **community centre** used for a wide range of activities such as learning music or playing sport.
- There are **no priests or ministers** because Sikhism **resists hierarchy**; the gurdwara is run by a committee of men and women.
- **Kirtan** helps worshippers to **focus on God** and not themselves – the aim of all Sikh worship.
- The **Ardas** is an **important Sikh prayer** and is said at or after a significant moment when a person asks God to assist them. God as **Waheguru** is called on to bless those who use His name.
- **Langar** expresses many very basic teachings of Sikhism, such as the following:
  - **Equality** – everyone is served the same food; men and women sit together.
  - **Sewa** – those who **prepare** the food learn about the value of **service to others**.
  - **Worship** – while the food is prepared God's name is recited.

Evaluating the gurdwara
Is a gurdwara essential for Sikh worship?
Points to consider:

- **On the one hand ...** worship of God can take place anywhere just by repeating God's name, by saying prayers at home and reading from the gutka. The gurdwara is useful, but not essential for worship.
- **On the other hand ...** the gurdwara is essential because it is where the Guru Granth Sahib can be given dignity and respect. There is no granthi at home and it is he who looks after the Guru Granth Sahib and takht.

Is the langar more important than worship?
Points to consider:

- **On the one hand ...** the langar is one of the most significant features of Sikhism. It is a great privilege to provide langar and a positive karmic act because it is showing concern for others in a way which worship does not.
- **On the other hand ...** Sikhism teaches that worship is more important than the langar because by putting God first then everything one does after that will be done to serve Him.

2.2 Prayer, reading and meditation

Knowing about prayer, reading and meditation

Prayer and worship at home

- Sikhs should aim to pray at **least three times** a day.
- Nitnem is a collection of poems used as prayers.
- Some poems are appropriate for particular days of the week.
- Before prayer the worshipper should **wash**.
- Then they say the **Japji** prayer of Guru Nanak.
- They may use mala or prayer beads.
- They may repeat **Waheguru** as they use the beads.
- The **gutka** is a shortened version of the Guru Granth Sahib.
- The gutka contains around **20 shabads** or hymns.
- It is used at home for **private prayer** and **worship**.

Reading – hukam

- **Hukam** means the **will of God**.
- It often refers to the practice of **reading a passage** from the Guru Granth Sahib after the **Ardas** prayer.
- The passage is chosen at **random**.
- The chosen passage reveals **God's will for the day**.

The Akhand Path

- The Akhand Path is the **continuous reading of the Guru Granth Sahib** from beginning to end.
- The Guru Granth Sahib has **1,430 pages**.
- It is read by a **rota** of Sikhs.
- It takes **48 hours** to complete the reading.
- The Akhand Path is used at **special** events such as **weddings** and **sports events**.

Meditating on the names of God

- **Nam japna** means **meditating** on the names of God.
- In the Guru Granth Sahib **God has many names**.
- **Repeating** one or more names in prayer is a form of meditation.
- The most popular meditation is **Waheguru** meaning 'wonderful guru or Lord'.

Understanding prayer, reading and meditation

- **Nitnem** ensures that God's presence is constantly kept in mind and helps the worshipper not to live a self-centred life.
- **Hukam** is a basic Sikh teaching about the way God's will is revealed through every event that takes place in the universe.
- The **Akhand Path** allows everyone to **listen** to and **reflect** on all the spiritual teachings and **discussions of the gurus** about God and the world.
- Although God is eternal and beyond all comprehension, by using **nam japna** the worshipper makes the mystery of God clearer.

Evaluating prayer, reading and meditation
Is prayer at home more effective than prayer in the gurdwara?
Points to consider:

- **On the one hand ...** as prayer at home should take place three times a day, it is constant reminder of a Sikh's commitment and devotion to God. Prayers can be chosen to suit a mood rather than set prayers in the gurdwara.

- **On the other hand ...** Sikhism places a lot of emphasis on the community, so it is more effective to worship together in the gurdwara and hear and listen to the same readings and prayers from the Guru Granth Sahib.

Is repeating God's names the best way of knowing about His will?
Points to consider:

- **On the one hand ...** repeating one of God's names focuses the mind on His nature, which tells worshippers about what He wills.

- **On the other hand ...** although repeating God's name may tell worshippers about what He wills, listening to the Guru Granth Sahib being read (as in the Akhand Path) and hearing a sermon opens the mind to greater understanding.

2.3 Festivals (gurpurbs)

There are many Sikh festivals (such as those that celebrate the anniversaries of the gurus), but you are only expected to know two of the following three: Vaisakhi, Divali and Guru Nanak's birthday.

- Most festivals include an ordinary **diwan** and **Akhand Path** (when the Guru Granth Sahib is read from beginning to end without stopping).

- Gurpurbs are festivals that honour the gurus.

- Melas are festivals that coincide with Indian festivals.

Vaisakhi

Knowing about Vaisakhi

- **Vaisakhi** is the **most important** Sikh festival and takes place in April.

- It is also the **Sikh new year**.

- The gurdwara is decorated.

- The **Nishan Sahib** (triangular flag) is washed and the old flag is replaced.

- There is a **procession** of the Guru Granth Sahib.

- It is **led** by those dressed traditionally as the **five Panj Payares**.

- **Martial arts** are performed.

- Individual and team **games** are played.

- Energetic dancing or bhangra **dancing** often takes place.

Understanding Vaisakhi

- The festival **commemorates** the foundation of the **Khalsa** in 1699 when Guru Gobind Singh called Sikhs together and tested their **courage**, **unity** and **loyalty**.

- It also celebrates the **Five Ks** and is therefore the foundation of Sikhism as it is practised today.

- The **Nishan Sahib** is **washed** in milk or yoghurt because in India the **cow is a sacred animal** and milk is considered to be **pure**.

- The martial arts and games celebrate the values of **unity**, **courage** and **strength**.

- Sikhism is an inclusive religion so people of non-Sikh faiths are encouraged to join in the festival.

Evaluating Vaishakhi

To what extent is the festival of Vaisakhi a model of how communities should work together?
Points to consider:

- **On the one hand ...** Vaisakhi is a model of how communities should work together because the Sikhs are encouraged to invite non-Sikhs to participate in the festivities as well as Sikhs from other gurdwaras. This helps break down social barriers.

- **On the other hand ...** Vaisakhi is just a time of having fun and showing off martial arts, games and dancing. To make communities work together requires a lot more understanding and hard work than a yearly festival.

Is sport more important than religion?
Points to consider:

- **On the one hand ...** for many millions of people supporting a football team, attending its matches and being a loyal supporter is more important than religion. Sport does not require belief in a difficult idea.

- **On the other hand ...** Sikhism teaches that sport is important to one's physical and mental life but it is not more important than religion because devotion to God gives a person ultimate meaning and purpose in life.

Divali

Knowing about Divali

- Divali takes place in **October/November**.

- It is a **festival of lights**.

- Homes are **cleaned** and candles and **lamps are lit**.

- **Presents** are exchanged.

- **Special services** are held in the gurdwara.

- **Kirtan** or singing from the Guru Granth Sahib takes place.

- **Fireworks** are set off in the evening.

Understanding Divali

- **Divali** is celebrated by **Hindus** as well as by Sikhs and as in the Hindu festival of Divali, **light** is especially important because it symbolises the **triumph of good over evil** (see page 135 on Hindu Divali).

- The festival commemorates the time when **Guru Hargobind** was **released from prison** and returned to **Amritsar**.

- The story tells how the **emperor allowed** 52 princes who shared Guru Hargobind's cell and held on to his **coat** to be **freed** as well.

- The story reminds Sikhs of the importance and centrality of **human rights** and **freedom**.

- **Light** symbolises **hope** and **freedom**.

Evaluating Divali

Is freedom more important than love?
Points to consider:

- **On the one hand ...** freedom is more important than love because without freedom a person is not able to express themselves fully, to explore all that life has to offer and to love properly.

- **On the other hand ...** without love, love of God, love of others and love of oneself, life and freedom are meaningless. Love is more important than freedom.

Does everyone have a right to freedom?
Points to consider:

- **On the one hand ...** everyone has a right to freedom because being free allows a person to express themselves fully as they wish.

- **On the other hand ...** people who abuse their freedom and threaten society do not have a right to freedom; freedom has to be earned not demanded.

Guru Nanak's birthday

Knowing about Guru Nanak's birthday

- Guru Nanak's birthday is traditionally celebrated in **November**.

- His **actual birthday** is on Vaishakhi Day in April.

- Two days before the festival the **Akhand Path is followed** – the whole of the Guru Granth Sahib is read.

- In the gurdwara on the day of the festival **hymns** are sung and a **sermon** is given.

- There is a procession of singing chants called the **Nagar Kirtan**.

- It is led by the **Panj Payares** in costume.

- The **Guru Granth Sahib** is **paraded** on its takht through the local area.

- **Music, singing and fireworks** form part of the celebrations.

- Gurdwaras gather together for a large community langar.

Understanding Guru Nanak's birthday

- Guru Nanak is the **founder of Sikhism** and so this is a very **sacred festival**.

- The procession of the Guru Granth Sahib commemorates how **Guru Nanak travelled thousands of miles** spreading his message of class, gender and race equality in relationship to the one God.

- The festival also **brings together different Sikh communities** to remember Guru Nanak's teaching on **cooperation** and **fellowship**.

Evaluating Guru Nanak's birthday
Should a major aim of all religions be to cooperate with each other?
Points to consider:

- **On the one hand ...** the main aim of all religions should be to worship God or a higher being. As each religion thinks it has the true understanding of God then there is no reason to cooperate as they think each other is wrong.

- **On the other hand ...** as the major world religions share so much in common (such as the need for prayer and worship), then they do need to make cooperation a major aim as there is strength to be found in cooperating with each other.

Did Guru Nanak found a new religion?
Points to consider:

- **On the one hand ...** Guru Nanak did not found a new religion because he developed Sikhism from many of the teachings of Hinduism and Islam – notably reincarnation, karma and mukti from Hinduism and the oneness of God and regular prayer from Islam.

- **On the other hand ...** he did found a new religion because he rejected the Hindu caste system and taught reincarnation which is rejected by Islam. Having a holy book as a guru is entirely new.

2.4 Rites of passage

Almost all religions have special ceremonies which mark important moments in a person's journey through life from birth to death. These ceremonies or 'rites of passage' also bring families together and remind members of the religion of key teachings and values. Sikhism is no different. Note the significant role of the **Guru Granth Sahib** in all these ceremonies.

Birth and naming ceremonies

Knowing about birth and naming ceremonies

Birth ceremony

- When a child is born the **Mul Mantra** is **whispered into the baby's ear**.

- A drop of **amrit** is placed on the baby's tongue.

Naming ceremony

- The Sikh naming ceremony is called **Naam Karan**.

- **The parents** bring the new **baby** to the **gurdwara**.

- The **baby** is **held above** the **Guru Granth Sahib**.

- Special **thanksgiving hymns** are sung.

- The **Guru Granth Sahib** is **opened** at **random**.

- The **name** of the child must start with the **first letter** of the **hymn on that page**.

- Sometimes a **kirpan** (sword) is dipped in **amrit** and **touched** on the **baby's tongue**.

- The **Ardas** prayer is said.

- The special **Karah Parshad** food is distributed.

- Often the parents will make a gift such as a **new cloth covering** (romala) for the Guru Granth Sahib in the gurdwara.

Understanding birth and naming ceremonies

- Birth and naming ceremonies are times when **parents think about their duties** to their new child.

- Placing **amrit** on the child's tongue reminds them of the **sweetness of the gurbani** and their duties to bring up their child in the teachings of Sikhism.

- In addition to their name, every **girl** is also called **Kaur** or princess and every **boy** is also called **Singh** or lion. This signifies that no Sikh is of **higher or lower status** than another Sikh.

- Some parents **pay for the Akhand Path** as a **celebration** of the birth of a new Sikh child into the world.

Evaluating birth and naming ceremonies

Should every child have a naming ceremony?
Points to consider:

- **On the one hand ...** having a naming ceremony marks a moment when a child becomes a member of the family and community. The child will have that name for life and so it needs to be celebrated.

- **On the other hand ...** giving a name to a child is important but a ceremony doesn't make it any more significant. It would be different if the child were old enough to remember the occasion and understand what it meant.

Should children be allowed to choose their own names?
Points to consider:

- **On the one hand ...** children should be allowed to choose their own names because there may be some names they dislike and some names which mean much more to them. Letting children choose their own name would be a way of giving them much more respect.

- **On the other hand ...** choosing a name for a child is a special role for parents and helps them bond with their child. Parents know more about their family history and are in a better position to choose a name that is meaningful.

Amritsanskar and the Khalsa

Knowing about Amritsanskar and the Khalsa

- Initiation occurs around the **age of 15**.

- Those wishing to become **Khalsa Sikhs** must show themselves willing to follow the Sikh way of life and wear **the Five Ks**.

- The ceremony is attended by **five Sikhs** or amrit-dhari who are **full members** of the **Khalsa**.

- They **wear** the **Five Ks** and **special saffron coloured robes**.

- The ceremony takes place **privately** in the **gurdwara**.

- The ceremony begins with a **reading** from the **Guru Granth Sahib**.

- Those being **initiated** are asked **various questions**, including 'Do you **believe in one God**?' and '**Will you live by Sikh teachings**?'

- **Amrit** is prepared by the **five amrit-dhari** Sikhs with a double-edged **sword**.

- The **candidates** receive the **amrit five times**. Each time they say, '**The Khalsa is dedicated to God. The victory belongs to God**.'

- The **Mul Matra** is said **five times**.

- The **rules** of **Khalsa** are **explained**, including not smoking, not taking drugs, not committing adultery, not cutting their hair.

- **Ardas** is said and there is a **final reading** from the **Guru Granth Sahib**.

The Five Ks

- Kesh – **uncut hair**: a sign of saintliness as hair is a gift from God.

- Kangha – **comb**: keeps uncut hair tidy. Men wear turbans.

- Kara – **steel band** on the right hand: a sign that **God is eternal** and a sign of the **unity** and strength of the Khalsa.

- Kachha – **shorts** (underclothes): a sign of **duty** to others and action.

- Kirpan – **curved sword**: a sign of **freedom** and a duty to **protect the weak**.

Understanding Amritsanskar and the Khalsa

- The Khalsa was **formed in 1699** by Guru Gobind Singh after he requested five Sikhs (the Panj Payares) to show their dedication, commitment and loyalty to God and Sikhism.

- The **Amritsanskar** is the most important ceremony in Sikhism because a Sikh becomes a full member of the Khalsa and take on responsibilities in the community.

- Some Sikhs do **not join** the **Khalsa** but **keep** to its **rules**. They are called **amritdhari** because they have taken amrit.

- Those who have not been through the ceremony but do **not cut their hair** and keep **many of the Khalsa rules** are called **kesh-dhari**.

- The **sahaj-dhari** are those Sikhs who do not keep the Five Ks but are **learning about Sikhism** and following its teachings.

- Allowing one's **hair** and **beard** to grow long naturally is to respect God, as nature and God exist in harmony.

Evaluating Amritsanskar and the Khalsa

To be a true Sikh should all Sikhs become full members of the Khalsa?
Points to consider:

- **On the one hand ...** a true Sikh is one who is fully committed to the Khalsa rules, wearing the five Ks and to the rules of the Rahit Maryada; anything less means that one does not fully believe in Sikhism.

- **On the other hand ...** there are different levels of religious commitment in Sikhism and not everyone has to be a full member of the Khalsa to live by Sikh principles. A true Sikh is anyone who fulfils God's will, not necessarily someone who has undergone a particular initiation ceremony.

Is Amritsanskar the most important moment in a Sikh's life?
Points to consider:

- **On the one hand ...** Amritsanskar is the most important moment in a young Sikh's life as it marks a key moment when they formally become part of the Khalsa and make important promises to live and practise as a Sikh.

- **On the other hand ...** initiation is just the start of a Sikh life and without everything else that follows – prayer, worship, carrying out the rules of the Khalsa – it would be meaningless. So, although Amritsanskar is an important moment, it is not the most important.

Marriage

Knowing about marriage

Betrothal

- At a **betrothal ceremony** the **girl's family** offers a **kirpan** and **sweets** to the boy as a sign of **commitment**.

- At the **Milni ceremony** the two families meet and **exchange gifts** and sing **hymns**.

Marriage ceremony

- The marriage ceremony is called **Anand Karaj** meaning 'ceremony of bliss'.

- The ceremony can take place in the **bride's home** or at a **gurdwara**.

- At the marriage ceremony, the **Guru Granth Sahib** must be **present**.

- The **bride** and **groom sit facing** the **takht**.

- The **groom** wears a **scarf of red and gold**.
- They are **told** about their **responsibilities**.
- A **blessing** is said for **them** and their **parents**.
- The couple **bow** to the **Guru Granth Sahib** as a sign of **agreement**.
- **Garlands of flowers** are given to them by the **groom's father**.
- The **groom's father** places the **groom's scarf** in the **bride's hands**.
- The **Lavan** or **marriage hymn** is **read**.
- The couple **circle** round the **Guru Granth Sahib four times** and **bow** to it each time.
- **Flower petals** are **sprinkled** over the **couple**.
- **Karah Parshad** is shared.
- **Sweets** are given to them by the **bride's parents**.
- **Money** is placed in the couple's laps by **guests**.
- Everyone joins in a **meal**.

Understanding marriage

- The **gurus** taught that families **were particularly important**, so Sikhs are strongly encouraged to marry.
- Marriages are **often arranged** but cannot take place unless both bride and groom agree to marry.
- **Circling** the Guru Granth Sahib shows that the couple **accept and will live** by its **moral** and **spiritual values** for the rest of their life.
- The father's **garland of flowers** symbolises the bride leaving her parents' home.
- Holding the **scarf** represents the couple's new life together.
- The **Lavan** hymn was written by Guru Ram Das and explains the relationship between the individual and God.

Evaluating marriage
Should a couple marry only if they are in love?
Points to consider:

- **On the one hand ...** marriage is about companionship and working together to help each other and to bring up a family. A couple need not be in love but they do need to trust and respect each other.
- **On the other hand ...** if a couple are not in love, they will not have that deep bond which will help them through the difficult times as well as the good.

Is a marriage ceremony necessary to get married?
Points to consider:

- **On the one hand ...** a marriage ceremony ensures the vows the couple make to each other in front of their family and friends are serious and important. The marriage ceremony lasts in the mind of the couple and reminds them of their promises.
- **On the other hand ...** what matters is that two people are committed to each other. Marriage ceremonies and rituals add nothing to the intention of the couple to remain faithful and committed to each other.

Practise answering questions with *Theology, Philosophy and Religion 13+ Exam Practice Questions and Answers* pages 23–24 and 97–100.

Test yourself ✓

1   Describe the main features of the diwan in the gurdwara.

2   How is Karah Parshad used in gurdwara worship?

3   Describe the Nishan Sahib and where it may be found.

4   Outline the significance of the langar.

5   What happens on the Akhand Path?

6   Describe kirtan in the gurdwara.

7   What is the name of the shortened Guru Granth Sahib?

8   What event does the festival of Vaisakhi celebrate?

9   Name three things that happen at the festival of Divali.

10   Who leads the procession at the celebration of Guru Nanak's birthday?

11   What are the names that all Sikh boys and all Sikh girls must be given?

12   Name all the Five Ks.

13   Explain the meaning of the symbols of scarf, flowers and circling in a marriage ceremony.

Glossary

Akhand Path The continuous non-stop recitation of the Guru Granth Sahib from beginning to end

amrit Sugar and water mixture used at Sikh initiation

amrit-dhari Sikhs who are full members of the Khalsa

bhangra A kind of energetic dancing

chauri Traditional, ceremonial fan waved over the Guru Granth Sahib

daswandh A tenth of one's income which is given to God

dhan Material service

diwan The hall where worship takes place

Five Ks The five items worn by members of the Khalsa

gurbani The book containing the teaching of the gurus

gurdwara Sikh place of worship

gurmukh Being God-centred

gurpurb Festivals associated with the lives of the gurus

guru Spiritual teacher

Guru Granth Sahib The Sikh holy book

haumai The idea of self-centredness or a person's ego

hukam Divine order

Japji Morning prayer recited everyday by all people

kachha Shorts worn by all Sikhs; one of the Five Ks

kangha A small wooden comb; one of the Five Ks

kara A steel bracelet worn by all Sikhs; one of the Five Ks

Karah Parshad Sweet dish made from flour, semolina, butter and sugar

karma Action with intention; the law of nature that every action has a consequence

Kaur The name 'princess' given to all Sikh girls

kesh The uncut hair and beard worn by Sikhs; one of the Five Ks

Khalsa The Sikh community

Kirat Karna To earn an honest living

kirpan Curved sword; one of the Five Ks

langar Community kitchen serving free food to visitors

maan Mental or intellectual service

mala Prayer beads used during chants or repeating daily mantras

manmukh Being self-centred

martyred Being killed for one's faith

melas Traditional fairs or festivals

mukti Freedom from the cycle of birth, life, death and rebirth

nam japna Meditating by repeating God's name

Nishan Sahib The Sikh flag

nitnem A Sikh book of prayers

palki Canopy over the Guru Granth Sahib

ragas The arrangement of the shabads into musical groupings

ragi A singer in the gurdwara

sewa Service to others, both within the Sikh community and beyond

shabads Hymns

Singh The name 'lion' given to all Sikh boys

taan Physical service

takht The throne on which the Guru Granth Sahib rests

Waheguru Wonderful God; the name in Punjabi given to God